James Walker

**Sermons Preached in the Chapel of Harvard College**

James Walker

**Sermons Preached in the Chapel of Harvard College**

ISBN/EAN: 9783337160944

Printed in Europe, USA, Canada, Australia, Japan

Cover: Foto ©Lupo / pixelio.de

More available books at **www.hansebooks.com**

# SERMONS

PREACHED IN THE

CHAPEL OF HARVARD COLLEGE.

BY

JAMES WALKER, D.D.

BOSTON:
TICKNOR AND FIELDS.
1862.

Entered according to Act of Congress, in the year 1861, by
TICKNOR AND FIELDS,
in the Clerk's Office of the District Court of the District of Massachusetts.

University Press, Cambridge:
Stereotyped and Printed by Welch, Bigelow, & Co.

# CONTENTS.

### SERMON I.
The Mediator . . . . . . . . . 1

### SERMON II.
The Everlasting Gospel . . . . . . 20

### SERMON III.
St. Paul, or the Scholar among the Apostles . 39

### SERMON IV.
Alleged Infidelity of Great Men . . . . 55

### SERMON V.
Inward Manifestation of Christ . . . . 74

### SERMON VI.
The Student's Sabbath . . . . . . 86

### SERMON VII.
Prayer . . . . . . . . . . 103

## SERMON VIII.
RELIGION AS AFFECTED BY THE PROGRESS OF THE PHYSICAL SCIENCES . . . . . . . . 119

## SERMON IX.
CONSCIENCE . . . . . . . . . 135

## SERMON X.
MOTIVES . . . . . . . . . 152

## SERMON XI.
CHARACTER . . . . . . . . . 168

## SERMON XII.
GOVERNMENT OF THE THOUGHTS . . . . . 182

## SERMON XIII.
DIFFICULTY, STRUGGLE, PROGRESS . . . . 199

## SERMON XIV.
SINS OF OMISSION . . . . . . . . 209

## SERMON XV.
NO HIDING-PLACE FOR THE WICKED . . . . 226

## SERMON XVI.
THOU SHALT SAY, NO . . . . . . . 239

## SERMON XVII.
THE HEART MORE THAN THE HEAD . . . . 252

## SERMON XVIII.
Compromises . . . . . . . . . 270

## SERMON XIX.
Conditions of Success in Life . . . . . 286

## SERMON XX.
On the Choice of a Profession . . . . 302

## SERMON XXI.
The End not yet . . . . . . . . 323

## SERMON XXII.
Faith and Works . . . . . . . . 340

## SERMON XXIII.
Salvation by Hope . . . . . . . 353

## SERMON XXIV.
Differences among Christians no Objection to Christianity . . . . . . . . 365

## SERMON XXV.
The Day of Judgment . . . . . . 380

# SERMONS.

## THE MEDIATOR.

FOR THERE IS ONE GOD, AND ONE MEDIATOR BETWEEN GOD AND MEN, THE MAN CHRIST JESUS. — 1 Timothy ii. 5.

THE sense of man's need of a Mediator did not spring up for the first time in Christianity. It seems to have had its origin in a feeling of the distance, the incomprehensibleness, the unapproachableness of the unseen object of fear and worship. Common men were afraid to speak to God; they did not conceive themselves to be in a condition to speak to him face to face. Accordingly, they looked round for some person or persons, bolder or holier than they, who would speak to God for them, — whether to ask his aid, or to acknowledge his goodness, or to appease his anger.

Hence, for the most part, the priesthoods of the ancient world; for it was out of this sentiment of ignorance, and awe, and human unworthiness, that nearly all of what was good or bad in the priestly office arose. We see its beginnings even in barbarous tribes, where there is almost always one or more who, in the character of magicians or necromancers, are resorted to by the rest, as having intercourse and influence with the invisible powers. In India and in Egypt the same idea was elaborately carried out in the organization of an hereditary sacerdotal caste, arrogating to itself the exclusive right of mediating between earth and heaven. And so of Greece and Rome; for though in their best days this assumption on the part of the priests was reduced and limited in many ways, it was by no means extinct. If Socrates would consult the Oracle at Delphi, he must do it through a priestess of the temple; if Augustus would know the will of the Gods as to the conduct of the war, there must be a diviner in the camp.

Turning next to the Hebrews, we find a people whose very form of government, a theocracy, made it necessary that almost everything should be done through mediators between God and men. Moses, by whom the Law came, was eminently "a mediator," and is expressly so denominated in the New Testament. He also says of himself in Deuteronomy, "I stood between the Lord and you at that time, to show you the word of the Lord." Hence, too, the appointment of Aaron and his posterity as a perpetual priesthood, to act as so many "mediators," through whom alone the people were to have access to Jehovah in the solemn and imposing service of the Temple. The people did not offer up their own sacrifices; they brought the victims or oblations to the priest, who made the offering in their name and stead. The people did not so much as enter the vestibule of the temple: even in the solemn atoning service, which was for the whole nation, the priests alone went in, while the people stood without. So likewise in great national emergencies, when it became necessary "to inquire of the Lord," it was through the High Priest, and by means of the Sacred Lot, that the response was expected and given. Such at least was the original provision; in later times this office seems to have devolved, for the most part, on the Prophets; always, however, it was by "mediators."

It is obvious, therefore, as I have said that, Christianity did not give birth to the idea of a mediator between God and men; neither was it the object of Christianity to extend that idea, or the agency representing it, but rather to purify, to exalt, and, in some respects, to limit both.

I shall begin by calling your attention to the *limitations* here referred to, as the first step towards a truly Christian conception of the Mediatorial Office.

In the first place, while other religions acknowledge a multitude of mediators, Christianity knows but *one*. So in the text: "For there is one God, and one Mediator between God and men, the man Christ Jesus." Also, in another place, the same Apostle says, if possible with still more explicitness, "For though there be that are called gods, whether in heaven or in earth (as there be gods many, and lords many), but *to us* there is but one God, the Father, of whom are all things, and we in him; and one Lord, Jesus Christ, by whom are all things, and we by him." Accordingly, the whole scheme of mediation, so far as it had depended on a ritual worship and the ministration of men like ourselves, became essentially changed. As Neander has said: "Such a guild of priests as existed in the previous systems of religion, empowered to guide other men, who remained, as it were, in a state of religious pupilage; having the *exclusive* care of providing for their religious wants, and serving as mediators, by whom all other men must first be placed in connection with God and divine things; — such a priestly caste could find no place within Christianity." * Instead of the many so-called "mediators," in whom men previously trusted, the Gospel has set forth one all-sufficient Mediator, —

---

* General History of the Christian Religion and Church, Vol. I. p. 179.

one, *because* all-sufficient. We need no other, and we are not at liberty to acknowledge any other. It is not enough considered that what the text forbids by implication is just as true, and quite as important, as what it expressly asserts. It warns us not to let any man, or any body of men, or anything whatsoever, save our Lord Jesus Christ, come between the soul and its Maker. Ministers, wise and pious friends, books, religious services, early training, — all these aids to faith and piety may help to put us into the way to God, but they are not the way itself. We must not suppose that it is only by them, or through them, that we have access to the Father, or that they can bar this access to the humblest of Christ's followers.

In the second place, not only has this way of access to the Father been opened to us by one Mediator, but by him *once for all*. This is intimated again and again. While the old priesthoods are represented as "daily ministering, and offering oftentimes the same sacrifices," it is expressly said that "we are sanctified through the offering of the body of Jesus Christ, *once for all*."

In order to understand the sacrificial language of the New Testament in its application to Christ, we must bear in mind that Christianity is not merely an absolute religion, that is, a religion all whose doctrines, when rightly construed, are absolutely true;

but also an historical religion. Christianity did not spring into being having no connections with the past: like every other great revolution, it has its place in history, and its historical antecedents, out of which it grew, to which it is accommodated, and without reference to which it can neither be comprehended nor explained. Historically considered, the New Testament stands related to the Old as the fulfilling of the Law, as the accomplishment of the prophecies, as the final realization of what was but "a shadow of good things to come,"—the gospel of Moses became the gospel of Christ. Accordingly, almost all its doctrines and institutions, almost all its modes of religious thought and religious expression, are at bottom Jewish, with only such modifications in terms or sense, or both, as fitted them to become the exponents of a universal and spiritual dispensation. Now one of the fundamental ideas in the Hebrew ritual is, that the people are not in a condition to approach their God, without first going through a process of purification and reconciliation by means of oblations and sacrifices; and that this process is to be renewed day by day, and year by year. Such was the Jewish idea, and it reappears in the Gospel, carried out and fulfilled under a Christian form, in the doctrine that whatever was understood to be done for "a peculiar people" by the sacrifices and oblations of the Old Testament, is now done for all mankind, and once for all, by the self-sacrifice of Christ. Through his sole mediation, that is to say, by his teachings and sufferings, by his life and death, he has broken down forever the legal and ritual impediments which were thought to separate man from his Maker, and thus opened a way of access to the Father "once for all." By a new and far more sublime revelation of grace and truth, and spiritual freedom, he has opened to the whole world a door of access to the Mercy-Seat, and *left it open;* and, blessed be God, it is a door which no man, or body of men, can shut.

Another circumstance distinguishing Christ's mediation is, that it aims to dispense with the necessity for all further mediation, by bringing God and man *together*, and making them *one*. Our Lord's words are: "That they all may be one; as thou, Father, art in me, and I in thee, that they also may be one in us." With the mediating priests and prophets of antiquity it was not so. What they in general undertook to do was merely to open between God and men a kind of *distant* communication or correspondence, by bearing to the former the offerings and requests of the latter, and bringing back the response. But Christ has done more. As the one Mediator he has opened, once for all, not only a way of communication with the Father, but a way of access to Him, — that "new and living way" by which, instead of *sending*, we *go*. It is the privilege, the distinction, the glory of Christians, that they have personal, direct, immediate access to the Father. I do not mean to deny that we owe this doctrine to Christ, — in other words, that all is *through him*. Nay, more, I do not mean to deny the continued presence and agency of Christ in the Church; nor that "he ever liveth to make intercession for us;" — all this, nevertheless, is not that he may still stand between God and man, in the sense of keeping them apart, but that he may bring them together, and make them one. "By whom," as our common version of the Bible renders it, "we have now received the atonement," — that is, the *at-one-ment*, or the being *at one*.

Thus far I have spoken of obvious and striking points of difference between the Christian notion of a mediator, and the pagan or Jewish notion. But the question may here suggest itself to some minds, Why *any* mediator?

In answering this question, I think it neither wise nor reverent to lay much stress on arguments drawn from human conceptions of the Divine nature and government. For example: there are those who think it enough to say that God *cannot* forgive sin, however sincerely repented of, or receive the repentant and reclaimed sinner into favor, without a mediator; that is to say, he cannot do it freely, and of his own accord. But why not? I certainly can see no reason why he *could* not, if he *would;* indeed, I cannot see any reason why he would not. All such confident assertion on the part of philosophers and theologians as to what God *can* do, or *cannot* do, resting on no better authority than their imperfect conceptions of the Divine attributes, must be extremely distasteful to serious minds; and besides, it comes, let me add, with an ill grace from those who on other occasions are among the foremost to condemn the use of reason in religion, and especially in speaking of God.

On the other hand, I can as little agree with those who think it an argument *against* the use and necessity of a mediator, that God is immutable and impassible, and therefore cannot be changed in his purposes respecting man by what a third person can say or do; and furthermore, that he is essentially merciful, and always ready to forgive, and therefore needs no change. For, in the first place, if we believe in the proper efficacy of prayer, we must not make God immutable and impassible in such a sense that he cannot be affected by Christ's intercessions in our behalf; and again, if we believe God to be a moral being, we must also believe him to be moved by the spectacle of Christ's sufferings. Add to this what we know of God's providence in this world. Are we not continually thanking Him for blessings, which, however, we do not receive from him directly, but through "mediators," that is, through the instrumentality of others? Accordingly, I cannot see anything unphilosophical, or improbable, or contrary to experience, in the doctrine that we are indebted for many hopes and privileges to Christ's mediation, *and to the effect of this mediation on God.*

Even, however, if it were not so, it would not materially affect the question at issue. You are aware that the reconciliation to be brought about by the mediation of Christ is everywhere represented in the New Testament as a reconciliation of man to God, and not of God to man. Thus it is said, "God hath reconciled us to himself by Jesus Christ." And again, "For if when we were enemies we were reconciled unto God by the death of his Son, much more, being reconciled, we shall be saved by his life." The question, therefore, is not whether *God* needed a mediator, but whether *man* needed one. When the Scriptures speak of the necessity and use of Christ's mediation, it is always with reference to its benefits to mankind, and especially to mankind in the condition in which they were at his coming.

What then are some of these benefits?

It is common to mention in this connection the *outward* and *public* benefits which are to be referred to Christ, as a great Teacher and Reformer. Christianity, as I suppose all will admit, is a manifest improvement on the religions which preceded it, — an onward step in human progress. Modern civilization has grown out of it. Here, then, are great and manifest benefits in which the whole community share at this moment, believers and unbelievers. And be not misled by this statement. Some may think to argue from it, that if these benefits are now shared by unbelievers, they do not require that Christ should be accepted as a proper Mediator, and ought not, therefore, to be taken into the account. But there is a fallacy here. You might just as well say, that because the solution of a difficult problem requires no study *now*, having become part of the common sense of the age, it required none *in the beginning*. We are tracing these outward and public benefits of Christianity to their source. And, viewed in this light, is it not plain that the benefits of the institution presuppose the establishment and prevalence of the institution, — which never could have been except on condition of faith in the proper mediatorship of Christ? All, therefore, is to be looked upon as the fruit of this faith, though now enjoyed, to a certain extent, by those who reject the faith.

Consider next the *inward* and *personal* benefits resulting from the mediation of Christ, which always suppose faith in the participant. In a community nominally Christian, where all enjoy the outward and public benefits of Christianity, what advantage have those of us who believe in a Mediator over deists and sceptics who do not?

In the first place, we not only have a Teacher who approves himself to our judgment, but one who came from God, speaking to us in the name of God. Here the question is not, whether we really have a Mediator acting in this capacity, but whether it is not well to have one, and to be assured of it. I am not now discussing the evidences of Christianity; I am simply answering the inquiry, Why have a Mediator? If we had one, what would be gained thereby? Certainly it is something to know *on authority* what is God's will and purpose respecting us. On this point there can certainly be but one opinion. You cannot find a single serious and thoughtful unbeliever, far or near, who would not consider it a great thing to have his guesses respecting God, eternity, and the human soul turned into well-authenticated facts. Intimations are sometimes thrown out, as if the doctrine of a revelation through a Mediator, though useful and perhaps indispensable in the early ages of the world, is gradually becoming obsolete, or at least comparatively unnecessary. But it is not so. A change in relation to this matter there obviously is. What was most wanted in the beginning was *information;* what is most wanted now is *evidence;*—not that we may be saved from our errors, but from our doubts. The need, therefore, though not precisely the same, is nevertheless just as real, and just as great, now as formerly.

And this is not all. The Christian doctrine of the Mediator is, "that God was in Christ reconciling the world unto himself." "The Word was made flesh, and dwelt among us." Unhappily the Church has taken this mystery of the incarnation, which as a mystery means a great deal, and turned it into an unintelligible dogma, which means nothing. The Bible never speaks of two natures in Christ, or of his being God and man at the same time; but it represents him again and again as being a manifestation of God,—"the brightness of his glory, and the express image of his person." And this view, this conviction, has important practical bearings, and never more so than in the existing state of the highest human thought. It is not enough considered that we have no proper manifestation of the Living God except in Jesus Christ. We are sometimes said to see God in nature; but it is not so, even figuratively; we do not see *Him* there, we only see his footprints,—we see where he has been. We do not see in the material universe the Divine wisdom and goodness, we only see their *effects;*

but in Christ we see the qualities themselves. We see, therefore, in Christ what we worship in God; so that, without confounding them together, we can worship God *in and through* Christ. To some minds the distinction here insisted on may seem less unique and significant, because other men are also said in Scripture to be "made after the similitude of God." But this similitude, when applied to men in general, relates to *capacities*, not to *attainments*; to what they *might* become, not to what they *do* become. It is still as true as ever, that Christ is the only being in whom it has pleased the Father that "all fulness should dwell."

At the same time, it is this very fact, namely, that the Divine Presence is vouchsafed to us in a person of capacities like our own, which constitutes the peculiar fitness of the Christian Mediator. What do men want? Not a confounding together, but a coming together, of God and man, a meeting, if I may so express it, half-way, to be attended by the double benefit of bringing God down, so that he can be included within the scope of human sympathies, and lifting man up, so that he can become a partaker of the Divine holiness. Add to this, that by recognizing God in Christ we are naturally led to contemplate and approach the Infinite One under the aspect of his *personal* qualities and relations; by which we may hope that the strong pantheistic tendency of modern thought will be counteracted. Science, with the ever enlarging sweep of its generalizations, is reducing all to order and unity; and the danger is, that men will stop there, that, filled with the spirit of science, and not with the spirit of faith and love, they will fall down and worship Order and Unity; at any rate, that a vague notion of a Pantheistic Mind, or of a so-called "Soul of the Universe," may take the place of a belief in the living and true God. Hence, I insist, the necessity, and the growing necessity, of a Divine Mediator, whose very coming reveals God to us, not as the order of the universe, but as its conscious Source and Lord, — a Divine Mediator through whom this God is continually pleading with us to be reconciled to him, not merely as order and law, but as a loving Father.

One question more. Supposing it to be conceded that we need a Mediator, and such a Mediator as has been described, why also a *suffering* Mediator? There can be no doubt that the language used in the New Testament, and especially in the Epistle to the Hebrews, in speaking of the sacrificial import of Christ's sufferings and death, must be interpreted with a constant reference to Jewish institutions and modes of thought. Accordingly, where no regard is paid to this caution, we must expect that texts true in a literal sense will often be mixed up with texts true in a figurative sense, from which inferences will be drawn not true in any sense. Still, it is no purpose of mine to detract aught from the merit or the significance of Christ's sufferings, undergone, directly or indirectly, for our salvation.

Consider, first, their effect on the Mediator *himself*. "For it became Him, for whom are all things, and by whom are all things, in bringing many sons unto glory, to make the Captain of their salvation perfect through sufferings." It is a narrow and low view of the purposes of our being, which makes it a wonder, or a perplexity, that the good should suffer. In this way the good are made better; nay, it is only in this way that the great virtues of a brave endurance, and a noble self-sacrifice, can be won, or the serene and unearthly peace and joy which these virtues alone can inspire. Accordingly, in reading the narrative of the Evangelists, I think we can see evidence of our Lord's character becoming more gentle and tender and self-sacrificing under the discipline of hardship and sorrow. At any rate, we must admit the fact, for it is expressly asserted by the Apostle: he was made perfect by suffering, thereby showing that even his wonderful life is no exception to the law which makes the baptism of Christian goodness to be a baptism, not of water, but "of the Holy Spirit and of fire."

Consider, also, the *moral power* which the sufferings of the Mediator have given him over his followers, and over the world. We lay stress on his miracles, and Divine authority, and perfect character; and we do well, for all these are essential to the completeness of our idea of one who is to lead us to God. These give *the right* to reign: after all, however, it is the thought that he voluntarily bowed himself to pain, indignity, and death for our sakes, which actually enthrones him in the hearts of men. There are those who will question his miracles, demur at his authority, mock his virtues; but never one who can be made to see and enter into the nature and extent and spirit of his sufferings and sacrifices, without being touched and melted by the appeal. It is thus that "through his poverty we are made rich."

If I were to stop here, enough has already been said to vindicate the ways of God, in appointing a Mediator who can be touched by a sense of our infirmities, — "a man of sorrows and acquainted with grief." But I cannot help thinking that the general tenor of the New Testament teachings on this subject, and the moral and religious instincts of the human heart, go further. They testify to the fact, that heaven as well as earth is moved by the spectacle of such sufferings, endured by so holy a being, and from such love. I have nothing to do here with dogmas which have been fiercely contested in the Church. I do not say that these sufferings were necessary to make God placable; for this would seem to imply that he had been implacable before. I do not say that they are necessary to make repentance and reformation available; for it seems to me, that all justice is satisfied on sincere repentance and real reformation except vindictive justice,— the justice of retaliation or revenge. But this I say, with all reverence and humility; a compassionate God may be, and I believe is, made more compassionate still by the intercessions of such a Mediator for the frail and erring beings whom he is said, in the emphatic language of Scripture, to have redeemed, ransomed, bought by his own blood.

You may insist that this whole subject is involved in mystery, and that you are tired of mystery. But you cannot get rid of mystery, even if you would; it attaches to every point of the higher life in man; life itself is a mystery, and death a still greater mystery. And besides, do not object to mystery from confounding it with what is not mystery. A mystery, as that term is here used, is not an unintelligible proposition, or a proposition of any kind. It is a fact comprehended but in part,— half understood, and half not understood. That part which we cannot understand, we leave with the secret things which belong to the Lord our God; that part which we can understand we use for instruction and edification; and it teaches us in this case, "that God was in Christ, reconciling the world unto himself, not imputing their trespasses unto them; and hath committed unto us the word of reconciliation. Now then we are ambassadors for Christ; as though God did beseech you by us, we pray you in Christ's stead, be ye reconciled to God."

# THE EVERLASTING GOSPEL.

UPON THIS ROCK I WILL BUILD MY CHURCH; AND THE GATES OF HELL SHALL NOT PREVAIL AGAINST IT. — Matthew xvi. 18.

VICISSITUDE, we often say, and with the daily proof of it before our eyes, is stamped on all earthly things. Is it so with Christianity? Customs and institutions, dynasties and nations, systems of government, systems of philosophy, and systems of religion, have passed away, or are passing away. Have we any reason to believe, or to fear, that Christianity must also submit to the same law?

This is not a new question. John the Baptist, having been left to languish in prison for several months, sent two of his disciples to Jesus with the inquiry, "Art thou He that should come, or do we look for another?" A momentary cloud of despondency would seem to have passed over the mind of our Lord himself when he said, "Nevertheless, when the Son of Man cometh, shall he find faith on the earth?" And so with many of his sincere followers in all ages. They have not begun by doubting the Divine origin of Christianity, or its essential reasonableness, or its moral beauty and sublimity, or its unspeakable importance in a practical point of view. Their distrust, their misgivings, have had another origin. They have looked — and, as they thought, in vain, or almost in vain — for the promised and expected fruit. Nearly two thousand years have elapsed since angelic voices chanted the hymn: "Glory to God in the highest, and on earth peace, good-will toward men." A cry was also heard: "Repent, for the kingdom of Heaven is *at hand.*" Nearly two thousand years, — a long period, even for the unfolding of such issues; yet what do we see. Is the promise fulfilled? Is the prophecy accomplished? Individuals, no doubt, can here and there be found, who are penetrated and filled with the Christian spirit; but when we look at society at large, when we look at what is called the Christian world, where is the nation, where is the community, where is the party or the sect, which as a whole, or even generally, is Christian except in name? Can we wonder, then, that good men, discouraged and disheartened by the slow progress of things, and by the ill success of many a well-devised plan of improvement or reform, should sometimes be tempted to fear that Christianity itself, at least in much that was expected from it, may turn out a failure, — in short, that it has had its day?

The common argument to prove the groundlessness of this fear may be stated in a few words. Christianity is *the truth*, and truth is indestructible; nay, as knowledge increases, all minds must by necessity gravitate towards it. Moreover, Christianity is of Divine origin, and is founded on miracles. We must presume, therefore, that the same Almighty Being who founded it will continue to uphold it, even though miracles should again be necessary for that purpose; especially as we have express assurance in the text to the same effect: "Upon this Rock I will build my Church; and the gates of hell shall not prevail against it."

Now it is no part of my plan to call in question the soundness of this argument; much less, that of the conclusion to which it leads. Still there are two considerations which make it proper not to rest in this argument, but to pursue the investigation a little further.

In the first place, what is here said of Christianity may also be said, with little or no abatement, of Judaism. Judaism is understood to be of Divine origin, and, in so far as it is so, *the truth*. Moreover, the old revelation is understood to be founded on miracles, as well as the new; and the promise that it should be perpetual is quite as explicit, and more frequent. Thus, to Abraham: "And I will establish my covenant between me and thee, and thy seed after thee, in their generations, for an *everlasting* covenant, to be a God unto thee, and to thy seed after thee; and I will give unto thee, and to thy seed after thee, the land wherein thou art a stranger, and all the land of Canaan, for *an everlasting possession.*" This promise is renewed again and again to Moses and Aaron, and afterwards by the mouth of the prophets, in such words as these: "Thy people also shall be all righteous; they shall *inherit the land forever.*" And again: "The Lord shall reign over them *in Mount Zion from henceforth, even forever.*" I am aware of the turn given to these passages by the commentators. They say, and no doubt truly, that this promise was made with a tacit understanding, with an implied condition; namely, that the Jews should be faithful on their part. The promise, therefore, has not been broken; for though it has failed, it has been through the unfaithfulness of the Jews. Be it so. Why then may not the same thing happen in respect to Christianity? God, of course, will not break any of his promises; nevertheless, may not the promise of perpetuity *fail* under the new covenant, as we know it did under the old, and for the same reason, — because an *implied* condition has not been fulfilled, or, in other words, through the unfaithfulness of Christians?

A second reason for not resting content with the

bare statement of the argument, as given above, is found in the natural desire to strengthen and fortify our faith, though founded on acknowledged Divine authority, by proofs and illustrations drawn from other sources. How many sermons have been preached to Christian congregations in order to convince men of the efficacy of prayer, or of a life to come! Yet all know that both these doctrines are expressly taught in the Scriptures; and all believe, or profess to believe, that the Scriptures are the Word of God. In such cases we are far from thinking that faith can be dispensed with; in respect to many things we must "walk by faith, not by sight," and the more entire and unreserved this faith, the better. Still, it unquestionably gives new force and vivacity to what we believe on authority, even though it be on the highest authority, if we can be made to see that what we thus believe on authority falls in also with what we know by our own reason and experience. As regards practical effect, quite as much depends on its *seeming* to be a fact, as on our believing it to be a fact; on its verisimilitude, as on its truth.

It is, therefore, from no distrust of the authority of Scripture, but for other reasons, that we would push the inquiry a little further, and ask whether there is not something in the very *nature* of Christianity, and *peculiar to it,* to reassure us that it will never be destroyed by the prevalence of irreligion, nor supplanted by any other religion purporting to be truer or more Divine.

In the first place, if we attentively consider the essential nature of Christianity, we can hardly fail to be struck with one remarkable peculiarity. Unlike every other historical and authoritative religion, not excepting Judaism, it is neither a political constitution, nor a prescribed ritual, nor a doctrinal system, nor a code of laws; but a body of *principles*, to act as the unfolding germs of a higher type of moral and spiritual life. Neither the purpose nor the tendency of these principles is to arrest society at any stage of its progress, but rather to help on that progress indefinitely, — partaking of the progress themselves, inasmuch as, though the principles remain the same, they will be better and better understood, and more and more wisely applied.

Let me explain what I mean; and first, as regards *worship*, including all those duties and hopes which spring out of our immediate relations to God, and our direct intercourse with Him. You know how it was, in this respect, with the great historical religions which preceded Christianity, — the religions of India, of Egypt, of Greece, of Rome. Each consisted, for the most part, of an outward ceremonial, the details of which were appointed and regulated to the minutest particular by law or custom, and any departure therefrom, whether consciously or unconsciously, was looked upon as more likely than anything else to incense the gods. Were their armies routed and slain by the enemy, was there evil in the city, was there famine or pestilence, the excited imagination of the people was almost sure to charge it upon some change or some neglect in the sacred rites. The same is true to a considerable extent of Judaism, as every one must see on turning over the pages of the Levitical code; neither is it any objection to a religion intended to be preparatory, and therefore to pass away, or be superseded by another. But in the New Testament an essentially different view of worship is inculcated. "Jesus saith unto her, Woman, believe me, the hour cometh when ye shall neither in this mountain, nor yet at Jerusalem, worship the Father. Ye worship ye know not what: we know what we worship; for salvation is of the Jews. But the hour cometh, and now is, when the true worshippers shall worship the Father in spirit and in truth: for the Father seeketh such to worship him. God is a spirit; and they that worship him must worship him in spirit and in truth." Accordingly, the triumph of Christianity is not to be regarded merely as the triumph of one ritual over another ritual; it is the triumph of religion over all rituals, except in so far as one or another may be thought useful for the decencies and conveniences of worship in a particular church. Under Christianity, the place, the time, the outward form, are nothing in themselves considered; it is enough if the worship is *true* and *spiritual*, these words to be interpreted according to the highest conceptions of the true and the spiritual that shall, at any time, have been attained.

Turning next to the *ethical*, as distinguished from the devotional, element in Christianity, the same peculiarity reappears. In the primitive and preparatory religions, morality is taught almost exclusively, when it is taught at all, in the form of certain outward actions enjoined, and certain other outward actions forbidden. The morality of the Mosaic dispensation, an admirable summary of which is given in the Ten Commandments, is of this kind. Scarcely a word is said in that compend about inward principles and dispositions, or about virtues and vices, as such; but the people are expressly told what *to do*, and what *not to do*;—doubtless the best and only practicable course to be taken in a rude age. In the more spiritual tone of the later prophets we behold the morning twilight of a better day; which they foretold, and to some extent anticipated, as one when God would "put his law in men's inward parts, and write it on their hearts." And that day has come. Of course you will understand me to speak in this connection of Christian morality; — not of the actual morality of Christians, but of what the morality of Christians ought to be according to the Gospel.

A glance at the Sermon on the Mount, and especially at the Beatitudes in which the doctrine and spirit of that sermon is summed up, must convince every unprejudiced mind, that we have here, not merely a higher cast and style of morality than had been hitherto known, but also an essentially different manner of moral inculcation. The stress is no longer laid, as before, on the outward act, or the specific and arbitrary rule, but on the *purpose*, the *intention*, the *thought*. The outward action is still as important as ever; but it is so, in a moral point of view, merely because it expresses or involves some good or bad inward principle or disposition. Accordingly, under the Gospel, the moral injunction is laid directly on the inward principle or disposition: in other words, it is not said, as it was "to them of old time," "Thou shalt not steal," "Thou shalt not kill," "Thou shalt not bear false witness against thy neighbor;" but rather, "Blessed are the meek," "Blessed are the merciful," "Blessed are the pure in heart." The inward principle or disposition is insisted on, and each individual is expected and required to manifest the same in such manner as the highest moral and spiritual culture for the time being may dictate or approve. The merciful man of to-day may live up to a higher conception of what mercy means and includes, than the merciful man of five centuries ago; still he is but a merciful man after all; he does no more than what is required; he does not, and he cannot, transcend or outgrow the Christian rule.

Thus does Christianity, as regards both worship and obedience, link itself to the great law of human progress, and partake of that progress. No real or possible growth of society and the human mind can ever have the effect to outgrow Christianity, inasmuch as the *actual* Christianity will grow along with it. I do not mean that Christianity, *considered in itself*, can ever differ from what it is, or from what it was in the beginning; but the *actual* Christianity may,—nay, *must*, in proportion as men understand its principles better, and enter more entirely into its spirit.

We shall also arrive at the same general conclusion, if, instead of considering the kind of piety and righteousness inculcated in the New Testament, we look at *the Example* we are to follow, or at the great practical *authority* which makes imitation of that example binding on the soul.

Cicero's complaint respecting the founders of pagan systems of religion and philosophy is well known. "Who is there among them all," he asks, "whose practical principles, temper, and conduct were conformable to right reason? Who ever regarded his philosophy as a law and rule of life, and not rather as an ostentation of his ability and learning? Who ever obeyed his own instructions, and made his precepts the model of his own daily practice?" But with Christ it is not so, infidels themselves being the judges. By universal consent his doctrine and life are one. His character was a living impersonation of what he taught, thus becoming of the nature of a new and supplementary revelation, because it shows how the various Christian graces should exist and act *together*, qualifying each other, balancing each other, complementing and perfecting each other. The need of some such authenticated pattern or presentation of the character required, not in its separate ingredients but *as a whole*, was felt long before the coming of Christ; and the Stoics thought to supply it by the fiction of what they called their Sage or Wise Man. But this well-meant expedient failed in two obvious particulars. In the first place, their Wise Man was not a reality, having authority over them, but a fiction constructed by themselves; and secondly, as it was nothing more than a fanciful embodiment of the doctrines of a particular sect in a particular age, it was sure to pass away with the age and sect which gave it birth. And so it did.

Widely different is it with the character of Christ, — the living, the absolute, the Divine pattern and standard set forth in the Gospel. This might be illustrated in a thousand ways; but the point of distinction to which alone I wish to call your attention now is, that the great Christian Exemplar can never become obsolete, can never lose either its use or its authority.

It is to no purpose to say that the character of Christ is what it is; that it represents a fixed quantity, a stationary object, while society and the human mind are constantly moving on. You might just as well say the same of Nature. You might just as well say that Nature is what it is; that it represents a fixed quantity, a stationary object, while society and the human mind are constantly moving on. But does Nature ever become obsolete? What become obsolete are *men's views* of Nature; and these become so, only because they are superseded and displaced by juster and more profound views. So it is with the character of Christ.

What more perhaps than anything else distinguishes the believing and earnest man of all times is his aspiration after an ideal good, an inextinguishable longing to *realize* his conception of *the highest* and *the best*. Now one of the purposes and one of the effects of the moral character exhibited in the life of Jesus is to help such persons not merely to realize this conception, but also to elevate and purify the conception itself, inspiring them with the idea of a *higher* highest, and of a *better* best, than they could have unfolded from their own minds, or from any merely verbal description. And this is not all. Though in a much nobler sense, and to much more exalted issues, it is the same with the study of the Christian model of holiness as with the study of the finest models in art. Not only are susceptible minds excited and instructed by the first impression of the model, but by the continual study of it, by a growing familiarity and sympathy with it, they are able to see more and more in the model itself. In this way the example of Christ, as well as his teachings, his life as well as his word, becomes not merely a perpetual revelation, but a perpetually *progressive* revelation, forever keeping pace with the progressive receptivities of those to whom it is addressed. Let the world grow as much wiser as it may, the wisest and best men in it will always be among the foremost to acknowledge, that "God, who commanded the light to shine out of darkness, has shined in our hearts, to give the light of the knowledge of the glory of God in the face of Jesus Christ."

Meanwhile, and for the same reason, the *moral*, the *practical authority*, of the Gospel, the authority which gives effect to the whole, must also be on the increase, and not on the decline.

When men refer to the authority on which Christianity rests, I believe they commonly mean its *historical* authority, the authority of the record as a genuine and trustworthy narrative of what actually took place eighteen and a half centuries ago. Restricting themselves to this narrow and unspiritual view of authority in things heavenly and Divine, we need not wonder if they should sometimes fall into the error of supposing that *this* authority must gradually, and in the lapse of ages, lose its hold on the human mind. One writer,* and he neither an enemy nor a sceptic, has gone so far as to make this process a matter of mathematical calculation, his conclusion being that the probability of the New Testament narrative will entirely cease at the end of 3,150 years, reckoning from the birth of Christ; and consequently, that this will be the epoch when the Son of God will come to judge the world, because then, according to Luke, chap. viii, ver. 8, there will be no more faith on the earth. Let such vagaries pass for what they are worth. I do not shut my eyes on the importance and necessity of the historical authority of Christianity; neither am I under any apprehensions that it will ever fail; but this I say, unless sustained, or at least concurred in, by the moral and practical authority, it would not, it could not stand. If the monkish

---

* John Craig, in his *Theologiæ Christianæ Principia Mathematica.*

legends of the Middle Ages, if the coarse and vulgar pretences to the supernatural in our own day, are urged upon us as entitled to credence, because supported by a greater amount of historical evidence than can be adduced in proof of some of the Christian miracles, my answer is, in the words of Locke, the praise of whose humble faith and sobriety of judgment is in everybody's mouth: "The miracles are to be judged by the doctrine, and not the doctrine by the miracles." *

So far as our faith in revelation depends on tradition alone, whether oral or written, there can be no doubt, I suppose, that time must do something to wear away its freshness and vitality. But nothing hinders this loss from being made up, and more than made up, in other ways;—in the case of Christianity, by the fulfilment of prophecy, by continued opportunity to submit its claims to a practical test, by its triumphs, by its fruits. In order to excuse our own doubts and misgivings we are apt to over-estimate the advantages which the early converts had over us, and to under-estimate the advantages which we have over them, as regards the Christian evidences. When the apostles were arraigned before the Council at Jerusalem, you remember the ground taken by Gamaliel, "a doctor of the law, had in reputation among all the people":

---

* Lord King's *Life of John Locke*, Vol. I. p. 234.

"And now I say unto you, Refrain from these men, and let them alone; for if this counsel or this work be of men, it will come to naught, but if it be of God, ye cannot overthrow it." Strange as it may seem, he does not appear to have been much affected, one way or another, by what had already taken place: he makes everything turn on the question, Will it stand? Now it *has* stood. More than that; whatever we may say or think about its inward triumphs, its outward triumphs are unquestioned and complete. At this very moment the whole civilized world are glorifying the advent of the Son of Mary, — of Him, who while upon earth knew not where to lay his head, the Crucified One. Who does not perceive that the men of that day, Jews and Gentiles, would have poured into the Church by thousands and tens of thousands, if they had foreseen, if they had even so much as suspected, what we *know?*

After all, however, the faith which is built on any form of external evidence, is a faith of the understanding, and not necessarily of the heart; a faith, moreover, which a man of a base heart may attain, his heart remaining unchanged. What we want is a living and saving faith in Christianity, which consists, not in believing or knowing that the Gospel is true, but in feeling the force of the truths which the Gospel teaches; and this cannot be, until our hearts are brought into communion and sympathy with them; and this, again, is the work, not of books on the evidences, but of Christian nurture. What is true of God in Nature, is true also of God in History and God in Christ;—to apprehend Divinity anywhere, in anything, so as to be vitally affected thereby, we must first be put into communication with it, through the development of what is divine in our own souls. Did our Lord mean nothing when he said: "My doctrine is not mine, but His that sent me; if any man will do His will, he shall know of the doctrine, whether it be of God, or whether I speak of myself"? Does any one suppose that holy and devout men, men who know Christianity from the life and have made great progress in that life, ask for any better evidence of its truth than they can find in themselves? Whence then this modern conceit, that we are growing so wise and good as to be in danger of outgrowing Christianity? Undoubtedly there is a culture of the understanding and of the taste, which will make a great scholar, or a great artist, or a great man of business, without bringing him any nearer to the kingdom of God; but it is because the culture is limited and one-sided. Make it to be the culture of the whole man, and the higher the culture, the stronger and the purer the faith.

If these things are so, it follows incontestably that Christianity is not a passing phase of society, a religion very well for its time, a single stage in human progress, which, like every other such stage, must have its beginning, its middle, and its end. It is "an everlasting possession." This I have shown to follow from the fact that Christianity is true and Divine, and from the express teaching of Scripture. But I have not stopped there. I have also shown it to follow from the nature of the religion itself, and from the character of its Founder, and from the adjustment of both to the essential and indestructible needs and capacities of the human soul. In proportion as Christianity educates men up to a level with its own teachings, they will find the witness in themselves. The deep intuitions of our spiritual nature, once awakened by the Gospel, will shine in their own light, and shine on forever.

Jesus of Nazareth is looked up to, not as the head of a new school in philosophy, not as the founder of a new dynasty, or a new state, but as the Father of a New Age. Modern civilization is built on the great movement which he began; and this civilization would be shaken to its base, would tumble into ruins, were faith in Him to fail. But it never will. We may wonder at the slow progress of things; but it is because they are in the hands of Him with whom "one day is as a thousand years, and a thousand years as one day." We may wonder at the errors and follies, at the divisions and strifes which have prevailed, and still prevail among Christians; but to say that all this struggle between good and evil, between light and darkness, is to end in nothing, would be worse than a belief in atheism; it would be atheism acted out. Everywhere, and over all is heard that voice at which the storms were hushed, and the dead raised: "Upon this rock I will build my Church; and the gates of hell shall not prevail against it." "Heaven and earth shall pass away, but my words shall not pass away."

# THE SCHOLAR AMONG THE APOSTLES.

I AM VERILY A MAN WHICH AM A JEW, BORN IN TARSUS, A CITY IN CILICIA, YET BROUGHT UP IN THIS CITY, AT THE FEET OF GAMALIEL, AND TAUGHT ACCORDING TO THE PERFECT MANNER OF THE LAW OF THE FATHERS.—Acts xxii. 3.

PAUL was the only one among the Apostles who can be said to have enjoyed the advantages of a liberal education, or to have moved before his conversion in the higher walks of life. I propose to consider the influence of this circumstance on his character, teachings, and success.

Let me begin, however, by observing, that I entertain no disparaging views either of the social or intellectual condition of the rest of the Apostles. Though they cannot be said to have been learned, in the sense of being scholars, like Paul, there is no ground for supposing that they were especially rude, ignorant, or even illiterate. They were not taken from the lowest class in society; in that case they would have had too much to learn: nor yet, from the highest class; in that case they would have had too much to unlearn. In common with a large proportion of the first Christian teachers, they were taken from the middle class; where almost all great moral revolutions have begun, as Protestantism in Germany, and Puritanism in England, and where such revolutions, for obvious reasons, must always be expected to begin.

Let me also, before going any further, anticipate a general objection to the very aim of this discourse, which may possibly occur to some minds. It may be thought that in making Paul's conduct in his apostleship to be modified or determined in any way by his previous culture, I forget, or virtually deny, that he was *inspired*. The Apostles may have differed, as other men do, in their natural and acquired tastes and abilities; still it may be thought that these differences could not have affected them as apostles, certainly not in their teachings, inasmuch as they all "spake as they were moved by the Holy Ghost."

In reply to this I hasten to say, that nothing is further from my purpose than to call in question the inspiration of the sacred writers, or to seek to resolve that inspiration into natural causes. I assume that they were divinely appointed, and divinely illuminated, in order to become infallible guides as to what is essential or important to Christianity. But we are not to suppose that inspiration annihilates personality, or differences of personal endowment, even as regards teaching. In fact, we know better. We cannot open the New Testament, at any rate we cannot peruse it with the smallest measure of discrimination, without perceiving that Matthew did not write like John, and that neither Matthew nor John wrote like Paul. From this we do not infer that all of them, or any of them, were uninspired men. We believe them all to have been supernaturally enlightened, and to have thus had before them a true conception of the religion they were to teach. Still in the act of teaching it, we believe, or rather we cannot help seeing, that one insists on one topic and another on another, that one illustrates the same truth in one way and another in another, that one considers it in one connection and another in another, according to the particular purpose he has in view, or his peculiar bent of mind, or his skill, or his want of skill, as a writer.

I return, then, to a consideration of Paul's condition in life and early training, and the influence they appear to have had on his conduct and success.

Though of Hebrew descent, he was born at Tarsus, in Cilicia, — "a citizen of no mean city." Strabo, a contemporary of Paul, says of the inhabitants of this place, who were mostly Greeks, that they "cherish such a passion for philosophy, and all the various branches of polite letters, as greatly to excel Athens and Alexandria, and every other place in which there are schools and academies of philosophy and erudition. But Tarsus differs in this; those who here devote themselves to the study of literature are natives of the country; not many come from foreign parts. Nor do the natives of the country continue here for life, but they go abroad to finish their studies, and when they have perfected themselves, they choose to live in other places: there are but few who return home."* The course pursued by Paul illustrates in a striking manner these statements of the old geographer. The first years of his life were passed in his native city, where he could not fail to profit by the facilities he enjoyed to become acquainted with Greek society, Greek literature and the Greek mind. His condition in life was evidently such as to bring these advantages within his reach; for he says expressly that he was "born" a Roman citizen,—a distinction his family is supposed to have obtained by purchase at an exorbitant price, or else as the reward of important public service: in either case it argues a family of consideration. Moreover, to have coveted such a distinction, the privileges of Roman citizenship, argues a family not shut up within the narrow bounds of Jewish prejudice.

---

\* *Geographica*, Lib. xiv. Cap. X. 13.

However this may be, it is certain that in due time, and before attaining to manhood, Paul followed the practice which Strabo says was so common with the students of Tarsus, he went abroad to complete his education. As "a Hebrew of the Hebrews," as "a Pharisee, the son of a Pharisee," he repaired, of course, to Jerusalem, still the centre of Hebrew tradition and Hebrew learning; where he joined the school of Gamaliel, the most distinguished at that time among the doctors of his nation, and was brought up at his feet, being "taught according to the perfect manner of the law of the fathers." Here, his proficiency and zeal were such as to attract the attention of the leading men at Jerusalem; so much so, that they did not hesitate to intrust him, soon afterwards, young as he yet was, with commissions which they must have known required not a little of resolution and address. Accordingly he says on one occasion: "I profited in the Jews' religion above many mine equals in mine own nation, being more exceedingly zealous of the traditions." And again: "I persecuted this way unto the death, binding and delivering into prisons both men and women; as also the High Priest doth bear me witness, and all the estate of the elders: from whom also I received letters unto the brethren, and went to Damascus, to bring them which were there bound unto Jerusalem, to be punished."

Some have wondered that Paul, after having had his mind enlarged and liberalized by study,—especially under such a teacher as Gamaliel, who appears to have counselled moderation and forbearance in respect to the new religion,—should have become so unwearied and relentless a persecutor of the Church. But they forget two things. In the first place, they forget that a spirit of moderation, is generally much more a matter of temperament, than of instruction or education. Again, they forget that persecution is of two kinds: some persecuting from policy, because their craft is in danger; others from an honest dread of what they believe to be pernicious error,—because they think that religion, morality, order, the best interests of mankind, are in danger. I am aware that, in practice, we seldom meet with either of these two kinds of persecution wholly unmixed with the other; still history affords some examples,—for instance, that of Sir Thomas More,—where the latter kind, which we may call *conscientious persecution*, was comparatively pure. And so with Paul; for he tells us, after his conversion, "I verily thought with myself, that *I ought* to do many things contrary to the name of Jesus of Nazareth." We also have the evidence of his after life to the same effect. The moment he was convinced that the new doctrine was from God, his love of truth showed itself to be stronger than his prejudices, or his party ties, or his worldly ambition; and from being the persecutor of Christianity, he became the most active and successful of its advocates and missionaries. I do not make these distinctions in order to *justify* the conduct of Paul, while a Jew;.he never thought to justify, or even to excuse it, to himself;—but simply to set it in its true light. It did not spring, like most persecution, from an essentially bad principle, but from the perversion of an essentially good principle;—a perversion, moreover, to which a young and ardent scholar, fresh from his studies, and burning with desire to signalize his zeal for what he had been taught, was peculiarly liable.

All are familiar with the miraculous circumstances which attended the conversion of Paul, while on his way to Damascus, and also with the fact, just intimated, that he " was not disobedient to the heavenly vision." And here it is difficult, if not impossible, to avoid the conclusion, that the preparation of Paul up to this time had been by the special ordering of Divine Providence; for an exigency had now arisen, calling for precisely such a man, with precisely such a training. As he was to be the great Apostle to the Gentiles, as he was to form the connecting link between the Jewish and pagan worlds, it was necessary that his education should be such as to make him acquainted with Jewish and pagan habits of life and thought, in order that he might be in a condition to understand and do justice to both.

First of all, we see the fruit of this culture in the *thoughtfulness* and *deliberation* with which he entered on his labors. Had Paul been an ignorant man, or even what is called a self-educated man, he would probably have deemed himself competent at once to the undertaking; as it was, he had the diffidence which belongs to men of large and comprehensive views. Accordingly his first step was to retire into Arabia, where he passed three years in comparative seclusion; being occupied, for the most part, as we may presume, in adjusting his mind to his new experiences and his new conceptions of truth, in maturing his plans and deepening the foundations of his own faith and piety. It was this earnest self-discipline, in conjunction with the cosmopolite character of his previous training, more perhaps than anything else, his miraculous powers excepted, which qualified him so eminently to become an Apostle to the Gentiles. His subsequent conduct testifies to this truth. Among all nations, from the most civilized to the most barbarous, with all people, from the most enlightened to the most ignorant, — among the wandering hordes of Arabia, in the beautiful country of Asia Minor, amidst the bleak and barren mountains of Thrace, with the sceptical and philosophizing Athenians, with the corrupt and effeminate Corinthians, in the Eternal City, in Spain, even among the poor and superstitious islanders of Malta, — there was scarcely a discovered spot on the face of the globe, where we do not find the footprints of this unwearied apostle, *everywhere at home,* everywhere prepared with views and arguments adapted to the habits and capacities of the people he addressed, everywhere preaching "Jesus and the resurrection," and becoming all things to all men, that he might at least save some.

We also see traces of Paul's scholarship, and general refinement of thought and manner, in his teaching; and especially in his *style of address,* where rude, but well-meaning, reformers are so apt to fail. He carefully abstains, as has just been hinted, from giving unnecessary offence. As far as compatible with conscience and his leading objects, he always seeks to accommodate himself to the customs and prejudices of the persons addressed, combining in a remarkable manner the severe independence and uncompromising purpose of a confessor and martyr with the adroitness, and oftentimes with the ease and urbanity, of a man of the world. Witness the exordium of his celebrated defence before Agrippa. "Then Paul stretched forth his hand and answered for himself. I think myself happy, King

Agrippa, because I shall answer for myself this day before thee, touching all the things whereof I am accused of the Jews; especially because I know thee to be expert in all customs and questions which are among the Jews: wherefore I beseech thee to hear me patiently." And, above all, in the noble burst of eloquence at the close of that discourse. "Then Agrippa said unto Paul, 'Almost thou persuadest me to be a Christian.' And Paul said, 'I would to God, that not only thou, but also all that hear me this day, were both almost, and altogether such as I am, *except these bonds.*'" Witness, also, his address to the Athenians. It appears that Paul, as his custom was, had been preaching "Jesus and the Resurrection," and this, by a natural misconception on the part of polytheists, had been construed into an unauthorized "setting forth of strange gods," which the laws forbade under penalty of death. Hence one of his objects was to undeceive them in this respect, and to do it in a manner which should be true in itself, and, at the same time, intelligible from their point of view. Mark how admirably he succeeds. "Then Paul stood in the midst of Areopagus, and said: 'Ye men of Athens, I perceive you altogether much given to religious worship. For as I passed by and beheld your devotions, I found, among others, an altar with this inscription, To the Unknown God. Whom, therefore, without knowing, ye worship, Him declare I unto you.'" I have no wish to exaggerate the literary merits of the sacred writers, or to put what they have done on a level, in this respect, with the great masterpieces of genius and art: nevertheless I do not wonder, that, in a fragment ascribed by some to Longinus, Paul of Tarsus is numbered among the celebrated orators of Greece.

Again, we see the influence of Paul's intellectual training and activity, in *the logical form* which the Christian doctrine took under his hand. The other writers of the New Testament look chiefly to practical wants; Paul alone represents the logical or purely intellectual want of the Church; and he represents it, because he alone, from his previous mental training and habits of thought, was likely to feel it. The other writers of the New Testament were content to give a *religion* to the world; he aspired to give a *theology*, that is, a philosophy of religion, — not only what is to be believed, but the reason why it is to be believed, and its connections with other truths, and especially with what is known of the human and Divine natures. I am aware that some persons are half-inclined to regret, that so early an example was set in the Church of an attempt to make the Gospel assume a logical or scientific form. While we have but one *religion*, they will tell you, that we have a multitude of *theologies;* that these theologies have only had the effect to distract and obstruct the religion; and that the Pauline theology was the first, and led the way to others, or at least to varieties of itself. But all such regrets are vain. A scientific spirit, a passion for comprehending things, and putting all knowledge in harmony with itself, in one word, *logical thinking,* with all its consequences for weal or woe, is a necessity to some minds. Very probably the majority of Christians would be content with the devotional and practical portions of the New Testament. But this to the Augustines and Luthers of all ages is "milk for babes"; they turn to the Epistle to the Romans and the Epistle to the Galatians, as the "strong meat for men." John was "the disciple whom Jesus loved": Paul is known by another distinction, which, in the view of many, is hardly less honorable, — he was *the great thinker* in the Primitive Church. From these personal differences we do not infer that the Gospel according to Paul differed from the Gospel according to John *in substance,* but only *in form;* and it was doubtless best that among those who were authorized to give a form, or, rather, some of its various possible forms, to the Gospel, every type of the human mind and character should find its representative.

We find still further traces of Paul's large and

generous culture in what may be called *the spirit of his teaching*. A large proportion of the intolerance and uncharitableness among Christians originates in narrow views. Enlarge men's minds, and you do not a little towards enlarging their policy, and sometimes even their hearts. Of this we have more than one illustration in the Apostle Paul;— in the readiness with which he gave up his Jewish repugnance to admit the Gentiles into the Church; in the magnificent eulogium on charity in his First Epistle to the Corinthians; and in the candor and liberality which he recommends in the treatment of weak brethren. "Him that is weak in the faith receive ye, but not to doubtful disputations. One man esteemeth one day above another; another esteemeth every day alike. Let every man be fully persuaded in his own mind. *I* know, and am persuaded by the Lord Jesus, that there is nothing unclean *of itself;* but to him that esteemeth anything unclean, *to him* it is unclean. We then that are strong, ought to bear the infirmities of the weak, and not to please ourselves." This, certainly, is the language of one, whom the study of men, as well as of books, has imbued not only with the love of wisdom, but with the wisdom of love. Hence in all the differences which grew up among the first Christians, we find Paul on the liberal side. He knew how endless and profitless were

most of the contentions which divide and estrange
mankind. He knew, too, that neither righteousness
nor piety was confined to one place, or one party,
or one creed. For he had travelled the world
over; he had seen men under every variety of climate and government and religion, and he had
found good men everywhere, and bad men everywhere. He felt, moreover, for his whole race, knowing that he shared with them a common frailty,
and they with him a common hope; that there was
one Father over all, who could not but love all his
children.

One remark more, which may be regarded as the
application of the whole subject. The education
and social position of Paul give new force to *the
argument for the truth of Christianity drawn from
his conversion*. We have dwelt on the education
and social position of Paul, not for the purpose of
proving that he was a good man, or an inspired
man, for they prove neither; but as evidence that
he was raised above many popular errors, and not
likely to be carried away by a mere popular excitement. With the rest of the Apostles it was not
so; much enlargement of mind, or much knowledge
of the world and its ways, was hardly, of course, to
be expected in persons of their condition in life.
Accordingly, had they alone, and such as they, been
wrought upon, it would, no doubt, have been pre-

tended that a little enthusiasm or a little craft was quite sufficient to account for the success of the delusion. But in Paul we have a man not so easily to be deceived and misled,— a man whose mind had been informed and enlarged by liberal studies and foreign travel,— a man who could reason with philosophers, and at whose eloquence kings trembled,— a man of whom Festus said, " Paul, thou art beside thyself; much learning doth make thee mad."

If we ever doubt the historical truth of our religion, I believe it is, generally, because we think that if we had lived at the time, and on the spot, we should have been able to detect some flaw in the evidence. But what right have we to think we could have done this, when we find it was not done by Paul? Have we any more penetration than he had, or more knowledge of the world, or of the weaknesses and perversities of human nature? Are we any more elevated than he was, by birth, education, and standing in society, above the delusions and credulities of the popular mind? Should we have been any more likely than he was to suspect fanaticism or hypocrisy, or to detect pious frauds? To all these questions we must answer, No. Yet this man, living at the time and on the spot, was converted; this man, from being a conscientious and thoroughly instructed Jew, became a Christian; this man, from being an enemy and persecutor of the new faith, became its most active and zealous advocate and missionary; this man, who, to all outward appearance, had everything to lose, and nothing to gain by changing his religion, changed it, nevertheless, on conviction, and lived and died in that conviction.

There is a tradition in the Church, that Paul was beheaded near Rome, and buried about two miles from the city, on the Ostian Road. A magnificent cathedral, dedicated to his memory, was built over his grave by Constantine; but his noblest monument is found in the churches which he planted, and, above all, in his immortal writings which "are read of all men." How instructive is this lesson from history! for it shows that the most enduring fame is to be found in the ways of the highest duty. If Paul had denied or stifled his conscience, if he had thought only of ease and present reputation, he might doubtless have taken his place among the most distinguished rabbis of his nation; but who would have cared for him now? His glory is this, that he devoted his talents and learning and life to the service of truth and the good of mankind, — a glory as imperishable as the objects for which he labored.

# THE ALLEGED INFIDELITY OF GREAT MEN.

HAVE ANY OF THE RULERS, OR OF THE PHARISEES, BELIEVED ON HIM?—John vii. 48.

WE sometimes hear insinuations thrown out against a belief in Christianity, as if it were a weakness, to which men of strong minds, especially if also men of science or men of the world, must by necessity be superior. Let this opinion prevail among the educated and ambitious classes, and there is an end to all hope that they will ever be deeply and seriously affected by the Gospel. They may find it prudent or convenient to pay an outward respect to it, as the religion of the country; they may even do so from a sincere regard to the best interests of the community; but that they should be deeply and seriously affected by it in their own hearts, while entertaining such views, is out of the question.

The friends of religion, from their jealousy of human learning and worldly distinctions, are sometimes betrayed into language tending to the same effect. I am aware that, in the latter case, when infidelity and irreligion are charged upon great men, it is with a view to detract from the great men, and not from the religion of which they have shown themselves unworthy. Still, if the topic is frequently returned to, and dwelt upon, without making the proper discriminations, it will insensibly give rise, at least in most minds, to the prejudice above mentioned. They will begin to suspect that as knowledge advances faith recedes; and, on the strength of this suspicion, their own faith will begin to recede. Ostensibly it may not take the form of an objection to the Gospel, but it will do the work of an objection; or, worse still, it will act as a secret, undefined, half-unconscious misgiving.

For this reason I propose to take up and examine the alleged infidelity and irreligion of great men. How far is this charge well-founded? and as far as well founded, what does it signify?

Reasoning from general considerations alone, it would be easy to show that there is no incompatibility between religion and true greatness.

Thus I might show, in the first place, that the very preparation of mind necessary to make it fully alive to the satisfactions, or even to the evidences of spiritual truth, must also have a tendency to refine, liberalize and enlarge the mind itself. I might show, in the second place, that the leading subjects of contemplation which religion brings into notice, are of such a nature that they cannot fail to communicate something of their own weight and dignity to the mind that is familiar with them. I might show, in the third place, that the feelings and dispositions, the purposes and aspirations, which religion excites and calls forth, are among the noblest properties of the soul, and as far as possible removed from all that is low, or mean, or ordinary. I might show, in the fourth place, that in a multitude of instances the direct influence of religious principle has been to lead men to acts of magnanimity and heroism, which have never been exceeded. And lastly, I might show, that the most illustrious names in history, the brightest ornaments of society and greatest benefactors of mankind, infidels themselves being judges, have been found among those who looked to religion as the source of their highest as well as purest inspirations, and considered themselves as never more truly great, than when in the act of acknowledging God as their infinite and loving Father.

But general reasonings of this kind meet the difficulty under consideration only half way. They prove indeed that there is no incompatibility between true religion and real greatness; and furthermore, that many great men have been humble and devout believers. Still the original charge may stand, to this extent at least, that the proportion of great

3*

men who have been infidels or sceptics, is larger than that of men in ordinary life.

Is it so, however, in point of fact?

Great men are either great actors, or great thinkers; they are seldom both. Now when great men are said to be sceptically inclined, I suppose the great men intended are the great thinkers: first, because they are the only great men who are likely to intermeddle with the difficult and perplexing questions at issue; and secondly, because they are the only great men whose judgment in such matters is of sufficient importance to be referred to.

The charge, then, is against the great thinkers; but, considered as made against them, several reasons may be suggested, which should make us slow to entertain it.

Great thinkers must be presumed to be sometimes in advance of the world in their thinking; else why are they called great thinkers. Merely to be able to defend by a subtle and refined logic a foregone conclusion argues ingenuity, it is true, but not the much higher faculty, that of original thought. Now everybody knows that a considerable departure from the popular faith, though it is merely by being *in advance of it*, is apt to be regarded by the multitude not simply as the giving up of one view of religion, but as the giving up of all religion. Hence the early Christians were denounced by the pagan world as "atheists," and persecuted under that name, and for that crime. So likewise in the case of Socrates, one of the most religious men in all antiquity. Very probably the leading politicians who were active in his condemnation, cared but little about religion in any way; still their success was mainly owing to the fact, that it fell in with the vulgar clamor against him as an over-curious sceptic, and impious innovator. First of all, therefore, I insist that the frequent charge against great men of infidelity and irreligion, when resting on no better foundation than popular clamor, is to be listened to in all cases with extreme distrust.

Consider next the antagonisms of religious systems, and the jealousies of system-makers, or system-holders, as giving rise to the charge in question. A system of philosophy or religion is neither more nor less than an attempt to sum up and reconcile the facts in the case, *as understood at the time*. Of course, as a man's knowledge of these facts is cleared up, or refined, or enlarged, his system must be modified; and sometimes the modification is radical, leading him to view all things from a new stand-point, and under new connections and relations. Whenever this happens, the partisans of the old way of looking at the subject are offended and perplexed; they hardly know what to make of it; and in their impatience are ever ready to charge the new system with being not merely a new exposition of what was believed before, but a real or virtual denial of it. Hence almost every philosopher who has attempted a new solution of the great problem of life, or of the universe, has been stigmatized by his opponents, at least in the beginning, as an atheist.

So it was with Descartes, the great reformer of the science of mind in the seventeenth century. By candid critics he has been thought to have done more for religious truths and realities than any other philosopher, by the clear and sharp line of demarcation he was the first effectually to draw between matter and spirit. And besides, to show how far he was from denying or doubting either the being or the perfections of God, it is enough to say, that one of the peculiarities of his system consists in making every form of human certainty, excepting that of our own existence,—even the certainty of mathematical demonstrations,—to depend on the Divine veracity. All this, however, could not save him from being persecuted and driven out of Holland as an atheist, at the instigation of a knot of Protestant divines.

The same thing was soon afterwards attempted in England against Locke, though by no means with equal success. Locke's whole life, and all his opinions, as far as developed by himself, were a living refutation of such a charge. Moreover, his celebrated "Essay concerning Human Understanding" gives what is there styled "a demonstration" of the being of a God, and lays down the principle that we have more certain evidence of the Divine existence than we have of the existence of the external world. His "Reasonableness of Christianity" is also one of the ablest defences of revelation ever made. All this, however, went for nothing with a party who were alarmed at some of the aspects of his system of philosophy, and the freedom of some of his speculations, and a cry was got up, that he was no better than an atheist or deist "in disguise."

Patience in speaking of such conduct would seem at first sight to be little better than treason to truth and right. And yet, on second thoughts, why all this surprise and indignation at a fault so easily accounted for and explained, and withal, in its various degrees, so common? Have we yet to learn how few there are, even among good men, the habits of whose minds will allow them to be just to the opinions of their opponents?—especially where, as in this case, the matters in dispute are felt to be of great practical moment. The reason of this is also obvious. We see the opinions of our opponents from our own point of view, and not from theirs; and the consequence is, that we, I might almost say, by necessity, misconstrue them. Thus in respect to the misrepresentations complained of above: every man's argument for the being of a God rests on certain principles, which to his mind are essential to the conviction. When, therefore, these principles, or any of them, are assailed, it seems to him as if a blow was struck at the foundations of all religion. He forgets that principles which are necessary to *his* faith, or at least are thought by him to be necessary, are not so to that of his neighbor, who believes in God on totally different principles, and yet believes in Him just as sincerely, and just as devoutly. Let us therefore put the most charitable construction on the *motives* of these traducers; only we must remember that they *are* traducers, which brings us to the same conclusion as before. It would be easy to show, on historical grounds, that a considerable proportion of the great men who have been stigmatized in the polemics of the Church as unbelievers, have done nothing whatever to warrant the reproach.

But there is another class of great men under charge or suspicion of unbelief, who cannot be disposed of so easily. I mean those who have indulged, more or less, in what seem infidel speculations, and are often claimed by infidels as of their number, yet do not themselves accept the name, nay, sometimes indignantly disclaim it. To this class belong several of the uneasy, questioning, and fiery spirits, who were thrown up into activity and consequence by the convulsions growing out of the Revival of Letters and the Protestant Reformation. I am not sure that any of these men deserve to be called great thinkers; but some of them were bold and original thinkers; and in their first attempts to go alone they often lost their way, and wandered into extravagances which can hardly be reconciled either with religion or anything else. For the most part, however, they indignantly repelled the charge of impiety or unbelief. One of the last of them, Vanini, burnt at Toulouse as an atheist, in 1619, on being asked at his trial if he believed in God, picked up a straw from the floor, and holding it out in his hand, said to his judges, " This straw, if there were nothing else, would constrain me to confess a Divine Author of Nature."

A similar remark is applicable to many of the great metaphysical thinkers in Germany, in recent times. It is common to hear these men referred to as the deniers and subverters of religion,— the modern Antichrist. On inquiry, however, it will be found that the professed, and, as far as I can see, the real purpose, of most of these writers was to supplant the shallow naturalism and rationalism already existing in the Church by a more profound and severe philosophy, — a philosophy, also, which would retain Christian ideas by showing that they enter into and make part of the highest thought of the age. Somebody, in defending the new philosophy, had presumed to institute a parallel between Kant's system of morals and that of Jesus. But Kant himself, to whom the manuscript was submitted, hastened to express a religious horror at the sight of his own name in such connection with that of Christ. He begs his friend not to publish the work; or if he should, he charges him to erase the offensive parallel, using these memorable words: "One of those names, that before which the Heavens bow, is sacred, whilst the other is only that of a poor scholar, endeavoring to explain, to the best of his abilities, the teachings of his Master."* Hegel, also, professed to the last his belief in the ordinary faith of the Lutheran Church, and held it to be a principal recommendation of his system, that it supplied a scientific basis for what are called "evangelical doctrines."

Here, then, is another view of the matter, which strengthens my conviction that the reputed number of great men justly chargeable with unbelief vastly exceeds the real number. Even of those who have done something to provoke, and, it may

---

* Stapfer's *Life of Kant*, a translation of which is inserted in the *Biblical Repertory* (1828). Vol. IV. p. 337.

be, to authorize the suspicion by the infidel look or tendency of their speculations, only a few, a very few, have *professedly* taken infidel ground. Professedly they have labored to reform, and in some cases to restate and refound the popular religion, in order to reconcile it with the progress of thought on other subjects, but not to overthrow it.

"What!" the objector will say, "is it not clear, that whoever accepts this or that doctrine, or adopts this or that system, cannot consistently believe in Christianity?" Grant that he cannot *consistently*; I submit that this is not the question. What hinders him from doing it *inconsistently*, — yet really and sincerely? Who does not know that mankind are full of inconsistencies? Certainly, therefore, it would be taking a strange, I had almost said a ludicrous position, to assume that nothing can be true of a man's faith, even in matters the most difficult, abstract, and remote, which involve an inconsistency on his part. In such a case, the real or alleged inconsistency is nothing to one who does not *see* it. To your eyes the faith is self-destructive, because self-contradictory; but to his eyes it is neither the one, nor the other; that is, the difficulty does not exist, at least so far as the reality and sincerity of his faith are concerned.

"But the system, as carried out by the school, has ended, in point of fact, in rank infidelity, perhaps in rank atheism." To this I reply, first, that for "school" in the statement under consideration we must generally, if not always, read "*some* of the school." The system of Locke, in the hands of his French followers, ended in the denial of all religion; but not so with the bulk of his English followers. The same is also true of the system of Hegel, the last and most extreme form of German idealism: while one wing of that school openly spurns the very thought of God, the other still adheres, like its master, not only to Christianity, but also to church orthodoxy. Besides, suppose that the system, when fully carried out, is seen by all to end in materialism, fatalism, pantheism,—I care not what. You have a right to charge the legitimate consequences of a system on *the system itself;* but not on the author of the system, any further than you have reason to believe that he foresaw and accepted them. It is but seldom that all the legitimate consequences of a new principle, or a new system, are foreseen or even suspected at the beginning. When, therefore, a religious man invents or adopts a system, which afterwards develops consequences subversive of religion, it is but fairness to assume, that he was not aware of these consequences, and that if he had been, he would have rejected the consequences, and the system too.

"Yes; but infidels claim these great men as being

on their side." Very likely they do, and for obvious reasons. Sylvain Maréchal, in his "Dictionary of Atheists," comprehends in his list almost every original thinker whom the world has known. In the same spirit, Jeremy Bentham refers, in his correspondence, again and again to private conversations with reputed Christians, including several dignitaries of the Church of England, from which he chose to gather, that not a few of them had as little faith in the popular religion as himself. But what does this prove? There are two ways of accounting for these absurd imputations,—absurd, at least, in the extent to which they have been carried. In the first place, narrow-minded and conceited men,—men who see clearly perhaps as far as they see at all, but want largeness of view,—are apt to think that whoever agrees with them in some things, must agree with them in everything. And, secondly, in the case under consideration, infidels are strongly tempted by the desire, consciously or unconsciously entertained, to make up for the want of numbers and popular sympathy by the prestige of great names.

My conclusion is, that there are no just grounds for the infidel taunt, that great men, on becoming great, outgrow Christianity.

At the same time, we must take care not to fall into the opposite error of making too much of greatness in this connection. The Scriptures, experience, common-sense, concur in protesting against the doctrine that men are always or generally religious or Christian *in proportion* to their abilities or worldly distinction. Remember our Lord's words: "I thank thee, O Father, Lord of heaven and earth, because thou hast hid these things from the wise and prudent, and hast revealed them unto babes." Remember also what was said by an apostle: "For ye see your calling, brethren, how that not many wise men after the flesh, not many mighty, not many noble, are called."

These passages are to be explained, it is true, and limited by reference to the times. At the first promulgation of the Gospel, the great men of the day were committed in a thousand ways, politically and socially, as well as intellectually and religiously, to the established worship. If they knew more than others, it only followed, as a general rule, that they had so much the more to *unlearn* before they were in a condition to receive the new faith. If, as was generally the case, they looked down with contempt or indifference on the faith and rites of their own country, they were not likely to entertain much respect for a new religious movement, of which they understood nothing, except that it was an offshoot from Judaism, and came up from the depths of society. We mistake the matter entirely, if we suppose that the great men of Greece and Rome troubled themselves to make up a serious and well-considered judgment on the merits or evidences of Christianity, at the time and on the spot. They rejected it without examination, just as we should have been likely to do in their place; and this being the case, their rejection of it, no matter what may have been their competency and opportunity in other respects, signifies nothing.

Accordingly, in looking back on the first preaching of the Gospel, we do not deny, we do not wonder, that it was the common people almost alone who heard it "gladly," while the bulk of what are called the higher classes, the really great and the would-be great, stood aloof. Nevertheless, we say, it was not for anything in greatness itself, but because their greatness placed them in circumstances which blinded their eyes to a revelation from heaven.

To a certain extent this remark applies, also, to the great men of succeeding times. Among the adverse circumstances in which they are almost always placed, we may mention, first, the press of worldly avocations, leaving them but little leisure to bestow on religion. It is so particularly with statesmen, professional men, merchants in large business, and men of letters,— even their hours of apparent leisure are filled with care. Strange as it may seem, it is nevertheless true, that men who read the most, often read the least on religious subjects. If a man has but one book in the world, it is commonly the Bible; and if he reads no other book, he is likely to read that so much the more. Accordingly, we must not be surprised if we often meet with men who are great and learned on other subjects, but whose *knowledge* on the subject of religion is exceedingly limited and superficial, — more so than that of many in the humblest walks in life.

Again, there are other circumstances incident to superior rank and learning, but adverse to religion. I may mention first, the pride of standing and intellect engendered by the consciousness of such superiority. Minds thus affected are slow to look with desire or respect upon gifts and graces which God, in his great mercy, has placed within the reach of all. There is also the secret feeling, no matter how unfounded and fallacious, that religion, though necessary perhaps to the bulk of the community, is not so to them, inasmuch as they have substitutes for it in a higher culture, in philosophy, and in a just sense of character and reputation. Then, too, there are the temptations of power, and opportunity, and prosperity. Great men, as well as others, are liable to prejudice, vice, and worldly ambition, " the lust of the flesh, and the lust of the eye, and the pride of life "; and these, like fevers in the strongest constitutions, are often found to produce the worst effects in the most richly endowed minds.

Add to this, that men are often accounted great, and justly so, because they are great in particular things, in single endowments, — for example, in mere intellect, or in mere force of will. Nobody denies that such men effect great changes in the world; yet in the qualities necessary to understand the nature of Christianity, or even to appreciate its evidences, they sometimes fall far below the average of mankind.

Putting all these things together, we can be at no loss to account for the fact, that some really great men reject Christianity, and that many really great men, though admitting its truth and obligation, are unfaithful to it. In no case, however, is it from their greatness in itself considered; on the contrary, true greatness always has favored, and always will favor a religious interpretation of nature and law, of human life and human destiny. If I were asked what is the radical difficulty in religion to most sceptics, I should answer, Because it transcends experience. But this difficulty will have comparatively but little weight with a really great man, because, by his discoveries, inventions, and conjectures, he is continually doing the very same thing. He is prepared for, he is continually expecting, new revelations of truth and reality.

Moreover, the really great man is eminently a man of faith. What made Columbus a great man was not, as it has been justly said, his discovery of a new world, but his sailing away into an unknown and trackless ocean, on the strength of his faith in an idea.

History will confirm everything I have said. I cannot recall a single individual of the very highest order of mind, who has set himself in opposition to religion. The active enemies of religion are mostly made up of men ambitious of greatness, but unable to achieve it. Stung by the failure, they have turned against the dearest instincts and the most sacred traditions of mankind, seeking, and sometimes finding, in this reckless course the vulgar substitute for greatness,—notoriety.

If then you are at any time tempted to abandon your principles and hopes as Christians, consider, I beseech you, before you take a step that may be irretrievable, into what connection and fellowship it will bring your name and fortunes. It will be with men who owe whatever consequence and notoriety they have obtained much less to any superiority of their gifts than to the wantonness in which they have misapplied what gifts they had; with men, who even when they have taken under their protection a good cause, civil liberty, for example, have afterwards almost invariably disgraced and ruined it by lawlessness and excess;—with men who have begun with denying their obligations to God, and commonly ended with making a jest of their obligations to one another;—with men, in fine, who would take from human nature its principal dignity in success, its principal support in trouble, its principal guard in temptation, leaving nothing in their place but the melancholy pride of thinking to be able to see what others cannot,— that we are without a Father, and without hope.

And you who are almost persuaded to become Christians, consider I beseech you, with whom an earnest and humble faith will bring you into communion. It will bring you into communion with the men to whom the world is indebted for almost every advance it has made in true civilization. It will bring you into communion with the men the monuments of whose benevolent enterprise are in every land, diffusing the inestimable blessings of truth and order and liberty. It will bring you into communion with the men who are pledged in a thousand ways to honor, virtue, and philanthropy; and all these pledges redeemed, the communion on earth will become a communion in heaven,—of all those whose names are written in the Book of Life.

# THE INWARD MANIFESTATION OF CHRIST.

JUDAS SAITH UNTO HIM, (NOT ISCARIOT,) LORD, HOW IS IT THAT THOU WILT MANIFEST THYSELF UNTO US, AND NOT UNTO THE WORLD? — John xiv. 22.

THE disciple who put this question to our Lord was still under the influence of that prejudice of his countrymen, which led them to expect that when the Messiah manifested himself, it would be by openly assuming the office of the Restorer of Israel. But this step, whenever he should take it, would have the effect to manifest him to his enemies and to the public, as well as to his immediate followers. What then could he mean, when he spake, as he had just been doing, of manifesting himself unto his disciples, and not unto the world?

No proper conception had as yet been formed, even by the Apostles, of that inward and spiritual manifestation of himself which Christ is continually making to his friends. And even since that time, the fate of this doctrine in the Church has not been much better. In the hands of the mystics, with whom it has always been a favorite topic, it has been made to assume so preternatural, so fantastic, or at best so vague and shadowy a form, as to induce sober-minded and practical men to have as little to do with it as possible. But this is not the way, as it seems to me, in which we should treat any solemn and emphatic inculcation of the New Testament; certainly not when, as in the case before us, it can be vindicated on rational grounds, and set in a clear light, from its conformity to one of those great laws of mind and life which all are concerned to know.

I can best indicate this law by the help of a familiar illustration.

Take two men of strongly marked characters, and of like tastes, dispositions, and pursuits,— two poets, for example, two men of business, or two philanthropists; let there be no occasion of jealousy or rivalship between them, and it is obvious that they will understand and appreciate and believe each other better than they otherwise would, merely because on the great subjects on which they think and feel most deeply, they think and feel in common. The poet will understand, appreciate, and believe the poet; the man of business will understand, appreciate, and believe the man of business; the philanthropist will understand, appreciate, and believe the philanthropist. Again, let the conditions of the supposed case be reversed. Bring together a poet and one who is the reverse of a poet, a business man and a recluse student, or an earnest philanthropist and a heartless egotist and trifler, and what will follow? Not only will they be "unequally yoked" in other respects, but they will find it difficult, if not impossible, to understand, appreciate, or believe each other, because on the great subjects on which they think and feel most deeply, they think and feel diversely. To persons of such different tastes, dispositions, and pursuits, not only the same words, but the same actions and the same things, have a different meaning, that is to say, they will suggest different and sometimes opposite ideas and trains of thought. In common and every-day affairs such men may get along well enough together, because here the distinctive peculiarities of neither party are much brought out; but let them be put into situations in which these peculiarities are brought out strongly, and the life of each will become a marvel, a puzzle, an insolvable mystery to the other.

The fact, I suppose, will be generally admitted, as here stated; and by penetrating a little deeper we shall find an explanation of the fact. Words, *of themselves*, reveal nothing. When we speak of colors or odors, pleasures or pains, it is always on the supposition that those whom we address have experienced these sensations: else we should not expect to be understood. The same is true when we speak of courage, pity, generosity, self-devotion: we presume that those whom we address have had some experience of these affections; otherwise, we should not expect to be understood. And this remark extends also to natural language, — to looks and gestures, — even to actions themselves, when considered as expressing the principles or emotions from which they spring. To those who have had some experience of these principles or emotions, who know what acting from them is, and what it means, these actions will be as *external signs* of the principles or emotions to which they belong: to others they will signify nothing. This is the reason why men who are conscious of acting from none but low and sordid motives, come at length to deny or doubt the existence of higher motives. Again, it is the reason why, in an age of formalism in religion and general profligacy of manners, if a prophet, a martyr, or a radical reformer appears, he is everywhere cried out upon as an impracticable man, a fanatic, and a " dreamer of dreams," — perhaps as insane. It is not *merely*, as some would seem to think, because his rebukes and warnings are offensive and irritating; but because his whole being is a moral enigma; because he cannot make himself to be understood by persons so unlike himself.

This then is the conclusion to which we are brought. *Conduct*, in the largest sense of that word, — conduct considered as including the principles of action, as well as the actions themselves, is properly and fully *intelligible* only in so far as men are educated up to the same level of moral progress. Where all participation stops, all sympathy stops; and where all sympathy stops, all true and living communication, all true and living manifestation, stops.

To all this it may be objected that "humanity is entire in every individual"; — that is to say, every individual has *something* of *every* human quality, enough in degree to prepare him to understand and believe in the existence of that quality in any degree in another person. But, in the first place, I deny that the higher virtues do exist even in a degree in all minds, if by this is understood existence in a state of *actual development*. The *germs* of all human qualities are to be found, I suppose, in every human soul; but it does not follow that all these germs have even so much as *begun* to be unfolded, and until this takes place the individual is not conscious of them; that is, they are to him as if they were not. Admitting, however, for the sake of the argument, that all virtues do exist in all minds, the only difference being a difference of degree, who does not perceive that this difference of degree is alone sufficient to give rise to a want of mutual understanding and sympathy? Of course a man who has actually felt compassion, for example, though in a low degree, must have some idea of what is meant by compassion in general, and even of compassion considered as existing in much higher degrees. Still it is found, in a practical view of the subject, that men are extremely sceptical, if not absolutely incredulous, as to the actual existence of any feeling or moral sentiment in a degree much above that to which they have themselves attained. Hence it is that selfish and narrow-minded men always suspect the disinterested virtues; and hence, too, cold and phlegmatic men are apt to suspect *the sincerity* of enthusiasts, and to look around for by-motives — how unreasonably, I need not say. Enthusiasts have their full share of imperfections, I allow; but it does not require much reflection to perceive that they are among the last people in the world to play a part. The cold and phlegmatic are much more likely to be insincere even in the little to which they pretend. Nevertheless, such is the constitution of the human mind that we find it extremely difficult, in practice, to believe in the actual existence of any feeling or virtue in a degree so much above that in which we possess it as to be beyond our sympathy. We may not choose to pronounce the feeling or virtue, so much above our own, to be a pretence, an imposture, an impossibility; still we shall be very likely to act under a vague impression that, somehow or other, it is in part at least unreal. As was said before, where all participation ends all sympathy ends, and where all sympathy ends all mutual understanding and all proper communication end.

This then would seem to be a universal law. I have taken some pains to set it in as clear a light as I could, on account of its wide and manifold practical applications; but of these the only one to be insisted on here respects the doctrine of the text: Jesus Christ manifesting himself to his friends, and not to the world.

By this manifesting of Christ we understand the manifesting of what is Divine in his doctrine, his person, and his life; causing it to be perceived, comprehended, and felt. But, according to the law just laid down, that we may comprehend and be assured of Divinity anywhere, it is necessary that what is Divine in our own nature should first be awakened and developed, so as to bring us into communication with it. To whom is manifested what is Divine in the outward universe? It does not depend on the perfection of the outward senses; nor yet on the acuteness or comprehensiveness of the pure intellect: for there have been men, all whose perceptive and logical powers were of the highest order, who yet could see nothing in the material world but the play of a mute and dead machinery, obeying the laws of a necessity as mute and dead as itself. And this, I suppose, would always be the tendency of our intellectual faculties if we had no other faculties, — if we were all head and no heart, — if we had not moral and spiritual sensibilities to be touched by the countless traces of a righteous rule, a beneficent purpose, and a Father's care. I might go further still: I might say, that it is only in so far as, in the language of Scripture, we become "*partakers* of the Divine nature" that we can enter into or even approximate, the full significancy of the Divinity of God. Many hold, and, as I believe, on good evidence, that there never was a people so ignorant and degraded as to have no object of worship, — no God at all; but how different that God, beginning with the rude fetich before which the savage mutters his incantations, and attaining at last to the Judge and Father of all whom the enlightened Christian loves, trusts, and adores. And this change is found to keep pace, in every country and in every age, with the progressive development of men's moral and spiritual ideas.

All this will be readily conceded, perhaps, as regards those who are left to depend for their moral and religious knowledge on the light of nature alone; "but not so," some will say, "with us who have the Bible in our hands, clearly manifesting God and Christ *to all*, — alike to the righteous and to the wicked, — to those who think, and to those who do not."

Nothing can well be further from the truth than such a statement. Need I say again that words of themselves reveal nothing; that the only meaning which any words have, or can have, is that which we give to them, and which we must first have in our minds in order to give. We can take up the language of Scripture, I know, and call God "holy," "just," and "good"; but what these words will really signify to our minds must depend on our own ideas of what constitutes holiness, justice, and goodness. Of course our conceptions of the Deity must still vary according to the degree of purity and elevation which, from a true Christian culture, our own moral and spiritual ideas have attained. Who then will pretend, though we do have the same Bible, that what is Divine in the teachings and life of Jesus is manifested alike to all? Take any part of his discourses, — the Beatitudes, for example, — and who does not perceive how much more meaning benevolent and devout men will attach to the words than others do or can? with how much more life, force, and distinctness everything will be apprehended, merely because the reader's mind is thoroughly imbued with the spirit which the passage breathes? Above all, who can enter into, or practically understand, the deep spiritual experiences of Christ, — his inmost springs of action, — the life of his life, — if he is a stranger to like aspirations? Or, take the holy Communion, — who will say that Christ is manifested equally and alike to all persons, whether devout or undevout, in that solemn service? Alas for us! take the best man that lives, and, from want of a like elevation of soul, how inadequately must he be able to sympathize with, or comprehend, in all its extent, that sublime spirit of self-sacrifice which moved the Sinless One to lay down his life for a guilty world!

But here a difficulty presents itself, which we must not pass over without a word of explanation. "We are to be made good by what the Scriptures reveal, and yet it now appears that it is only in proportion as we have become good that we can enter fully and entirely into the meaning and spirit of what is there revealed. Is not this making the effect to come before the cause?" I answer: In most things we must first know, in order to love and practise; but in morals and religion the rule is often reversed, — we must first love and practise in order to know. "What, then, is to induce us to love and practise?" I answer again: By our trials and failures, by meditation and earnest prayer, there is awakened in us a deep sense of moral and spiritual wants, which are feebly represented by the physical cravings of hunger and thirst, — wants which we feel and know the world cannot satisfy; and this leads us to look beyond and above the world. Christianity proffers us, while in this state of mind, the means of the great salvation, which we must accept, in the first instance, walking, for the most part, by faith, and not by sight; for it is not until we have *experienced* their adaptation to the soul, and their harmony with eternal truth, that our trust is changed into assurance, and our hope into fruition and peace. Nor does it end with beginning. Every new moral and spiritual aspiration prepares the way for a new revelation of moral and spiritual truth; and this again elevates us, so to express it, to a higher level of the soul's progress, from which still higher aspirations may commence. Thus it is that Jesus is continually manifesting himself, and manifesting himself more and more unto his friends, and not unto the world.

Behold why it is that Christianity, with the same Bible to define and expound it, is so different a thing in one age from what it is in another, in one country from what it is in another, to one person from what it is to another. Behold also the element of progress in Christianity, linking it indissolubly, by the ties of a mutual dependence, to the progressive civilization of the world, and the progressive education of the human race. Behold, moreover, how much less the highest manifestations of revealed truth depend on the exclusive culture of the sciences of logic and interpretation, than upon the actual progress which a whole people has made in liberty, holiness, and love. After all, there are depths in the divinity of our Saviour's teachings and life, into the full significancy of which we cannot hope to enter, so long as our spiritual vision is dimmed by the mists of earthly prejudice, earthly passions, and earthly care. "What I do," said our Saviour, "thou knowest not now; but thou shalt know hereafter." The revelations of eternity must come in to solve the enigmas of time. "It doth not yet appear what we shall be; but we know that, when Christ shall appear, we shall be like him"; and *because we are like him,* "we shall see him as he is. And every man that hath this hope in him, purifieth himself, even as He is pure."

# THE STUDENT'S SABBATH.

THE SABBATH WAS MADE FOR MAN, AND NOT MAN FOR THE SABBATH. — Mark ii. 27.

WHEN it is said that "the Sabbath was made for man," the meaning is, that it was made for his use and benefit. It does not mean that he has a right to use it, or not; nor yet that it is his in such a sense, that he has a right to put it to whatever use he pleases. It still supposes that the Sabbath has its appropriate and legitimate uses, and that it is the duty of every individual to ascertain what these uses are, and avail himself of them.

They are reducible, as it seems to me, to two: rest from secular labor, and opportunity for moral and religious culture.

Some have thought to add to these a third, namely, the favor and content of the people, secured by giving part of the day at least to social pleasures and recreations. This appears to have been the policy of the Catholic Church from remote ages. It was adopted by the Anglican Church in its early struggles with the Puritans, and did as much, perhaps, as any other one thing to drive to extreme measures that austere and uncompromising sect. At this moment on the continent of Europe this policy is understood to be almost universal among Christians of all denominations.

We have a right to ask, Has it worked well? Certainly not, if we are to find the answer in the results. All agree that in those countries where it has most prevailed there has been a lamentable falling away from the ancient strictness of faith and practice. I know it is common to ascribe this defection, so far as Protestant countries are concerned, to the sceptical or unspiritual writings of critics and philosophers. But whence these writings? Why there more than here? As a general rule it will be found that they have but attended and reflected, step by step in the downward course, the sceptical or unspiritual state of the public mind. The writings have not, to any considerable extent, *caused* the evil; they have only *reflected* it. The cause, as it seems to me, is still to be traced, in no small part, to the neglect or misappropriation of holy time; first, by the higher classes only; at last, by all classes.

Could anything better have been expected? Undoubtedly it is desirable that Sunday should be the happiest day of the seven; but then it should become so by our loving its appropriate and legitimate uses, and not by our turning it to other and inconsistent uses. But what, you may ask, is to be done for those who have no taste, as yet, for religious exercises, and no inclination for self-communion, or moral and spiritual culture?

I answer, that Sunday, and the whole of Sunday, should be devoted to giving them this taste, and this inclination. I do not deny that there are such things as gloom and asceticism; these we are to avoid in our Sabbatical observances, as well as in everything else. But gloom and asceticism do not come from giving too much time to religion; they come from false views of religion.

Besides, I cannot help observing generally, in this connection, that modern sentimentalism has a little too much to say about *happiness* in religion, — happiness as pertaining not only to the mature life of the Christian, but also to the process by which that life is formed. In looking to the promises of Scripture it is apt to overlook the conditions on which these promises are suspended. We are told, it is true, that "*perfect* love casteth out fear"; but the love of most persons, and even of most Christians, is far from being "perfect"; hence that other Scripture, "Work out your own salvation *with fear and trembling.*" We must take things as they are; we must take man as he is. When we consider how much the best of us have to look back upon each week that ought to humble us, and fill us with regret and anxiety, every one must perceive that the duties of Sunday, which consist pre-eminently of self-examination, and the offices of penitence and prayer, cannot, if faithfully performed, dispose men to merry-making of any kind, or be reconciled with it. There is a serious joy which accompanies every well-directed effort for self-improvement; this joy belongs especially to Sunday, and with it we should be content.

Still the question may be pressed, "Is it not better that the irreligious part of the community should be accustomed to connect Sunday with agreeable rather than with disagreeable associations?" Undoubtedly it is; provided only, that the appropriate and legitimate uses of the institution, to themselves or others, are not frustrated or essentially compromised thereby. But remember, our principal objection to the intrusion of worldly cares and recreations into consecrated hours is not, that they take up the time needed for more important objects, though this alone would be insuperable, but that their tendency is to dissipate the mind, and divert it from that profound seriousness, without which the exercises of religion, however punctiliously and sanctimoniously gone through with, degenerate into a form of godliness without the power. Christianity was not given in order to multiply amusements for the irreligious part of the community. God forbid, that we should try, or wish, to make the sinner happy in his sins, or in the neglect or misappropriation of one of the principal means by which he is likely to be reclaimed from his sins.

I return, therefore, to the position taken in the beginning of this discourse. The benefits resulting from the Christian Sabbath are reducible to two, — rest from secular cares, and opportunity for moral and religious culture.

It is common to dwell on these with special reference to the wants of the uneducated and laboring classes, meaning by the laboring classes those who labor with their hands. Here it may not be amiss to reverse the practice, and consider this whole subject with particular reference to the duty and the needs of men who labor with their minds, — the scholar's Sabbath day.

In the first place, it is obvious that students, professional men, and men of letters, from the very nature of their occupations, are peculiarly in danger of neglecting the duties and losing the advantages of a weekly day of rest. The husbandman pursues his calling in the open fields; the mechanic in the noisy workshop; the mercantile classes in the market-place, and the thronged city. *Their* work, therefore, must be suspended. Its continuance would arrest public attention, and neither public opinion nor the laws of the land would allow it to go on, as it would interfere with the proper observance of the day by others. But no such external restraint is felt by the scholar, or the professional man. Neither the law nor public opinion follows him home, to pronounce judgment on what he reads or thinks; and consequently there is nothing but his own sense of propriety to hinder him from reading the same books, and pursuing the same investigations, on Sunday as on other days. Nor is this all. Even his own sense of propriety will be apt to be blinded or misled on this particular question by a vague notion, not unfrequently entertained, that Sunday, as a day of *rest*, was intended for what are called, by way of distinction, the *laboring* classes; and again, that Sunday, as a day for *moral and religious instruction*, was intended chiefly for the *uneducated* classes.

Both these assumptions, I think it will not be difficult to show, are unfounded.

First, as to the benefits of a day of *rest* to those who labor with their minds, and not with their hands. In reply to the objection sometimes made, that it is a loss of so much time, at least as regards men's worldly occupations, it has been proved again and again in respect to bodily labor, that more work is probably done in the course of the year *with* this occasional respite, than would or could be done *without* it. The same is also true of mental toil. None of our faculties or organs appear to be so constituted as to be able to bear a long-continued strain. The brain may be overloaded and overworked as well as the stomach or the limbs; and this overworking depends quite as much — nay, I think I may say, a great deal more — on its being *unremitted*, than on its being intense for a time. Who has never gazed at an object until all clearness and distinctness of vision was lost? Who has never studied a subject day after day without being able to master it; but upon giving his mind a little time for relaxation, and then returning to it again, has been able to master it at once?

I grant that persons raised above the necessity of manual labor belong, as a general rule, to that portion of the community which can best afford to live at ease. On this account it is true perhaps, as a general rule, that they are less likely, than the humbler classes, to overtask themselves, or be overtasked by others; and hence it may be inferred that they do not stand so much in need of an appointed and legalized day of rest. But in estimating the value of an institution like this to a class, it is not enough to know whether many or few will be affected by it *directly*. Only a few may be benefited by it directly; and yet through them the benefits resulting from it indirectly to the whole community may be immense. Let it be that but a small proportion of students and professional or public men stand much in need of the *physical* relief which Sunday brings, or ought to bring, to the overworked mind; still we should remember that, small as this proportion is, it will probably comprise the *élite*, — those from whom the world has most to hope. Though they do not constitute the majority of the class, they probably constitute those who have most influence in the class; — in proportion of numbers not more, perhaps, than one to a hundred, yet in proportion of merit and public promise it may be as a hundred to one. Any institution, therefore, which tends to keep eager and earnest minds of this description from premature death, or from lingering disease which is the death of their prospects and their usefulness, is an incalculable good, not only to them, but to the whole class and the whole community.

Imperfectly as the day is kept, there can be no doubt that it prevents much evil in this way; if it were kept as it ought to be, it would prevent much more. I have no occasion to press any argument beyond what it will easily bear. I am willing to suppose that the early decline, not infrequent in the class of young persons of whom the highest hopes are entertained, is often to be traced to that peculiar sensitiveness of the nervous system, or that peculiar delicacy of organization, which belongs to precocious minds. Still physical differences of this description can only be regarded as predisposing, and not as proximate, causes of disease. Even in such cases, therefore, it is still true, that the proximate cause of disease is almost always over-exertion, — over-exertion for such a constitution; and this over-exertion would certainly be less likely to take place if secular studies and secular thoughts were not allowed to encroach on holy time.

And so in after life. Here, too, the most valuable lives are most in jeopardy, because most likely to be pressed and importuned by important business and public cares. There is good reason to believe that a proper observance of the Lord's day would have saved many such lives from a premature and melancholy close. Mr. Wilberforce, after hearing that Lord Castlereagh had destroyed himself, wrote as follows in his diary: "He was certainly deranged, — the effect probably of continued wear and tear of mind. But the strong impression of my mind is, that it is the effect of the non-observance of Sunday, both as abstracting from politics, from the constant recurrence of the same reflections, and as correcting the false views of worldly things, and bringing them down to their true diminutiveness."

Again, writing to a friend, and referring to a similar catastrophe in the case of another eminent individual, Sir Samuel Romilly, he says: "I am strongly impressed by the recollection of your endeavor to prevail on the lawyers to give up Sunday consultations, in which poor Romilly would not concur. If he had suffered his mind to enjoy such occasional remissions, it is highly probable the strings would never have snapped, as they did, from over-tension." *

Thus much in proof that eager and faithful students, including also all men of large cares and earnest thought, stand in need of Sunday as a day of rest from mental toil. They also stand in need of it as a day of *religious instruction and moral and spiritual culture.*

And, first, as regards *religious instruction.* Because a man knows one thing very well, we are apt to presume that he knows other things; but this by no means follows. For example: because a man is an eminent naturalist, it does not follow that he knows everything, or anything, about ethics or political economy. And it follows less now than at any former period. The sciences have become so multiplied, and each is pursued so far, that an individual, if he wishes to distinguish himself in any department of human inquiry, must give himself to it almost exclusively. The day for universal scholar-

---

\* *Life of William Wilberforce,* Vol. V. pp. 134, 135.

ship is past, never to return. We find no fault with this state of things, for we see that it is an inevitable condition of human progress; but we contend that an exception ought to be made, for obvious reasons, in favor of morality and religion. All, especially in the educated and influential classes, whatever else they know or do not know, should know something about morality and religion. For this, therefore, adequate provision should be made in the arrangements of society; and such provision is made by the institution of the Christian Sabbath; during which the theory certainly is, whatever may be the practice, that all secular and professional cares and studies should be suspended, the thoughts being mainly turned upon those questions which belong to our eternal peace.

Such provision, always needed, even by liberally educated men, is becoming more and more so for another reason, — I mean the change which has taken place in the spirit and aim of education itself. We can go back to the time when almost all the learning in the world was in the Church, and for the Church. Our boasted system of common schools grew mainly out of the Puritan principle, that every individual should be put into a condition to read the Bible for himself. What first led to the founding of this college was the fear that otherwise the succession of learned and faithful ministers would fail. Yet we have lived to see the day when the question is gravely discussed, whether the Bible ought to be read in common schools. Also, in this college, still purporting to be dedicated to Christ and the Church, the Greek New Testament, though for more than a century the only text-book in the language, has dropped at last entirely out of the academical course. I do not mention these changes in order to condemn them. For anything I have to say at present, they may all be for the better, and not for the worse. One thing, however, is plain: in so far as religious instruction is excluded from general and professional education it follows incontestably, that the so-called educated classes are not any more likely than others to be well informed in religious matters.

And do not facts sustain this view? When the conversation turns on questions calling for familiarity with Scripture, or with the grounds and limitations of disputed doctrines, or with the history of the controversy with unbelievers, or with different sects, I do not find that scientific or professional men are any more at home on such topics than intelligent farmers or mechanics. And not only so. When unauthorized and crude novelties are broached under the name of religion, or, which is just as bad, when a temporary reaction takes place in favor of cast-off errors and superstitions, I find that a full proportion of educated men and women, and of the so-called higher classes, are carried away by the folly. Does not this prove that a full proportion of those classes have yet to be "rooted and grounded" in what "be the first principles of the oracles of God"? From all which I think we have a right to conclude, that, regarding Sunday merely as affording opportunity for religious instruction, the great body of what are called the higher and the educated classes stand in need of it, as well as others, and as much as others.

But the benefits resulting from Sunday in respect to Christian knowledge are inconsiderable when compared with the benefits resulting from it in respect to Christian morals and piety, to *Christian nurture*. Those who think to class the observance of the Lord's day under the head of outward forms and ceremonies entirely mistake the nature and purpose of the institution. It is not a form or ceremony of any kind, but an appointed season, a set time, which we are to give, as we best may, to the means of moral and spiritual culture. You might just as well rank under the head of outward forms and ceremonies the four years spent at college, or the three years spent in the study of a profession. The education of the heart is just as much education, as the education of the head; and for the former at least, all, I suppose, will agree that frequent opportunities are as indispensable to the learned as to the unlearned. There is some connection, it must be confessed, between strength and activity of intellect on other subjects, and strength and activity of intellect on the subject of religion; but there is no necessary connection whatever between either, and that devotion of heart and life which God requires. A giant intellect is no more the substance or the sign of moral superiority than a giant frame. On the contrary, the very consciousness of great mental power, co-operating with the pride and selfishness of man's heart, is of the nature of a temptation, and on this account needs especially to be kept under by the frequent discipline of self-examination and prayer.

To such as object to keeping particular days holy, on the ground that every day should be kept holy, there are two answers: one assuming that the objection is made in good faith; the other, that it is a mere pretext.

I have no doubt that the *early* Quakers were perfectly sincere in what they said on this subject; but then it should be remembered that they *did* keep every day holy. Whoever takes up with their doctrine respecting the Sabbath, ought, at least, in order to be consistent, to take up with their practice on other days, abstaining from all worldly amusements, and also from all worldly occupations of a questionable character or tendency. Even then, however, we should not be satisfied. Not that we would not have every day kept holy; but this is our position. We would have Sunday kept holy in *one* way, that is, by giving it to public and private worship, and to serious reading and meditation, and the rest of the week kept holy in *another* way, that is, by giving it to the faithful and earnest discharge of duty in the business of society and the world. Nay, more; we are persuaded that, unless one day in the week is kept holy in the way first mentioned, the other days are not likely, in the end, to be kept holy in *any* way. And for proof of this I would refer to the history of Quakerism itself. Spiritually-minded men who are tempted to think lightly of consecrated times and places, and outward ordinances, would do well to consider that those sects which maintain these fixtures and bulwarks of the religious sentiment stand as strong as ever, while those, on the contrary, which began by abandoning them have either faded away, or, to prevent this, have been constrained essentially to modify their original plan.

As for those who talk about one day being as good as another, without taking care to make any day what it ought to be, I suppose we have a right to regard the whole as mere pretext, resorted to as an excuse for religious indifference. In arguing with such persons, it would, perhaps, be out of place to appeal to the highest principles of human action, for they do not recognize these principles. But as some who take this ground are not unwilling to acknowledge the moral and social benefits of Christianity, it may not be without avail to urge that all these are put in peril by the neglect of the Lord's day. It is a significant fact, that, in speaking of our frontier settlements, travellers agree in this, that, whenever they have found themselves beyond the reach of the Sabbath, they have also found themselves beyond the reach of Christian civilization. Even in the most favored regions, the best men deplore their inability to keep the day as they would. And what is the reason? It is because the six days given to the world are more than a match for the one day given to heaven. If it were not for this one day given to heaven, the world would swallow up every thought, every care.

My friends, as a general rule we are not wont to trifle with our important *temporal* interests: let us not trifle with our moral and religious interests, merely because they are *eternal*. "Remember the Sabbath day, to keep it holy." As educated men, we need it; — we need it for our own good, for our own safety. We owe it also to others; for it is only in this way that the genius and learning of the country are likely to be elevated and purified by the Christian spirit. And what the Scriptures affirm of the individual is pre-eminently true of the community: "if the light that is in thee be darkness, how great is that darkness."

Think not, because I have said that something is to be *done* on the Christian Sabbath, that I would compromise its benefits as a day of rest. To the mind change is rest. And, besides, if the day is spent as it ought to be, it will lead us to take another view of the entire work of life, — dignifying it by a higher significance given to its responsibilities, and making the whole a service of freedom and satisfaction, because of choice and love.

# PRAYER.

IF YE THEN, BEING EVIL, KNOW HOW TO GIVE GOOD GIFTS UNTO YOUR CHILDREN, HOW MUCH MORE SHALL YOUR FATHER WHICH IS IN HEAVEN GIVE GOOD THINGS TO THEM THAT ASK HIM? — Matthew vii. 11.

SUPPLICATION, or prayer, is the natural language of weakness, dependence, and fear. When in trouble and perplexity, when the danger is pressing, and we from any cause feel unequal to the exigency, it is as natural for us to cry out for help, as to groan when in pain, or weep at scenes of distress. If any one is near who can save us, who is thought to hold our fate in his hands, or is looked up to as greatly our superior in wisdom or station, our cries are spontaneously directed to him. Thus it is that the child often turns to his parents, the sick man to his physician, the slave to his master, the subject to his prince, in the language and look, as well as in the spirit, of prayer. In the appropriate circumstances it is as natural for us to pray as to speak. When there is occasion for it, our language takes the form of petition or entreaty as readily and naturally, as it takes that of question or command when there is occasion for that. Prayer is the fit, natural, and spontaneous utterance of those who need help, when in the presence, or in the supposed presence, of those who can render it if they will. A sense of propriety, self-respect, pride, reserve, and a multitude of other causes, may induce a man to keep silence at such times; but it can only be by restraining one of the most distinctly pronounced tendencies of human nature.

Thus far I have spoken of prayer *in general*, — of prayer as it might exist, and would exist, if there were no such thing as religion.

Passing now to prayer *in religion*, the first remark which occurs to me is, that it differs not from prayer as above described in occasion or form, nor essentially in its nature or spirit, but only in its object. Prayer in religion is addressed to an Invisible Being. It supposes a communication between the visible and the invisible worlds. It takes for granted two facts: first, that a being, or perhaps that many beings exist of a higher order than ourselves; and, secondly, that he or they can be moved by our supplications. Deny these facts and you deny religion, and, of course, all foundation for prayer in religion. Admit these facts, and prayer, as a *religious* act, becomes as natural and spontaneous as it is for the hungry to ask for bread, or for the drowning to cry out for help.

We may therefore say of prayer in religion what was just said of prayer in general. It is the fit, natural, and spontaneous utterance of those who need help, when in the presence, or in the supposed presence, of One who can help them if He will. Under these circumstances, to pray is as natural as to breathe. Under these circumstances, to restrain prayer is not to follow our nature, but to do violence to it; so that all occasion for argument is with those who neglect or withhold prayer. In other words, the question with us should not be, Why pray? but, Why *not* pray?

But if prayer is so natural and spontaneous an act, it would seem to follow that it must be *universal*. And is it not so in fact? One of the best informed of the pagans has said: "Survey the face of the globe. You may find whole tribes and nations without fortified places, without letters, without a regular magistracy or fixed habitations, without property or the use of money; but never one without a God, without altars, without prayers." * Neither was this a mere state contrivance for state purposes, — the craft by which a few would subdue and control the many. We have the testimony of several of the early Christian fathers to the general prevalence throughout the pagan world of a disposition among the common people to appeal when in trouble

---

\* Plutarchus: *Moralia. Adversus Colotem*, Cap. XXXI.

or alarm to a higher Power. It is also remarkable that in the deepest emotions of their minds they never directed their invocations to their false gods, but employed such expressions as these: "As truly as God lives!" or, "God help me!" Moreover, at such times they did not turn their eyes to the Capitol, but lifted them to Heaven.\*

And how is it at the present day? Far am I from supposing that piety, considered as a predominant or abiding trait of character, the piety required by the New Testament, is universal or general. But where will you find a man who *never* prays! You may find men without morality, without natural affection, without any proper or steady faith; you may find plenty of doubters and deniers, scoffers and blasphemers; but where will you find one who never prayed! Throughout the wide world, where will you find one whom the consciousness of peril, anguish, impotence, or sin never betrayed into some such ejaculation as this: "God help me!" or "God have mercy on me!" Yet all these are of the nature of prayer. I do not think I should be very extravagant were I to assert, that it is as impossible to find a man who never prayed, as to find one who never shed a tear.

---

\* Cudworth's *Intellectual System* (Harrison's Ed.), Vol. II. pp. 157 *et seq.*

Still some may think that such prayers, however natural and common, are worthless, are not proper prayers, as they do not spring from gratitude, but from a sense of our needs and our helplessness. But why this objection? What better or more suitable spirit is there, from which prayer, as prayer, can proceed, than from this very consciousness of our needs and our helplessness. Here indeed breaks upon us, as it seems to me, one of the most important views to be taken of those trials and afflictions which bring man's insufficiency to light. They make us *feel*, what is true whether we feel it or no, that we are nothing without God, and so *lead* us to God as our only refuge and stay. Other wise purposes are answered, I doubt not, through our exposure to trouble and calamity; yet none of these are of so direct and high benefit as the one we are now considering, impressing on the human mind, as it does, a sense of entire dependence on God, and making prayer to be the natural and only resort.

What man is there whose own experience does not come in aid of this doctrine? Those especially who have felt the crushing weight of a great sorrow, will they not testify that they found no peace until they gave over struggling with Providence, until they gave over struggling altogether; until they yielded themselves unreservedly to the Divine disposal, something whispering that it was to bring about this happy state of mind that the sorrow was sent? There are prayers, as every one knows, which are *not* prayers; but this can hardly be said of the earnest cry which is wrung from men in their extremity, when every other hope has fled, and they cast themselves wholly on God. I cannot help thinking that many a solemn-sounding litany has been chanted by priestly lips in consecrated places, to waste itself on the air, while the whole ear of heaven was intent on some poor sailor's "God help me!" as it went up amidst the howlings of the tempest from the parting wreck.

Again, it may be objected that these natural, spontaneous, and often ejaculatory appeals to God, when we are in difficulty or trouble, amount to nothing as they are not founded in reason, but in some illusion of the imagination. "Forgetting," such objectors will say, " the essential distinction between the Divine and human modes of acting, we call upon God, as we should call on a man if he were near, and expect the Divine interference as we should expect that of a friend, of a father, if he were standing by." And why not? Either you must say that God is not our friend and father, which is to deny the truth of religion; or that, though our friend and father, he will not *act* as if he were, which is to make it of no importance to us whether religion is true or not. Why are we glad to be assured that God is our friend and father? Simply and solely because we thence infer that he will *be* a friend and father to us; that is to say, do for us what a friend and father would in like circumstances. Undoubtedly we should guard against the not uncommon error of pushing too far the analogy between the human and Divine modes of conduct. For example, we must not expect from God many things which we might expect from the *folly* or *weakness* of a friend or father; but certainly we may expect from God what we should expect from the *wisdom* and *goodness* of a friend and father. If these titles when applied to God do not mean this, I would fain ask what they do mean. Is it not plain, not only that they mean this, but that they can mean nothing else? God is not our friend in the same way in which a man is our friend, that is, by mutual sympathy and reciprocity of favors; neither is he our father in the literal sense of that word. The terms are not intended to denote a physical, but a moral relationship. That is to say, we call God our friend and father, because, and only because we suppose he will do for us what the wisdom and goodness of a friend and father would do for us in like circumstances. Calling God our friend and father means this, or it means nothing; it means this, or it does not afford us the shadow of ground either of comfort or trust.

Accordingly, the Scriptures, both the Old Testament and the New, abound in instances in which the paternal character of God is expressly set forth as a reason for expecting his help in time of need, and especially in answer to prayer. "Like as a father pitieth his children, so the Lord pitieth them that fear him; for he knoweth our frame; he remembereth that we are dust." "Can a woman forget her sucking child, that she should not have compassion on the son of her womb? Yea, they may forget; yet will I not forget thee." The parable of the Prodigal Son is also a beautiful and most impressive illustration of what may be expected from the paternal relationship of God, showing that no degree of ingratitude and sin will shut his ear against our prayers, should we ever afterwards turn to him with an humble and contrite heart. And so our text: "What man is there of you, whom if his son ask bread, will he give him a stone? or if he ask a fish, will he give him a serpent? If ye then, being evil, know how to give good gifts to your children, *how much more* shall your Father which is in heaven give good things to them that ask him?"

The first practical lesson to be gathered from what has been said is, that we should *cherish* this natural and spontaneous disposition to look upon our Heavenly Father as always near, watching over our conduct, and ready with all needed succors. A man is not religious because he believes in the existence of God, but because he recognizes and feels His continual presence and agency. The Epicureans did not deny the existence of the gods; but they denied the fact of a Providence; they denied that the gods had any care or pity for mortals, and so subverted the foundations of all religion in the soul. Not much less fatal to worship and a devout habit of mind is a doctrine held by some at the present day; namely, that God made the world, and then abandoned it to the action and control of physical laws, retiring himself from all supervision and interference in human affairs. The ground and life of prayer depend on our believing, not merely that there *was* a God once, the Creator of the world, but that there is one *now* and *here;*— a living and personal God, witnessing everything which we do, and hearing everything which we say.

Men, I repeat it, are not religious in proportion to the strength, the clearness, or the soundness of their faith, but in proportion to the hold which this faith, whatever it may be, has gained over their feelings and imagination. A serious and spiritually minded man, though of but little faith, is often more religious than one who never knew what it was to doubt, the difference in conviction being more than made up by the difference in feeling and imagination. I do not mean that we should look to the feelings and imagination as sources of truth. To find out what is true, we should use our reason; but having found it out, if we would give *effect* to it, we must call in the aid of the feelings and the imagination, by which alone what is true to the understanding is converted into a present reality to the heart and the life. Reason may assure us of the *existence* of "Him who is invisible;" but this is not enough. This conclusion may be accepted by the intellect alone, in which case we shall hold it without being affected by it. In order to be affected by it, and to become personally what it requires, we must live, we must act, we must enjoy, we must endure, "as *seeing* Him who is invisible," which cannot be done without the help of the feelings and the imagination.

Let me add, that this is hardly more necessary to religion than to a high and strict virtue. A great deal too much has been said about the self-sufficiency and the all-sufficiency of virtue. Virtue *with* religion makes a man contented and happy, I allow; but virtue *without* religion only makes a man more painfully alive to the unequal distributions of this world, and the hopelessness of oppressed innocence. Besides, what security have we for the thoroughness and endurance of such virtue without religion? Little does the world know about the thoughts of those who are accounted upright, and who generally are so; little does it know what they do, or are tempted to do, when withdrawn from the public gaze; little does it know what the best of them would be tempted to think and do, if they could divest themselves of the secret impression that the eye of the Invisible Witness is upon them at all times.

Another practical lesson to be gathered from what has been said is, that we should not only look upon our Heavenly Father as always near, but accustom ourselves to make known our requests to him, asking that we may receive, and thus cultivating a direct and habitual intercourse with him. I am not ignorant of the speculative difficulties respecting prayer, by which some minds are troubled; but it is a mistake to suppose that these difficulties are generally at the bottom of their neglect of prayer. What hinders a vast majority of such men from praying is the want of a devout habit of mind. With their present dispositions, nine out of ten would not pray, habitually and from the heart, even if these difficulties were removed; and nine out of ten, if they could be induced to cultivate a devout habit of mind, would soon begin to pray notwithstanding these difficulties. The worst that can be said of these difficulties is, that they supply the unspiritually disposed with an excuse or pretext for not so much as trying or caring to *cultivate* a devout habit of mind.

To this some may reply: We have no objection to a devout habit of mind; but we think this can be cultivated and evinced by acknowledging God in all his ways, by submitting to every affliction as appointed in mercy, by referring every blessing to his gift, — in short, by religious thoughtfulness and meditation, quite as well as by selfish importunities under the name of prayer. If I find difficulty in dealing with those who make this objection, it is because I find difficulty in believing it to be made in good faith. Is it true, do you think, that those who take this ground against prayer are among those who are most addicted to religious thoughtfulness and meditation? Nor is this all. I can hardly conceive it to be possible that a devout man should become familiar with the thought of God as a loving Father, and accustom himself to recognize his constant presence and agency, without being often irresistibly impelled, by a sense of insufficiency or sin, to cry out for help or pardon. As it has been justly said: "To repeat desires in our minds, being at the same time sensible that the Supreme Disposer of our lot stands by and observes them, without ever directing them to Him, or looking to

Him for the accomplishment of them, — this implies a neglect of the Giver of all good, so repugnant to the sentiments of the human heart, and so criminal, as to be absolutely incompatible with right dispositions."* To ask whether a man can be religious without prayer, is like asking whether a man can be sociable without the use of speech. It is bringing together incongruous, irreconcilable ideas. Besides, for other reasons, I do not admit that any form of religious thoughtfulness or meditation is as likely to bring about a devout habit of mind, as prayer. The very posture which the soul assumes in prayer opens it and predisposes it to the reception of Divine influences. In private prayer especially, supposing it real and not mere form or routine, when the soul is alone with its Maker,— this is felt to be no time nor place for dissembling, or vain parade, or side purposes. Conscious that the eye of the Omniscient is upon him, and that no record is made of what he is doing but that which will be sealed up until the judgment of the great day,—if man is ever sincere and in earnest, if he is ever touched by a sense of his relationship to the Divinity, if his heart is ever warmed and melted by the spirit of humble and childlike trust, it must be then.

---

\* Price's *Four Dissertations*, Fifth Edition, p. 282.

There is one more practical lesson to be gathered from what has been said. We are not only to cultivate the spirit and the habit of prayer, but we are to do it from belief *in the direct efficacy of prayer.* I have just alluded to the difficulties on this subject which exist in some minds. Time would fail me to speak of them in detail, but they are mainly resolvable into this: that God will do for us what is fit and best, whether we ask him or not. True; but is it not plain that it may be fit and best for us to receive many things in answer to humble and devout prayer, which it would not be fit and best for us to receive on any other condition? Besides, these are difficulties to trouble a deist; and we are not deists. They ought not to trouble a Christian. The worst that can be said is, that, with our very inadequate conceptions of the Divine nature and government, reason cannot *see* how prayer can alter the course of events. Still the believer knows that the fact is revealed, and insisted on as much perhaps as any other in the New Testament; and under these circumstances the misgivings of his bewildered and baffled understanding are overruled by the sublime principle of faith. Moreover, these doubts about the efficacy of prayer do not originate in the best parts of our nature; neither do they manifest themselves in the best moods of the soul; they are born of our selfish and worldly experiences, and that almost exclusive culture of the understanding which leads to unspiritual views of nature and God.

Most persons find no difficulty in believing that prayer exerts a happy and desirable influence on the worshipper himself; but even this can hardly be, if it is generally understood that this is *all*. Indeed, I cannot help thinking that conscience itself would dissuade many from resorting to prayer, if brought to look on it as no better than a kind of well-meant cheat which we practise on ourselves for its moral uses. Prayer, to have much effect on ourselves, must be believed to have an effect on God. It is too solemn a transaction by far to be made use of as a kind of spiritual strategy. No; make not our prayers to seem one thing and be another. Strike not our devotions dead by the sceptical sophism that they can only have an effect *on ourselves*. They will have an effect *on God;* for he has said that they will, and the promise has been ratified and confirmed in the experience of holy and devout men in all ages. They will have an effect on God, for He who is " in the bosom of the Father" has said that they will. "Ask, and it shall be given you; seek, and ye shall find." Again it is said: "Let us come boldly unto the throne of grace, that we may obtain mercy, and find grace to help in time of need." And more affectingly still in the words of the text: "If ye then, being evil, know how to give good gifts unto your children, how much more shall your Father which is in heaven give good things to them that ask him." Wherefore, "Be careful for nothing; but in everything by prayer and supplication, with thanksgiving, let your requests be made known unto God: and the peace of God, which passeth all understanding, shall keep your hearts and minds through Jesus Christ."

# RELIGION AS AFFECTED BY THE PROGRESS OF THE PHYSICAL SCIENCES.

AND THERE SHALL BE SIGNS IN THE SUN, AND IN THE MOON, AND IN THE STARS; AND UPON THE EARTH DISTRESS OF NATIONS AND PERPLEXITY; THE SEA AND THE WAVES ROARING; MEN'S HEARTS FAILING THEM FOR FEAR, AND FOR LOOKING AFTER THOSE THINGS WHICH ARE COMING ON THE EARTH; FOR THE POWERS OF HEAVEN SHALL BE SHAKEN.—Luke xxi. 25, 26.

IN the language of Scripture the overthrow and destruction of nations are represented under images borrowed from unusual and terrific appearances in nature. We need not suppose that the Prophets, in resorting to such expressions, really meant that the physical phenomena here referred to would attend or usher in the events foretold. The expressions were not intended as descriptive and historical, but merely as suggestive and emblematic of the impending calamity.

But in the early popular superstitions of every country a mysterious connection is supposed really to exist between remarkable appearances in nature, especially when in the heavens, and remarkable changes in the affairs of men. On this fanciful idea arose that mighty superstructure of omens and portents and prodigies which plays so important a part in the religions of the ancient world. A day of unusual darkness, the shooting of meteors noticeable either for their number or magnitude, a singular conjunction of the planets, the appearance of a comet, or an eclipse of the sun, was sure to be attended by "distress of nations and perplexity," "men's hearts failing them for fear, and for looking after those things which were coming on the earth."

If the question should be asked, Why are not the multitude affected in the same way now? — the answer is on everybody's tongue. It is because the wonders of science have gradually and imperceptibly expelled the marvels of superstition. Who now believes in the pompous trifling of astrology? Who now thinks to read in the heavens the fate of nations, or of individuals? No doubt the sudden apparition of a comet, an earthquake, a total eclipse of the sun, or any other unusual and startling occurrence, will still arrest attention, and fill men with awe; but they are no longer looked upon as prodigies, as omens or portents, or as being in any sense preternatural. On the contrary, they are known to be resolvable into the operation of the same system of physical laws according to which the fire burns and rivers flow, the flowers expand and an apple falls to the ground.

Here, however, several questions arise, by which thoughtful and serious minds have been troubled not a little. Granting that the progress of science tends to lessen the number of popular illusions and mistakes, is there no reason to fear that it also tends to lessen the number of popular interests and securities? The intellect will doubtless be a gainer by it; but is there no danger that the imagination and the sentiments will suffer? Superstition will be rooted up; is there no ground for the apprehension that religion itself is also gradually losing its hold on the public mind, and from the same cause?

The writings of men who are distrustful of the times abound in doubts and misgivings of this kind, — so much the more mischievous because barely hinted at. To be forever asking sceptical questions as to the drift of human thought, and to stop there, can answer no good purpose. Let us, therefore, take up some of these inquiries, and pursue them as far as the narrow limits of a single discourse will permit.

In the first place, is it true that the progress of science threatens to leave us with nothing *to wonder at?* There are those who seem to think that, in proportion as the processes of nature are explained, that is, referred to established and known laws, so that they can be foreseen and predicted, everything must become tame and commonplace;—no objects to call forth some of the finest and noblest properties of our nature; no play of the imagination: man will look down on everything; he will look up to nothing. But it is because these alarmists make wonder to be of one kind only, when in fact it is of two kinds. There is a stolid wonder and an intelligent wonder; the wonder of bewilderment, and the wonder of admiration; wonder at what we do not understand, and wonder at what we do understand, and see to be so true and simple and perfect. Undoubtedly a savage will stand aghast at appearances in the heavens, which, if he were better instructed, would not affect him at all, or affect him in a very different way. But this is not the sole, or the highest form of wonder. What is most likely to fill a thinking mind with astonishment and awe, is not the disorder, but the order, of the universe; not the occasional convulsions of the elements, but the fact that a few simple laws reign throughout all this apparent diversity and confusion, and give unity and stability to the whole.

Still many will insist that a scientific view of nature is not a religious view of nature. And this is true; but only in the sense in which it is also true, that a scientific view of the Bible is not a religious view of the Bible. A scientific view of nature is not a religious view of nature, any more than it is a poetical view of nature; but this does not assume or imply that it stands in the way of either. A *religious* view of nature supposes two things; first, a heart alive to religious impressions, and, secondly, an eye to see in the visible universe the presence and activity of " Him who is invisible." And these, of course, do not originate in a science of nature, nor in a science of anything, but in our moral constitution, in religious culture, and the grace of God.

Let us try to make the proper and necessary discriminations on this subject. The whole discussion about the bearing of scientific study on religious character has been needlessly embarrassed and perplexed by the false issues which have been raised and argued. No enlightened advocate of education will pretend that the physical sciences, or that any science, even the science of theology, will make a man truly religious. Scientific men, to become truly religious, must become so in the same way in which other men do;—that is, by availing themselves of the means necessary to induce a devout habit of mind.

The point in dispute is therefore narrowed down to this: are scientific men less likely than others to resort to these means? or do they resort to them under less favorable circumstances? In other words, to be still more explicit and direct, the whole inquiry resolves itself into two questions. In the first place, is there anything in a scientific study of nature to hinder a man from *becoming* religious in the usual way? And, in the second place, supposing him *to be* religious, is there anything in a scientific view of nature to hinder him from taking, at the same time, a religious view of nature?

Before taking up the first of these questions, let us glance, for a moment, at the facts in the case. From the language often used on this subject one might presume, that nearly all the scepticism in the world can be directly traced to the progress of physical science. But it is not so. The great irreligious movements, so far as they have originated in study of any kind, have originated, for the most part, in the study, not of physics, but of metaphysics. So it was with the Greek sophists. So it was with English deism in the seventeenth and eighteenth centuries. And so pre-eminently with German pantheism, which is the offspring, not of German physics, but of German metaphysics. Even the materialism, so common among the French physicists of the last generation, was not the consequence of studying nature in itself considered, but of studying nature in the faith, and under the lead of a materialistic philosophy, that is to say, of a bad metaphysics. Moreover the religious character of a multitude of scientific men has never been questioned. Such names as Kepler and Newton, Boyle, Pascal, and Leibnitz, and a host of others like them, ought at least to save the physical sciences from being singled out for the reproach of necessarily tending to infidelity. And how is it in England and this country, at the present day?

Of course it would be absurd to say, that every student of nature is a religious man. But what evidence is there that the class itself has not, at this moment, its full proportion of such men, if compared with any other class as exclusively devoted to purely intellectual pursuits? We must not presume that a scientific man lives and dies without any regard for religion, merely because he does not see fit to introduce it into his scientific publications, or thinks, perhaps, with Bacon, that final causes have nothing to do with physics. Few names eminent in modern science are so frequently claimed on the side of infidelity as that of Laplace: it is instructive, therefore, to learn what his final sentiments on this subject were, from the following record of a conversation, which an English scholar of note had with him not long before his death. "Among other subjects he inquired into the nature of our endowments, and our course of academic study;

which I explained to him at some length. He then dwelt earnestly on the religious character of our endowments, and added, as nearly as I can translate his words, 'I think this right; and on this point I should deprecate any great organic changes in your system; for I have lived long enough to know, what I did not at one time believe, that no society can be upheld in happiness and honor without the sentiments of religion.'"*

Let us now return to the question, Is there anything in the scientific study of nature to hinder a man from becoming religious, in the only way in which any man can expect to become so?

Nobody understands, I suppose, that the scientific study of nature, alone considered, will *make* a man religious, any more than the scientific study of language or of law. Religion, I repeat it, is not the fruit of a scientific study of anything;—not even of theology or the Bible. For this reason we are to be neither surprised nor troubled on finding that there have been eminent theologians and Biblical critics, who were not religious men. Why *should* they have been so for that reason alone? that is to say, merely for knowing how a passage in the Greek Testament is to be read, or how religious systems are to be framed and defended?—in one word,

---

* Sedgwick's *Discourse on the Studies of the University of Cambridge*, Fifth Edition, p. 129.

merely because they are good linguists or good
logicians? Because a man is a good linguist or a
good logician, it does not follow that he is a good
Christian. Those who are fond of insisting, and
with truth, that religion is not a distinct and foreign substance, to be patched on the character,
must remember, nevertheless, that it is a distinct
development of character; that it may be, or may
not be, developed with the rest of the character;
and furthermore, that its development calls for distinct and appropriate means.

What is *to be religious?* I do not now ask,
how a man *begins* to be religious? for this would
bring up a multitude of unsettled questions. But
what I ask is simply this, let a man begin to be
religious as he may, when can he be said to have
become religious, in the sense of having a religious
character? I answer: when he shows himself to
possess a devout habit of mind, and not before.
How then, I ask again, is a devout habit of mind
to be acquired and maintained? Obviously, so far
at least as it depends on human means, in the
same way in which all other habits are acquired
and maintained; that is, by a repetition of the
thoughts, the feelings, the actions, which go to make
up the habit. Hence the institution of stated times
and modes of worship, the main purpose of which
is to keep up in men of every walk in life a relig-

ious consciousness, that is to say, an habitual sense of the presence and agency of God everywhere and in everything. As means to the same end, we may also mention faithfulness to the duty of secret prayer, the reading of devotional books full of the inspiration of a religious genius, and especially, of the Bible,—not as a critic, but for its practical and devotional uses; and last, though not least, the society of religious men, and well-written lives of the religious men of other countries and other times, considered as the means of quickening and enlarging our religious sympathies. Common sense, as well as the Scriptures, teach us that it is only in some such way that a religious habit of mind can be generated and upheld,—I do not say, in this, or that condition of life, but in *any* condition of life: in the scholar, the artisan, the day-laborer; in the man of business, and in the professional man; in the artist, and in the man of science. To expect it to be generated and upheld in any other way, is to expect an effect without the cause, a state of mind without the antecedents, the preparation on which it depends.

Now I insist that the principal, if not the sole danger religion has to apprehend from the physical sciences, even in those most devoted to them, is to be found, not in the sciences as such, but in the fact that they are apt to take up and engross the whole mind. A man may become a mathematician or a naturalist, and nothing else, just as he may become a lawyer, or a merchant, or a mechanic, and nothing else, — that is, to the forgetfulness, or at least to the serious neglect, of other cares and duties, and especially of his own social and moral and religious culture. But it would be neither reasonable nor fair, in such cases, to ascribe the evil to the *nature* of the pursuits; — it comes from exclusive devotion to them, and comes whatever may be the pursuit.

There is nothing, then, in the scientific study of nature to hinder men from resorting to the usual and necessary means of becoming religious, or to prevent these means from being effectual. And this brings us to the second question: Supposing a man *to be* religious, is there anything in a scientific view of nature to hinder him from taking, at the same time, a religious view of nature?

Science has to do with laws, and with phenomena as they illustrate, fall under, or help to establish these laws. An impression, I believe, prevails in some quarters, that these laws, in a scientific mind, take the place of God, and exclude him from the universe. But is it so?

Need I repeat here what has been said so often? Even if it were possible to resolve every phenomenon of nature into what are called the laws of nature, it would not be to take a single step towards dispensing with the necessity of an All-sustaining Energy, and an All-controlling Mind. For, in the first place, the existence of these laws would still have to be accounted for; and, in the second place, supposing them to exist, they are not a force; they are not the proper cause of anything; they are not an agent, but only the rules, or conditions by which the real Agent is pleased to govern himself; and this Agent is God. Nay, who does not see how much less inconsistency there would be in supposing the universe the work of chance, if it were *not* governed by general laws, and according to a fixed plan; because, though in this case we should still want a power to account for the motion, we should not want an intelligence to account for regular and concerted motion. Indeed, the moment we fully recognize the fact that the world *is* governed by laws; that order, adaptation, unity are everywhere apparent; that there are unmistakable traces of a plan, extending to all things, comprehending all things, — there springs up in the mind, unbidden and irresistibly, the conviction of purpose and thought, that is, of an Intelligent Author. Thus what to the scientific mind are but the laws of nature, become to the same mind, if religious, what, in the expressive and sublime language of Scripture, are called "*the Ways of God.*"

I say, "to the same mind, *if religious*"; for I must remind you once more, that precisely here is the great difficulty, not only in men of science, but in all men devoted to intellectual pursuits. As a general rule, I believe that men of action are more inclined to religion, than men of study; and the reason is obvious. It is not, as some would interpret it, because a superior education has raised the latter above religion, but because a one-sided education has made them incapable of it, or, at any rate, comparatively unsusceptible to it. It is because their habits and predispositions lead them to look at religion under a speculative point of view, where all its difficulties, and almost none of its chief attractions, are found. Be this, however, as it may, one thing is clear: a man must be religious in himself, before he can be expected to carry religion into his daily work, whether of body or mind. Unless a man will take some pains to acquire a devout habit of mind, in other words, unless he will take some pains to quicken and develop that part of his nature to which religion is addressed, it is certain that no amount of physical knowledge will make him properly sensible to the manifestations of God in the material world. He may open the book of nature where he will, and it will be to him, under a religious point of view, a blank page; while to those who have not neglected their consciences and souls in the exclusive culture of the intellect, and who therefore read it with a prepared mind, it will be written all over with lessons of adoration and praise, of solemn awe and humble trust.

Nay, more; these "laws of nature," from which so much danger to religion is apprehended,—when rightly viewed, they not only do not remove God further from us, but have the effect to bring him strangely, startlingly near. They not only prove arrangement, contrivance, a plan,—that is to say, connected and intelligent thought,—but, in proportion as we succeed in comprehending them, they enable us to enter into that thought. The human mind is conscious of being where the Divine Mind has been before,—perhaps I ought to say, where the Divine Mind *is now*. And besides, a world not governed by fixed laws would be a chaos, not a creation. Accordingly it is only by tracing these laws that we can attain to a conception of a Creative Mind, and put ourselves into communication with it. Nothing is to be feared, everything is to be hoped, from the progress of scientific culture, provided only that moral and spiritual culture goes along with it, hand in hand. To a religious mind God is best seen, not in that part of nature which is least understood, but in that part of nature which is best understood.

Let me add, that whoever begins by thus recognizing in nature a personal and living God, will not be likely to stop there. There is nothing in the study of the laws of nature by a devout mind to exclude the idea of a Revelation, though this Revelation be a miracle, and authenticated by miracles. God acts in and through laws; not however from necessity, but because, as a general rule, it is obviously important and indispensable to the safety and happiness of his children, who otherwise would not know what to depend upon. If then an exigency should arise, in which the safety and happiness of his children require a deviation from the usual order of things, from his ordinary rule of action, in all such cases the rule must give way to the principle which dictated the rule. There is no inconsistency or contradiction here; no change of purpose; no disregard even for *law*, for he still obeys the law of all laws, the law of his own nature, which is, to do in every instance what is wisest and best.

Moreover, what we know of religion by the study of nature has the effect to create in us an earnest longing to know more. A curiosity is awakened, which is not appeased; problems are suggested, which are not solved; a mysterious hand is laid on the veil, and we wait in humble, awful expectation to see that veil lifted up. Once believe, no matter on what evidence, in a personal and living God, and that he is a loving and tender Father of all men, and after that, the wonder is, not that he has interposed at times, but that he does not interpose oftener. Thus it is, that the recognition of God in nature prepares the way for the recognition of God in Christ. We accept the declaration, "God, who at sundry times and in divers manners spake in times past unto the fathers by the prophets, has in these last days spoken unto us by his Son." How then can we resist the appeal? "See that ye refuse not him that speaketh. For if they escaped not who refused him that spake on earth, much more shall not we escape, if we turn away from him that speaketh from heaven."

# CONSCIENCE.

AND PAUL, EARNESTLY BEHOLDING THE COUNCIL, SAID: MEN AND BRETHREN, I HAVE LIVED IN ALL GOOD CONSCIENCE BEFORE GOD UNTIL THIS DAY.— Acts xxiii. 1.

The Apostle Paul began his defence before his countrymen with this noble declaration, and though but his own testimony in his own favor, it is abundantly confirmed by what we know of his character from other sources. We have every reason to believe that he was what is called "a conscientious man" before he became a Christian, as well as afterwards. By his own confession, he "was before a blasphemer, and a persecutor, and injurious; but I obtained mercy," he adds, "because I did it ignorantly in unbelief." Again he says: "I verily thought with myself, that I *ought* to do many things contrary to the name of Jesus of Nazareth."

But if it be conceded that Paul was a conscientious man before his conversion, the question very naturally arises, How then can his conversion be said to have made him a better man? I answer, in one word,— because it made his conscience a better conscience. A man may be no more observant of conscience than formerly; but he may have a better conscience to observe.

Nothing has done so much to perplex men's speculations about conscience as certain fundamental mistakes respecting its proper nature and functions.

In the first place, conscience is not a law, but a *faculty;* not the decision pronounced in a particular case, but the faculty which pronounces the decision. As reflective beings, we are constrained to endure our own review of our own conduct, including our dispositions and intentions. Such, also, is our mental constitution, that we cannot knowingly do ill without feeling that we deserve ill, or knowingly do well without feeling that we deserve well. Hence we are said to have not merely a sensitive and intellectual nature, but also a moral nature; and the peculiar faculty by which this moral nature manifests itself, as far as it is manifested, is called *conscience.*

Again; this faculty is susceptible of *instruction* and *improvement*, like other faculties of the human mind; like the understanding, for example, or the taste. Of course, I do not mean that conscience is wholly a factitious thing, that education *makes* it, any more than it *makes* the understanding or the taste. Every faculty, properly so called, depends for its *existence* on the original constitution of the human mind, and, considered under this point of view, must be regarded as "the inspiration of the Almighty." But then it is also true, that every such faculty, and conscience among the rest, depends mainly for its *development*, for both the *manner* and *degree* of its *development*, on education, including under this term all the influences which are intentionally or unintentionally brought to bear upon it. And this being the case, who does not see that one man's conscience may be better than another's, just as one man's understanding or taste may be better than another's, and again that the same man's conscience may be better at one time than at another?

There is also another important distinction to be made in respect to conscience. Its authority is sometimes said to be *supreme* and *final*. And so it is, in a certain sense; that is to say, it is supreme and final over every other *kind* of human motive and inducement; should a conflict arise, our sense of what is right ought to prevail, in all cases, over our sense of what is expedient or agreeable. But the authority of conscience is *not* supreme and final in such a sense as to forbid conscience itself from revising, and, if need be, reversing, its own past decisions. I may appeal at any time from my conscience less instructed to my conscience more instructed, and under these circumstances what was right to me yesterday, may become wrong to me to-day; and what is right to me to-day, may become wrong to me to-morrow. Indeed, it is hardly proper to speak of this as something which may be; it ought to be, and must be, as men advance in wisdom and virtue. All will agree, I suppose, that self-culture, including moral progress, is a duty; and also that one of the most essential parts of this duty is the duty of clearing up our conceptions of right and wrong, especially in reference to the more complicated rules of duty, and to the application of these rules to the more complicated affairs of life. Preachers may say what they will, still the fact is indisputable, that good men, even the best men, are often at a loss what to do, — at a loss what course to take. The perplexity here referred to does not arise, certainly not in all cases, from unwillingness to face the difficulty, or to make the sacrifices, attending the right course, but from real ignorance or doubt as to which is the right course. This, to be sure, is not likely to happen in simple and plain cases of duty; but simple and plain cases of duty are not met with in life as often as they are in books. In life things are jumbled together very unscientifically. More than half our duties relate to matters only indirectly connected with morals; or to measures, customs, or institutions, where the moral question is so mixed up with other questions, as to make it easy for us to deceive ourselves, or be deceived by others, and easier still to take up with the current opinion without examination. Hence our need not only of a conscience, but of an enlightened conscience, — of a conscience willing to revise its old decisions under new lights, and to correct them if necessary.

But if conscience itself is an improvable faculty, and if, in its legitimate action to-day, it can revise and reverse its own decisions of yesterday, the question naturally arises, Is there anything in conscience which is fixed and absolute?

I answer, Yes. The things which are fixed and absolute in conscience — that is to say, the things which are the same in all consciences, and the same in every conscience at all times — would seem to be these three. In the first place, all consciences make a distinction between actions as being right or wrong; secondly, the notion of right, as such, or of wrong, as such, is identical to all minds; and, thirdly, all concur in the feeling that they ought to do what they believe to be right.

So far conscience is fixed, absolute, infallible. But let us understand ourselves. In saying that all consciences make a distinction between actions, classifying some as right and others as wrong, we do not mean that all make the same distinction in the sense of making the same classification. The simple conception of right and wrong is identical to all minds; when, however, we are called upon to apply this conception to complicated actions and dispositions, nothing hinders us from differing from one another, and even from ourselves at different times, on the question, under which head a particular action or disposition, a particular institution or measure, is to be classed. Strictly speaking, we never differ as to the distinction between right and wrong, but only as to the application of this distinction in certain cases; and here, too, the difference arises, not from our not understanding the distinction between right and wrong, but for the most part from our not understanding the measures, the actions, or the states of mind to be judged.

Moreover, though all concur, as I have said, in feeling that we ought to do what is right, nothing hinders that this feeling should exist in different minds, and in the same mind at different times, in very different *degrees;* — in some hardly appreciable; in others, so intense as to make the pains and pleasures of conscience their chief happiness or misery. Still the feeling itself never changes its essential character. Under no circumstances whatever can the moral sentiments with which *acknowledged* virtue and vice are respectively regarded be made to change places. We may approve a wrong action, mistaking it for a right one; we may also incline to a wrong action, notwithstanding it is wrong, from motives of interest or self-indulgence; but no perversion of nature or education can make us feel that we *ought* to do what we know to be wrong, or that we *ought not* to do what we know to be right.

I dwell on these distinctions, because I would not be thought to suppose or imply, in speaking of conscience as an improvable faculty, that conscience is wholly *factitious*,—the creature of circumstances, of training, of caprice. I believe no such thing. If there is a mutable, there is also an immutable element in conscience. In its principle and essence, conscience is not an arbitrary thing; it is not something which experience and education *put into* men, but something which they *bring out*, by bringing out his moral nature,—though, in different men, in very different degrees and proportions. The conscience of each individual is a *special* development of our *common* moral nature;—a more or less perfect development, but still a development of our common moral nature, and therefore always manifesting, more or less perfectly, the essential and unchanging properties of that nature, and so far always the same. It is only necessary that we should avoid confounding a man's conscience with his moral nature, just as we avoid confounding a man's actual taste with his æsthetic nature. They are two things distinct in themselves, and always to be kept so in our thoughts. A man's moral nature is his innate capacity of moral discrimination; it is part and parcel of our common human nature, and, for anything known to the contrary, is the same in all men. But this moral nature, this innate capacity of moral discrimination, may be wholly *latent*, as in the case of infants, who cannot be said to have any consciences, though they have a moral nature; and it is more or less so in adults. What we insist upon is, that a man's conscience, properly so-called, does not include that part of his moral nature which is still latent; it consists of that part only which has been put forth, which has come out into consciousness and activity. In other words, the conscience of an individual is, as I have said, a special development of our common moral nature, more or less true, more or less complete, but not likely to be identical in any two persons.

And so the Scriptures. They speak, indeed, of conscience as "showing," as "bearing witness to," as *revealing*, but not as *being* "the work of the law written in men's hearts." While they represent some as acting from "a *pure* conscience" and "a *good* conscience," they say of others, "But even their mind and conscience is defiled;" and again, "Having their conscience seared with a hot iron." They also ask, "Yea, and why even of yourselves judge ye not what is right?"—clearly implying two things; first, that our consciences may judge amiss, and, secondly, that they often do so from defects which we might ourselves supply by reflection and discipline.

I return, therefore, to the position taken in the beginning: whether we consult reason, or experience, or Scripture, we come to the conclusion, that conscience is an improvable faculty. It is a mistake to suppose that all men share a common conscience; they share, and perhaps equally, a common moral nature, but this common moral nature becomes *conscience,* as the very name imports, only in so far as it is put forth into consciousness and activity, only in so far as it is developed and made effective in the individual. Each man's conscience is a *special* development of our common moral nature; and each man's duty in respect to it is, to take care that this special development shall be more and more complete, and more and more effective; in short, that he may have a better conscience to obey, and obey it more faithfully.

It only remains to consider the means and appliances by which this twofold improvement, this progress, at the same time, in conscience and in conscientiousness, may be promoted and secured.

The first condition is, a habit of attending to the moral aspects and bearings of things, and especially of our own dispositions and conduct; in one word, *moral thoughtfulness*. This would be true, even if we started in life with a conscience ready formed. We are affected by what we at present know or believe, only in so far as *we attend to it;* and hence an apparent anomaly often noticed. Some men are a great deal better, and others a great deal worse than their principles, meaning thereby the moral and religious principles really held by them, *but not attended to*. And this remark applies with tenfold force, where the principles, as in the case of a man's conscience, are not only to be held, but developed. Why is it that among savages the animal instincts and passions are developed so disproportionately? Because there the animal instincts and passions are almost the only things thought of, or appealed to. Why is it that during long periods of moral and social degeneracy almost every manly and unselfish quality of human nature seems to die out? It is simply because these qualities are not put forth; and they are not put forth because they are not cared for or appreciated. And how are the great epochs of awakening and reform to be explained? Simply by the fact that, somehow or other, the public attention is thoroughly aroused to the public needs, often by a sense of the very depths of the public infamy and despair. At first the thought seizes hold of here and there a leading mind; gradually it becomes the ever-present thought of the community, of the age; and human nature reasserts its noblest qualities once more. Why is it, that on some points, such, for example, as peace, temperance, and human rights, our consciences are evidently in advance of the consciences of our fathers, while on many others it is equally evident that the reverse is true? Simply and solely because the former points are more attended to by us: we are more alive to them; they are more in our thoughts. It is moral thoughtfulness, taking the special direction given to it by the age.

A second necessary condition of the twofold moral progress required — of progress in both conscience and conscientiousness — is found in a determination to do right, cost what it may; in other words, to moral thoughtfulness we must add *an invincible moral purpose*. We often hear it said, that men mean well enough when they start in life, even though afterwards led astray by temptation; but this remark is true only in a very limited and qualified sense. I do not suppose that many start in life with a determination to become murderers, robbers, rogues, or drunkards; their error consists, not in starting with a *bad* moral purpose, but with *no* moral purpose; at least, with none that is controlling and effectual. They are looking to ease, pleasure, success: the best that can be said of them under a moral point of view is, that they hope and perhaps expect to gain their objects without falling into crime. Not one man in a thousand, in choosing his profession, or laying down his plan of life, is influenced solely or mainly by a purpose to make himself as perfect as possible in the sight of God.

And this is not all. Much of what passes for fidelity to conscience is nothing but fidelity to prejudice or to party. A man is educated in a set of principles, which may be right or may be wrong, or, more probably still, partly right and partly wrong, or he is converted to such a set of principles, and afterwards deems it sufficient to be true to these principles; as if duty were nothing but an *inexorable consistency*. The double progress incumbent on all men makes it necessary for us to put to ourselves, at least at every important turn of our affairs, not one question only, but two, — Am I faithful to my principles? and, Are my principles what they should be? Neglect of the latter is as much of an immorality as neglect of the former. Remember, the moral purpose, of which I speak as being at the foundation of a good life, is not a purpose *to obey our consciences as they are*, whether well or ill-advised, but a purpose *to do right;* and this involves the purpose, to endeavor to find out what is right, that we may do it; and this, again, the still rarer and more difficult purpose, to bring to the subject that fairness and earnestness of mind which is indispensable to practical wisdom; and, above all, to shun those illusions, deceits, self-indulgences and sins, by which so many are given over to a reprobate mind, " to believe a lie."

The progress insisted on in this discourse supposes another condition; namely, that we not only obey conscience, but obey it as an echo of the Divine will: in other words, to moral thoughtfulness and a moral purpose we must add *a sense of the authority and sanctions of religion*. Our moral nature is what God has made it to be; so that when conscience is a legitimate development of this nature, it may be regarded as a Divine utterance,— the voice of God, speaking in and through our moral nature. Disobedience, therefore, becomes not merely an offence against conscience; it is also an offence against God, bringing us under the judgment of God. The penalty begins, I allow, in the hurt done our own moral nature,— in shame and remorse; but it does not end there: if it did, constitutional dulness in some, and blindness and hardness of heart in others, would make them careless and indifferent about it. I do not go to the extreme of holding that there would be no conscience without religion, no foundation for morality without some recognition of the will of God. Suppose all sense of the Divine being and agency to be blotted out of the human heart, I believe that conscience would still lift up its voice against baseness and crime; but in the presence of sore trial and temptation, in the stress and din of conflicting interests and passions and opinions, who would regard it? What gives effect to conscience is the mysterious and salutary dread, never entirely effaced even from the guilty soul, that there is an Almighty Vindicator and Avenger of conscience. This feeling, this principle, all should guard and nourish; not indeed as a substitute for conscience, but as re-enforcing conscience, and practically indispensable to its unfolding life and power.

One condition more. To make us more observant of conscience, and, at the same time, to make conscience what it ought to be, we must *take our standard of righteousness from the New Testament.* To moral thoughtfulness, a moral purpose, and the sanctions of religion, we must add a heart penetrated and filled with the spirit that was in our Lord Jesus Christ. Without sympathizing at all with those who are sometimes tempted to speak of Christianity as a failure, I still cannot help thinking that its good effects, at least on the moral and social condition of mankind, have not been so great as might naturally have been expected. This is doubtless to be ascribed, not to Christianity, but to Christians, who have always been more disposed to consider the Christian scheme of salvation in its relations to God, than in its relations to themselves, — *his* part in that scheme rather than *ours*. Most clearly we are not to be saved by the scheme, or by knowing and believing the scheme, except through its effect in fitting us for the kingdom of Heaven, in making us capable of the Christian salvation. We are to be saved by the truth only in so far as we live the truth. Let no one be turned aside from this conclusion by fear of the senseless clamor, that this is making salvation to depend on morality, a ground on which pagans might be saved as well as Christians. I am not speaking here of morality, simply considered; much less of pagan morality; but of the morality of the Gospel, the morality of the Sermon on the Mount. I am not speaking of mere righteousness, but of "the righteousness which is of faith;" not of obedience to conscience, whether well or ill instructed, but of obedience to conscience enlightened and sanctified by the Holy Spirit; — "till we all come in the unity of the faith, and of the knowledge of the Son of God, unto a perfect man, unto the measure of the stature of the fulness of Christ."

Look again at the example of Paul. What a noble declaration was that with which he was able to begin his defence before his countrymen: "Men and brethren, I have lived in all good conscience before God until this day." Still he was not content with this, and therefore he says, in another place: "Not as though I had already attained, either were already perfect; but I follow after, if that I may apprehend that for which also I am apprehended of Christ Jesus. Brethren, I count not myself to have apprehended; but this one thing I do: forgetting those things which are behind, and reaching forth to those things which are before, I press toward the mark, for the prize of the high calling of God in Christ Jesus." Here lay the secret of his greatness. He did not rely on a morbidly sensitive conscience, the vain refuge of fanatics; nor yet on the hard rigor of an obstinate conscience, the still vainer refuge of bigots; but on a conscience as quick to learn as to feel, — a conscience speaking with the authority of God, and therefore listening reverently to every new revelation from God, insisting on the law of progress, and therefore the more ready to be itself included under that law, accepting life as a struggle, and turning that struggle into a victory. Hence the triumphant words with which he could look forward to his death are nobler even than those with which, in the text, he had looked back on his past life. "I am now ready to be offered, and the time of my departure is at hand. I have fought a good fight;

I have finished my course; I have kept the faith. Henceforth there is laid up for me a crown of righteousness which the Lord, the righteous Judge, shall give me at that day; and not to me only, but unto all those also that love his appearing."

# MOTIVES.

**WHILE I WAS MUSING THE FIRE BURNED.** — Psalm xxxix. 3.

WHEN we witness the performance of a noble deed, when we become acquainted with a noble character, when we read the life of a great and good man, we are tempted to ascribe his superiority, in great measure at least, to a difference of circumstances. "He has had facilities, incentives, motives," we are apt to say, "such as have not fallen to the lot of most men. Give us the same facilities, give us the same incentives and motives to virtue, and we should be glad to do as he has done. The difference in his moral attainments is mainly owing to the different influences under which he has acted. He has felt motives which we have not."

Undoubtedly there is a sense in which this is true. He has felt motives which we have not. But *why* has he felt them?

To answer this question, we must begin by answering several others on which it depends. What are motives? What gives efficacy to one motive over another in particular cases? And why is it, that while this man is alive to the highest motives of human conduct, that man is alive only to the lowest? We must press each of these questions home, and then, perhaps, it will appear, that what is often set forward as an excuse, is only another ground for humiliation and self-reproach.

In the first place, then, *what are motives, externally considered?* All will agree, I suppose, that they do not act on the mind as impulse acts on bodies; that is, by virtue of a power or momentum which they possess in themselves, and independently of the persons moved. Neither is it a mere transference of motion from one body to another; as when one ball strikes another ball, and causes it to move. Motives act on the mind, it is true, but not until the mind has first acted on them. They act on the mind accordingly as they affect the mind; but then they affect the mind according to the view which the mind is led by its prevailing habits and dispositions to take of them. Set before a promiscuous collection of men a great variety of motives,— such as ease, pleasure, wealth, influence, fame, conscious integrity,— and you will soon perceive that the law of elective affinities holds as good in the moral as in the natural world. Each individual will be affected mainly, if not exclusively, by that class of motives which falls in with his prevailing habits and dispositions. One will give up everything to enjoy ease; another will risk everything to indulge in pleasure; a third will do anything and everything to obtain wealth, influence, or fame; a fourth is only anxious that he may do what is right. Thus one man is influenced and determined by one motive, and another by another; and yet none can complain, that *all* the motives were not *set before him*.

Motives, then, are considerations set before a rational being, not to move him, in the strict sense of that word, but to induce him to *move himself*. After all, the principle of motion is not in the motive, but in the man himself. Strictly speaking, in our voluntary acts we are never moved; we always move ourselves. The motive, externally considered, is the reason or consideration for acting, or not acting, in a particular way; which, of course, will be attended to and appreciated very differently by different persons, and so affect them very differently.

Let us next consider, *what gives efficacy to one motive over another in particular cases?* An opinion prevails on this subject, which, though true to a certain extent, may be pushed too far. It is said that motives affect us through the concurrence of good or bad dispositions previously existing in our own minds. Of course, nobody will deny that where the motive *falls in* with a strong propensity already existing in the mind, it is much more likely to prevail on that account. But we should remember, there was a time when this propensity had not begun to manifest itself, and that it never would have manifested itself at all except on condition of some motive which had power to awaken it,— to call it forth. Now what gives to motives this power to call forth a latent propensity, or disposition of the soul, *in the first instance?* We might say, in general, that it is owing to a certain correspondence or mutual adaptation between the motive and the disposition,— one to excite, and the other to be excited. But this does not explain the difficulty, why it is that the same motive does not have the same effect on all men, and on the same man at all times. Therefore, to answer the question more explicitly, we should say, that it is the *actual feeling* or *perception* of this correspondence or mutual adaptation between the motive and the disposition to be awakened thereby. It is not enough that the quality exists; the individual must *feel*, must *perceive* that it exists, or else *to him* it does not exist. Those who perceive it, and attend to it, and give themselves up to it, are affected; those who do not are not affected.

And now we are prepared to take up the third question, *Why is it, that while one man is alive to the higher motives of human conduct, another is alive only to the lower motives?* Something doubtless is attributable to difference of organization and temperament, but not the whole. If it were, how should we be able to account for material and essential changes in moral and religious sensibility, which the same individual often undergoes? In the case of repentance, involving a real change of heart, it will hardly be pretended that this alters a man's organization or temperament; and yet how entirely it alters his sensibility to moral and religious motives. These motives were always before him; but he did not see them, or at least he did not feel them, as he does now. In this respect he differs from his former self, just as all good men differ from all bad men; nevertheless, organically considered, he is the same man he always has been. So likewise of acquired habits, considered as predisposing men to be affected by certain motives. If we say, that a man is alive to the highest motives merely from his acquired habits and predispositions, then the question arises, how it is that, under the influence of motives, these habits and predispositions were acquired in the first instance; and again, how it is, that, under the influence of new and counteracting motives, they are sometimes radically changed. In the case of a rational, moral, and free being there must be something which modifies and rules mere organization and habit; and this something would seem to be the power of certain external incitements or motives to evoke slumbering elements of the soul, to bring out latent principles of action in the first instance, and thus to give, as it were, a *new pitch* to the whole character. And, other things being equal, this power is felt by the individual just in proportion as the incitement or motive is *attended to*,—attention being the means through which it is brought into connection with the mind, and acts on the soul.

There is no exception to this law. Even what has just been conceded to organization and predisposition, natural or acquired, resolves itself at last into this law. Why is it that motives have more influence over the mind in proportion as it is in any way predisposed to be affected by them? The chief, if not the sole reason, is, that such a mind *gives them more attention and thought*, enters into them more fully and entirely as realities, returns to them more frequently, and dwells upon them to the exclusion of other things. It is not that such a person is moved without attending, but only that he is more sure to attend; for his heart is in it, which is the great condition of earnest and undivided attention.

Hence it follows, that serious and earnest attention to the highest motives of human conduct awakens and calls out the highest and best affections of the soul; and again, it is only by renewing this attention from day to day, that these affections are kept alive and rendered more and more intense. In the words of the text: "While I was musing the fire burned." For this reason the Scriptures everywhere lay great stress on meditation and holy contemplation, on communing with God and our own souls, and having our conversation in heaven, as the conditions of "newness of life." "Beholding as in a glass the glory of the Lord, we are changed into the same image from glory to glory, as by the spirit of the Lord."

If, then, we do not feel the highest motives of human conduct, it is not because they are not set before us, nor yet because we are incapable of feeling them, but because we *do not attend to them*.

To this, however, an objection will be likely to occur to most minds, which I hasten to notice. It will be said, that there are those who have made the highest motives of human conduct, that is, moral and religious considerations, not only objects of attention, but the study of their whole lives, and thus have become eminent philosophers and theologians, who nevertheless do not *feel* these motives any more, if indeed they do as much, as many an ignorant and simple-hearted Christian who never entered into an inquiry on the subject, and never had a doubt.

The fact is admitted; but in order to reconcile it with what has been advanced, it is only necessary to point out an obvious distinction between *speculation* and *meditation;* between that reflection which is the act of a *questioning* spirit, and that reflection which is the act of a *believing* spirit. It is the principal business of the philosopher and theologian to prove the truth and reality of the moral and religious motives; but this is to attend to the *evidence* of the motives, and not to the motives themselves. How can a man be said to attend to a motive, as a motive, until he is prepared to take for granted its truth and reality? for if it is not true and real, it is not a motive; it does not exist to be the object of his attention as a motive. He is only inquiring whether there is such a motive or not. Nay, more; if he has spent much time in *discussing* the truth and reality of the higher motives, even though he should at last decide the question in the affirmative, as often as he returns to the subject the old habit will be apt to be revived, and he will find himself considering, not *what* these motives are, but *whether they exist.* This is the penalty, or at least the danger, of an inquisitive and speculative turn of mind, and accounts for the alleged moral and religious coldness and insensibility of some philosophers and theologians, without making it to be an exception to the law laid down above. If the simple-hearted Christian is more alive to moral and religious motives, it is because these motives are more frequently and intimately present to his soul, *as realities;*—not perhaps as *questions*, but as *realities*. The law, therefore, holds good, as before. A peculiar connection or correspondence subsists between certain motives and considerations, and the dispositions and affections which they are adapted to awaken and evoke. It is only necessary for us to give our minds and hearts to these motives and considerations, until we enter into their nature, and then that nature, the grace of God consenting, will do the rest. "While I was musing the fire burned."

Taking this principle along with us, we shall not find much difficulty in explaining some of the greatest perplexities of the Christian life.

In the first place, it will help us to define, with sufficient distinctness at least for all practical purposes, the office of *free will*. Whatever may be true in theory, there can be no doubt that, in practice, we are generally disappointed, when we expect a great deal from man's self-determining power. The reason is, not that this power does not exist, but that it is not applied at the right time, and in the right place. No doubt I may say, it depends on myself whether I see a particular object, or not, because it depends on myself whether I open my eyes, and look in that direction, or not. But supposing me to keep my eyes shut, or to look in another direction, then certainly it does not depend on myself whether I see that object, or not. Just so in respect to the influence of the higher, that is to say, the Christian motives. I may say, and say with truth, that it depends on myself, under God, whether I feel, and am affected by, these motives, because it depends on myself whether I attend to them, and put myself in the way of them, and seek to enter into their spirit, and bring them, as it were, into contact with my nature. But if from any cause I refuse or neglect to do this, then, of course, I shall not feel these motives, nor be affected by them, let me desire it or will it ever so much. In the action of any motive three conditions are implied: first, the nature of the motive; secondly, our own nature considered as adapted to be affected thereby; and, thirdly, attention on our part, by which the motive and our nature are brought together. Now the first two of these conditions are given quantities in all cases: the third is the only one which remains to be determined; and that we may either determine for ourselves, or, like many, drifting with the current of events, we may allow it to be determined for us.

K

Again; the same principle will help to explain why it is, that when men become decidedly religious it is often in consequence of some startling or impressive event, — the death of a friend, a remarkable escape, a pungent discourse, a striking remark, a dream, a thought. It may be said that such an occurrence does not add one iota to the number or the strength of the motives to a Christian life which these persons had, and which they knew they had, before. And this is true; but it calls *attention to those motives;* and this, as we have seen, is all that was wanted. As a general rule, men are not insensible to religious motives because they are ignorant of them, or because they do not believe in them, or because they think them of secondary importance; but simply and solely because they do not *attend* to them. Their minds are taken up with other things. And if you ask again, how it happens that their minds are taken up by other things, though confessedly of less importance, the answer is ready. Though these other things are confessedly of less importance on the whole, and in the long run, they are nevertheless much more obvious, and more immediately pressing. Common and worldly motives are spread, if I may so express it, on the outside of things: they are obtruded on our notice; we cannot shut our eyes upon them if we would; we can hardly help attending to them, and attending to them continually. On the contrary, spiritual considerations, those which address themselves peculiarly to Christians, lie deeper: they are not forced on our regards by the necessities of our physical condition; we can attend to them, or not, as we please. Nay, to attend to them as we ought, to enter into their full significancy, to make them intimately present to our souls,— in one word, to make what is unseen to be real to the eye of the mind, so that it shall affect us as if it were seen by the eye of the body, — this supposes a degree of abstraction from earthly things, and an ascendency of reason or conscience over sense, which, in the present state of human culture and public morals, are hardly to be expected in the bulk of mankind, unless their attention is aroused by some startling event.

Once more; the view here taken of the manner in which men become alive to the highest motives will also account satisfactorily for local and temporary excitements in morals and religion. These are sometimes referred to sympathy and imitation, and even to causes less pure. Much of what is superficial and transient in them, and many of the attendant circumstances, are doubtless to be explained in this way; but not the whole. What is real and lasting in these movements has its origin in the *general attention to the subject* which, somehow or other, has been awakened. No new motives are discovered or invented. It is not pretended that any new motives are discovered or invented. The selfsame motives and considerations are urged which have been urged for a thousand years: the difference in the effect is owing to the greater attention which is paid to them; and this attention is more likely to be fixed, earnest, and continual, from the fact that the whole community is attending to the same subjects at the same time.

Take as a familiar illustration of this law the Temperance Reform. It is not pretended that men have found out any new motives for being temperate, or any new means of resisting temptations to intemperance. All the topics, all, at least, which are of much real weight, are old and trite, perhaps beyond those of any other subject which can be named. The movement, the marvel, the miracle, as some are disposed to account it, is to be ascribed to the increased attention which is given to these topics; and what may be termed the machinery of the movement is valuable only in proportion as it has a tendency to arrest and hold this attention.

The same is also true of what are called Revivals of Religion, affecting whole churches and whole communities. So far as they may be resolved into sympathy, imitation, or nervous excitability, they are nothing in a moral and religious point of view.

But it is hardly to be presumed that men can meet together to talk about religion, and go home to think about it, day after day, that religion should thus become the one object of interest in public and private for a long time, and yet that no minds should be affected by it deeply and permanently. Still, in this case, it is not because any new considerations are set before them: the considerations, the motives, are not new; the interest, *the attention*, — that only is new.

This, then, would seem to be the true theory of motives. God, in his works and Word, has set before us all reasons, inducements, considerations fitted to call forth the best parts of our nature, and so to lay the foundation of the noblest traits of character. But in order that these reasons, inducements, considerations may have any effect, they must be brought into contact, so to speak, with our nature; and this can only be done by our attending to them, — voluntarily, solemnly, earnestly; and attending to them, not in a questioning, but in a believing spirit. It is not enough that the motives really exist: before they can be said to exist *for us*, we must believe them to exist. Nay, it is not enough that we believe them to exist, for we are not affected by the simple fact that they exist, but by what they are in their own nature; which is such that we cannot attend to it and dwell upon it without feeling our own nature to be touched and transformed. "While I was musing the fire burned."

Let me then, in concluding, ask you to revert once more to the plea so often set up by the undevout, the indifferent, the worldly-minded:—to wit, that they do not feel the motives to virtue and piety which good men do. The fact is admitted; but when we come to analyze it, we find that, in most cases at least, it turns out to be, not an excuse, but a part of the wrong. As we have seen, they do not distinguish, they do not believe, they do not feel, because they do not *attend*. But attention is pre-eminently a voluntary act, and one, therefore, in respect to which all are pre-eminently free and responsible. Undoubtedly some men have more outward changes than others,—more admonitory and startling providences to arouse attention and direct it to higher and more enduring objects. But these things are not indispensable; neither is it in this way that the virtue of the eminently good is usually built up. It is enough for the latter if reason and conscience pronounce the course to be fit and right; they do not require to be dragooned into duty. Besides, who is willing to say, or to believe, that he is always determined from without, and never from within. That there are such men I do not deny, men who practically disown and abdicate the power to choose for themselves even what they will attend to, that is to say, in what direction they will look. But who, I ask again, would consent to take his place in such company, — the seaweed and driftwood of society, collecting here or there just as the wind, the tide, or the eddy happens to set? We must take care, and not seek self-justification in what must bring with it self-scorn.

The way, then, is open. You complain that you do not feel the higher motives of human conduct as good men do. Depend upon it, it is because you do not *attend* to them as good men do; and this again is because you do not *try* to attend to them as good men do, — I do not mean, as matters of speculation, but as matters of reality and holy trust. The unutterable love of God, the gentleness, the sinlessness, the self-sacrifice of Jesus, the peace and dignity of virtue, the anticipated bliss of heaven, — it is not in human nature that we should be practically familiar with such thoughts without being touched and transformed. I do not say, in a moment; for the change is not a mechanical wrench, but a living process: the words of the text express the law, "While I was musing the fire burned," — the true, sacred fire of the earth, which kindles the aspirations of struggling virtue, which glows in the heart of the patriot, the philanthropist, and the Christian, and which the many waters of death cannot quench.

# CHARACTER.

WHEREWITH SHALL A YOUNG MAN CLEANSE HIS WAY? BY TAKING HEED THERETO ACCORDING TO THY WORD. — Psalm cxix. 9.

IN modern discourses on practical religion much is said about *habits* and *character*. It is remarkable that neither of these words is to be met with in the Bible. But though the words are not there, the sense is. The Bible has as little as possible to do with abstractions and generalities. What we call a man's habits, the Bible calls his *ways;* and what we call a man's character, the Bible calls his *life.*

The text, interpreted by the light of this principle, introduces the question, How is a young man, or any man, to form his habits? and also the still more important one, How is he to mould these habits into character, so as really to have *a character* and a *Christian character.*

What is *character*, as that word is here understood?

Not surely *reputation;* for a man may have a reputation, that is, be distinguished and notorious, for the *want* of character. And besides, reputation is not what a man is or has in himself, but what he is *said* to be or to have. By character, as the term is used in this discourse, we mean a man's actual state;—not the opinion, true or false, entertained respecting him.

In what, then, I ask again, does it consist? Not surely in passion, propensity, predisposition. A man who acts from the feeling which happens to be uppermost at the time may have good or bad *impulses;* but he cannot be said to have a character. Sometimes, in common parlance, a man of strong natural aptitudes and proclivities is called a man of strong character; but it is a mistake, or, more properly, a misnomer: the utmost that can be said of such a person is, that he has the materials of a strong character. It is indispensable to character that a man should act from habit, and not from passion. The passion may give rise to the habit, and act through it; still character supposes something more stable than passion; there must be habit to determine us, even when the passion is not felt.

Hence some have made character to be *the sum total of a man's habits.* Will this definition satisfy all the conditions of the case? I think not. A jumble of habits will no more make a character than a jumble of passions. Habits often grow up blindly and indeterminately, without a single care or thought on the part of the individual acquiring them. Such habits have no more to do with the formation of character, properly so called, than the blind and indeterminate action of the passions themselves. Take, for example, indolent or intemperate habits, which men do not so much form as *fall into*. The truth is, such habits are but passions under another form, — just as blind and indeterminate, only more constant. And this is not all. A man may be addicted to inconsistent and contradictory habits, just as he may be the slave of inconsistent and contradictory passions. Of course in such cases one set of habits will exclude the other for the time being, but not from taking its turn as the scene shifts. Have you never met with a man who seemed to act from one set of habits when things went well with him, and from another set of habits when things went amiss, — from one set of habits when in society, and from a totally different set when alone? If then the sum total of a man's habits, any how constituted, is all that is wanting to character, you would make such a man to have two, or three, or four characters; which is the very reverse of what we mean by having *a character*, — that is, something by which he is always known.

Character, therefore, in the highest and truest

sense of that word, supposes not one thing only, but two things. In the first place, it is made up of *habits;* and, in the second place, these habits must be shaped and moulded into *a consistent and harmonious whole.* The character is more or less *complete* and *perfect* according to the degree of its consistency, and the entireness with which the whole is filled up and rounded out.

Adopting this definition, it would plainly be most unreasonable to expect a person to begin life with a character already formed. He cannot do it. We are not born with a character, good or bad, but only with a capacity to form one. However widely children differ from each other in their aptitudes and predispositions, that is to say, in the elements of a future character, they agree nevertheless in this, that the character itself is yet to be formed. All, therefore, that we have a right to require or expect of a young person growing up into maturity is this; — that he should look on the formation of an upright, honorable, Christian character as the great business, the great success of life.

*How* is such a character to be formed?

This question is not only proposed but answered in the text: "Wherewith shall a young man cleanse his way? By taking heed thereto according to thy Word." That is to say, an upright, honorable, and Christian character is to be formed by watching over our habits, and bringing them into conformity with the highest, that is, the Christian standard of truth and duty.

In the first place, we must *watch over the habits we are forming from day to day.*

To inculcations of this nature it has sometimes been objected, that the health of the soul, as well as that of the body, may be hurt by too much looking after. And there is doubtless a sense in which this is true. We do not want moral dyspeptics who are always thinking about cases of conscience, any more than physical dyspeptics who are always thinking about symptoms of indigestion. To weigh out everything one eats or drinks at every meal by grains and scruples would make him an invalid, if it did not find him one. And so in morals. But all this applies to a minute and painful scrupulosity as regards *particular actions;* it has nothing to do with a general watchfulness over *the formation of habits.* Nay, one of the principal reasons why we should be careful to form good habits is, that having made sure of them, there will be the less occasion to be anxious about single actions. The habit of doing right will lead us to do right spontaneously. It is as in learning to speak a language. In the beginning we have to think of every word we are going to utter, and even with this precaution speak but poorly and hesitatingly. After we have thoroughly mastered the language, that is, have grown into the habit of speaking it, the words may almost be said to come of themselves.

From this it also appears that in watching over the habits we are forming from day to day, our whole duty is not done by seeing to it, that no *bad* ones are contracted. You will sometimes hear it said of a man, that he has no bad habits, as if this were all that could reasonably be required of him. But not so. The absence of bad habits is but the negative side of a good character, what it is *not;* the positive side, in other works, that which makes it to be what it *is*, is found in the good habits which go to make up its substance and form. It is a great thing, I allow, not to have any bad habits,—more, I am afraid, than is true either of you or of me, our only hope being that we have some good habits to weigh against the bad. A man is not good, merely because he is not bad. A great deal too much is made to depend on the mere absence, real or supposed, of bad habits. Even if we had no bad *habits*, we should still be liable to bad and dangerous *impulses;* and what is to hinder these from breaking out, from time to time, into acts of license and crime, unless they are restrained by one good habit at least, that of self-control? And besides, what reliance can be placed on the best of impulses, considered merely as single, unregulated impulses? Take generosity, for example. Who has yet to learn that it is almost as likely to do harm as good, until it has been trained to obey the rules imposed upon it by reason and experience? that is to say, until it has ceased to act as a blind impulse, and become a habit? For the same reason, all dependence on the sentiments of honor, or the sentiments of virtue, or the sentiments of religion is worth but little, if these sentiments are understood to end with being mere sentiments; if they do not grow into habits; if from being a mere force or impulse they do not become a direction and a self-imposed law; in short, if from being a part of our undisciplined nature, they do not become a part of our disciplined character.

We are further to consider, in watching over the formation of our habits, that actions, the most trivial in themselves, if often repeated, become of great and decisive importance. You have been told again and again that the morality of a man's actions depends on his motives; and so it does, if you are considering the morality of *particular actions*. But if you are considering the effect of the whole on his character, on the *man himself*, on his moral progress, you must take into account consequences as well as motives,—not merely how the action finds him, but how it leaves him. How, in other words, are his habits of thought and feeling and conduct affected thereby? And under this point of view it is not the great, but the trivial and often repeated delinquency, from which we have the most to dread. Great crimes not unfrequently have the effect to startle and arrest the sinner in his downward course, and bring him to a pause; at any rate, they never induce the habit from which they flow. A man does not contract a habit of murder; he contracts a habit of malice and cruelty, almost always little by little, and murder is incident to this habit. It is almost always some venial form of the offence, renewed day after day, looked upon as indifferent or at least as allowable, and therefore exciting no compunction or alarm, provoking no indignation, stealing over us under cover of outward decorum and worldly respectability, which is most likely to fix and rivet the accursed habit.

This, then, is the first step towards the formation of a truly Christian character, — namely, to watch over the influence which our daily conduct is having on our habits. Of course, we must look to our actions too, for they *express* what we are, but still more to our habits, for they *make us* what we are. Habits, of some sort or other, every one will have, — habits of thinking, habits of feeling, habits of acting; the only question being, of *what* sort. A grown-up savage is sometimes said to be still in a state of nature; but it is not so: he is just as much under the dominion of acquired habits as you are. His dark superstitions, his stoical indifference to pain, the point of honor of his tribe, his very mien and gait, are not nature; they are all acquired habits,—as much so as the fashions and conventionalities of the most refined courts in Europe. And so of much that is said against education, considered as forestalling the mature judgment of the individual. Certain zealots for what they call the free development of mind object to early moral and religious training, because, forsooth, they would have the child grow up into life without any prejudices or leanings one way or another. But have these persons yet to learn, that, whether you strive to prepossess the child in favor of religion or not, a thousand causes are at work to prepossess him against it, or what in practice amounts to nearly the same thing, against the conditions on which it depends. The question is not whether something or nothing shall grow in your fields; but whether it shall be corn or weeds. And not only so. "One being asked, what could be the reason why weeds grew *more plentifully* than corn, answered, Because the earth was the mother of weeds, but the step-mother of corn; that is, the one she produced of her own accord, the other not till she was compelled to it by man's toil and industry."\*

---

\* Jortin's *Sermons on Different Subjects*, Vol. III. p. 6.

Once more, therefore, let me inculcate the duty incumbent on every one that lives, to watch over every change in his habits, however slight, with an untiring vigilance. Do not suspect me of pressing the doctrine of works to the extent of excluding or undervaluing the doctrine of grace. I do not forget that faith is the spring of Christian holiness, and that the Spirit must "help our infirmities" in order to make this faith effective. But these necessary and merciful provisions, to be of any avail to us personally, *must be accepted by us personally;* they must become ours in the sense of entering into our proper life, that is, into the inward and outward habits in which our proper life consists. What our habits are, we are. If they are Christian, we are Christian; if they are pagan, we are pagan;—no matter what may be our professions, no matter what may be our connections, no matter what may be our single and unconnected actions. "Many will say unto me in that day, Lord, Lord, have we not prophesied in thy name? and in thy name have cast out devils? and in thy name have done many wonderful works? And then will I profess unto them, I never knew you. Depart from me, ye that work iniquity." It is, I repeat it, a question of habits; of habits, too, which are changing every hour; and what makes the danger a thousand-fold greater is, that these changes are often brought about by influences, concessions, delinquencies, of so little moment, singly considered, as to attract no notice at the time, yet by constant repetition giving a radical and fatal bias to the whole character.

Depend upon it, we do not muster our defences at the most exposed points, if it is against the commission of great single crimes. I cannot, I will not believe, that any here are on the brink of outraging the laws or public opinion by deeds of flagrant injustice or infamy. But there is not one among us all so wise, so circumspect, so generally well-disposed, as not to be in danger of an insensible decay of his good habits, or an insensible strengthening of his bad habits, through the frequent repetition of what are looked upon as allowable indulgences. What I most fear for you, is what I most fear for myself. It is, that the treating of sacred things with lightness, or even with unconcern, or seeing them frequently so treated by others, will grow up into habits of irreverence. It is that a propensity to color and overstate in conversation, merely to please, or for effect, will gradually weaken and confuse our abiding sense of the sacredness of truth. It is that obstinacy in trifles, or giving way to slight impulses of impatience or anger, or the indulgence of ill-humor, or the use of sharp expressions, will insensibly generate a temper at once passionate and self-willed.

Here, I insist, — precisely here, and not in great single temptations or in great single crimes, — our principal danger lies. It will not do to say of the small sins in question, that they are nothing. Taken singly, they may not be much; but taken together, and in their connection and repetition, they go to make up our habits, and our habits are everything. Neither will it do to say of our minor faults, that they are trifles because the first appearance of an earnest purpose will scatter them to the winds. Whoever takes this ground forgets two things. In the first place, he forgets that these minor faults, if repeated and persisted in, will eat out the very heart and life of that on which all earnestness of purpose depends. And, in the second place, he forgets that the earnest purpose, even though it should come, may come too late. While we are sleeping in a false security, the faults in question, pigmies though they are, will have time to pin us down by innumerable threads, so that when we awake, we shall find ourselves as effectually bound as if by strong cords, as if by fetters of iron.

I have left myself room but for one more suggestion. As was intimated before, a jumble of habits, even of good habits, will not make a character. These habits must be so shaped and moulded as to form a consistent and harmonious whole; and to be a Christian character, this whole must express the Christian ideal of goodness. It is not enough that a young man takes heed to his ways; it must be with a view to realize, as far as human infirmity will permit, the Christian conception of a perfect man. Every one knows that the pagan type of character is a very different thing from the Jewish type of character; and again, that the Jewish type of character is a very different thing from the Christian type of character. In each case the character required is made up, for the most part, of good habits; but the habits are combined in different proportions, so that the whole expresses a different idea, exhibits a different style, of goodness.

Hence, as it seems to me, one of the first things to be attended to in Christian nurture is, to keep before the minds of the young, and before the minds of all, *the Christian conception of a perfect man.* How much better it would be if the primers of the Church, instead of attempting to define what are called "the mysteries of faith," would aim to show what are the qualities of heart and life by which a Christian is known. Here, also, as I cannot help thinking, is the true and only practicable ground of union among Christians. You cannot make men agree in the abstract principles into which the Christian character should be resolved; it is enough if they agree in the character itself, and manifest that character in their daily conduct.

By taking this course, we do but follow in the steps of our Lord. Read his discourses; read his Sermon on the Mount: it is impossible not to see that his main object is to teach men, not how to speculate, but how to live; to impress it upon us, that unless our righteousness "exceeds the righteousness of the Scribes and Pharisees," we "cannot enter into the Kingdom of Heaven," and to point out as precisely as may be wherein the difference should consist. Need I add, in conclusion, that by taking this view of the subject we impart a new value and a new significance to the example of our Lord. Not content with giving the Christian character in description, in idea, he has given it in fact, that "we all, with open face beholding as in a glass the glory of the Lord," may be "changed into the same image from glory to glory;" till we all come, in the only practicable unity of the faith and of the knowledge of the Son of God, "unto a perfect man, unto the measure of the stature of the fulness of Christ."

# GOVERNMENT OF THE THOUGHTS.

BRINGING INTO CAPTIVITY EVERY THOUGHT TO THE OBEDIENCE OF CHRIST. — 2 Corinthians x. 5.

I suppose there are few prerogatives which men would be less inclined to part with than the absolute secrecy and independence of their thoughts. The tyrant may fetter my limbs, and seal my lips; but there is one thing which he cannot do by the utmost stretch of his power. He cannot hinder me from thinking as I please; neither can he know what I think, unless I please to tell him.

But this very fact, as it shows that neither the law nor public opinion can take cognizance of our thoughts, only makes it the more indispensable that we should take the proper regulation and government of them into our own hands. What others cannot do for us, or even help us to do, each one should feel the more bound to do for himself, — taking care to keep himself inwardly as well as outwardly pure, " bringing into captivity every thought to the obedience of Christ."

Here, however, an objection is sometimes raised, which, if allowed to stand, must make the inculcation in the text of no effect. Our thoughts, it is said, succeed each other according to fixed and unalterable laws, one thought bringing up another in a constant train or current, over which the will has no more power than over the current of blood in our veins.

What there is of plausibility in this error arises, as is usual in like cases, from a mixture of truth. Unquestionably it is not for our will of itself, directly and immediately, to determine what we shall think of at the moment; neither can we, merely by willing it, stop thinking altogether. Thus much is true; but it does not follow that we have no control whatever over our *trains* of thought. All those who concede anything to human freedom must allow, that we are free to make any particular thought which comes up in one of these trains an object of special attention. We can arrest it and hold it before the mind for this purpose; which will have the effect, not indeed to stop our thinking, but to give a new direction to our thoughts. Obviously, therefore, *the turn* which our thinking takes depends, for the most part, on ourselves. Suppose, for example, that I am thinking of a sinful indulgence; I am free to think of that side of it which invites, or of that side of it which repels;

I can think of it as an *indulgence* merely, or as a *sinful* indulgence; and the train of thought to which the whole will give rise will vary accordingly. When I say I can do either one or the other, as I choose, it is no objection to reply that I cannot do it without some reason or motive. Certainly not. But the question is, whether, having a reason or motive to give my thoughts a particular direction, that is to say, believing it to be expedient and right, it is not within my power to do so.

There is also another way in which a man's will exerts an indirect, but yet an important and decisive, control over the tenor of his thoughts. As has been said, we are competent at any moment *freely and deliberately* to select out of a train of thoughts that one to which we will attend. But we will suppose this selection made, not freely and deliberately, but *spontaneously*, or from *the impulse of the moment*, as is probably the fact in most cases; still what we do spontaneously, or from the impulse of the moment, depends on the state of our minds, and this again depends, for the most part, on what we have chosen to make it, or allow it to become. What we call acting impulsively or spontaneously originates, in nine cases out of ten, not in our nature properly so called, but in some *habit* which has been superinduced;—not in our nature as it came from the hand of God, but as it has been developed and shaped by a long series of our own voluntary acts. Hence it is, for the most part, that different persons are affected so very differently by the same objects, — what will suggest vicious and impure thoughts to one having no such effect, perhaps the opposite effect, on another. The same book, for example, which will do incalculable injury to a man of bad principles, or of no principle, may be read with much less danger, perhaps with perfect safety, by one whose innocence is guarded, at every point, by discretion, a pure taste, and the fear of God.

Say not, then, that it is of the nature of certain objects to *force* on us bad thoughts. Say, rather, that the thoughts which any object will suggest to us, are those only which we, from the existing state of our minds, are led to associate with it; and that out of these we can select which we will make the object of special attention; and further, even if, in making this selection, we are more determined by habit than deliberate choice, we should remember that this *habit* is our own work. Our abiding and predominant trains of thought depend, therefore, on some act of the will, either present or past, or, at any rate, on a series of voluntary acts which have resulted in our existing habits or biases of character.

Accordingly it will not do to disown all responsibility respecting the government of our thoughts, on the plea that they are not subject to our control. Let our circumstances be what they may, if we take into view our conduct from the beginning, it depends on ourselves what shall be the general complexion and tendency of our thoughts, almost as much as it does what shall be the general complexion and tendency of our words and actions. Who does not know that a good man's upright purpose extends to his motives and his dispositions; that it penetrates and subdues his inward as well as his outward life?

Thus far, the aim of my reasoning has been to prove that *no* object is likely to suggest bad thoughts, except through the concurrence of a weakened or depraved mind.

But, in a practical view of the subject, this is taking higher ground than is necessary, or perhaps judicious. Let us admit then, that, in the present condition of humanity, there are some things so adapted of themselves to excite bad thoughts that they will have this effect on the best minds. Still this does not hinder us from being able to govern our thoughts, for it by no means follows that we are obliged to put ourselves in the way of such things. The government of our thoughts is as much in our own hands as ever; only it is on the condition that we do not expose ourselves to those particular temptations. Take, for example, the influence of bad books. A book may be so very bad, so thoroughly and insidiously bad, that it cannot be read without unsettling or defiling, more or less, the best minds. But the best minds are not obliged to read that book, or to look into it, or to touch it; nay, will not be disposed to do so, for the very reason that they are the best minds. And so of company, and conversation, and scenes. Undoubtedly there are situations into which a good man may thrust himself, if he will, where his tone of thinking is almost sure to be lowered, and in the end utterly corrupted, whether he will or no. In a certain companionship the bad thoughts are forced upon him; but the companionship itself is not forced upon him; so that he is still free, even as regards his thoughts. He is not free to avoid the thoughts, if he does not avoid the companionship, but he is free to avoid *both*.

Here, however, a distinction should be made between mere neighborhood, mere proximity, and real *companionship*. Men are often constrained to live together in the same vicinity, and it may be in the same house, or the same room; but companionship implies something more. It implies confidence and concert, a certain community of feeling, of tastes, of pleasures; and *these* cannot be forced. You know how it is in schools and colleges, in a ship or in camp: there all live together, and must live together, but each selects for his companions whom he will; and if he chooses to select those whose intercourse tends by necessity to corrupt and debase his mind, it is his own fault; he has incurred an evil which he might have avoided if he would; and therefore he has nobody to blame but himself.

Let me add, that the control which every man has, or might have, over his thoughts does not consist in *prevention* alone. We will now suppose that objects suggesting bad thoughts suggest them alike to all minds, and again, that we are necessarily exposed to these objects; in other words, we will suppose, (though, as a general rule, nothing can be further from the truth,) that bad thoughts force their way into our minds unbidden, no power or prudence on our part being able to keep them out; — still, even on this supposition, it must certainly depend on ourselves what reception we give to the intruders, and also how long we allow them to stay. Bad single thoughts may flit, from time to time, through the minds of good men; but it is bad men only who encourage, or even tolerate, their stay; — who welcome them; who recall them; who suffer their imaginations to dwell upon them until the moral taint they convey has had time to sink into the very substance of the soul. I do not mean that we can expel bad thoughts by no thoughts, leaving our minds entirely empty. If we would expel bad thoughts, it must be by the preference we give to good thoughts, that is, by introducing good thoughts into their place. However beset and haunted by bad thoughts, if a man is sincere and in earnest in his wish to rid himself of them, a single fervent ejaculation, a single turning of his whole soul to God, will be sufficient to rebuke or scare them away. The old Catholic superstition, that to pronounce the name of Jesus and make the sign of the cross would put to flight evil *spirits*, was doubtless fostered by the fact, if it did not grow out of it, that they were found to put to flight evil *suggestions*, by diverting our thoughts into another channel, and lifting them into a higher and holier region.

Away, then, with that subtile but most inconsistent form of fatalism, which teaches that we can help our actions, but not our thoughts. What is *to choose* but to think; and without freedom of choice what freedom of action could there be? *All* freedom, therefore, begins and ends with freedom of thought. As we have seen, it depends on ourselves, in no small measure, whether our minds are in a state to be accessible to bad thoughts; and again, it depends on ourselves, for the most part, whether we are thrown in the way of bad thoughts; and finally, even when, from any cause, bad thoughts find their way into the mind, it depends on ourselves whether we allow them to stay, or drive them out. Within certain limits, therefore, and as far as morality goes, we have as real a control over our thoughts as over our actions or our limbs.

This being conceded, nothing remains but to consider some of the reasons and motives which should induce us to exert this power wisely and effectually, "bringing into captivity every thought to the obedience of Christ."

Consider, in the first place, how much the thoughts have to do in forming and determining the whole character.

"Thought," says an eloquent writer, "is the rudder of human action. As the thought is wise or foolish, good or bad, vicious or moral, the cause of action is noxious or salutary. When, therefore, I am told it is *but a thought*, I am told that it is the most important of all things." Tell me what are a man's thoughts, and you do not tell me what he will actually do, but you tell me what he would *like* to do. Tell me what are a man's thoughts, and you do not tell me what he is in the judgment of the world, for the world judges by the outward appearance, but you tell me what he is in the judgment of God, who looketh on the heart. Thoughts have been called "the seeds of conduct;" but they are more than this. They are seeds which have already begun to germinate under ground; they have begun to develop their natural and essential properties, whether for good or for evil, though they have not come as yet to the light of day. In this way the whole character may be covertly undermined; the rot which began at the core may thus spread through the whole substance before it appears on the surface; so that a man may not begin to be suspected, nay, may hardly begin to suspect himself, until he is well-nigh lost. Melancholy and startling instances of this description occur, from time to time, in what is regarded as *the sudden fall* of men who have hitherto enjoyed the entire confidence of the community. There is no such thing as a sudden fall from virtue,—from a high and strict virtue. These men have been falling for years in the slow decay of all upright purpose and thought.

It will help us to understand how this can be, and at the same time strengthen our general conviction as to the necessity of controlling our thoughts, if we consider, in the second place, that every sin *begins* in a sin of thought; that is to say, in some vicious purpose or intention, and often in meditating, over and over again, what at length we are emboldened to do. The last suggestion is one which I wish to impress upon you. As a general rule, it is only after frequently revolving crime in their minds that men find the resolution, or rather the hardihood, to commit it. When sinful thoughts are spoken of, I believe it is common to suppose that a particular class of sins are referred to,—those, I mean, which offend against purity. But I make no such limitation here. I believe it to be true, in general, of *all* crimes, that they are *rehearsed*, so to express it, again and again, in thought, before they are brought out into act. Take, for example, the crimes of envy, jealousy, and malice; who does not know how often a man will *wish* evil to another, and *imagine* ways in which he would like to do him evil, before he arrives at the point of putting any one of his fancied schemes in practice? The same is also true of acts of fraud and dishonesty. A man does not belie at once, or in a single day, a whole life of just and honorable dealing, but the process of his demoralization, in most cases at least, is something like this. In his haste to be rich, or more likely still in this perplexity, if his circumstances become embarrassed, a questionable expedient occurs to his mind, — *if* he could only bring himself to feel that it would be right, or even allowable or safe. At first he cannot, and the thought is dismissed. But that thought returns again and again, under the same or a like form, and every time it returns a growing familiarity makes it seem less strange and less repugnant, until he is not only ready for that step, but for worse things.

The history of sin in such an individual, while it affords ample and melancholy evidence of human frailty, is one of the best vindications of human nature itself against the charge of a native and intrinsic bias to evil. It shows that actual transgression, *when first proposed*, is never in itself agreeable to our nature, but always more or less offensive and revolting. A strong instinctive aversion must be overcome before we can go on; and this is commonly done, not by reconciling us to the crime, as such, but by causing our repugnance to it to be less *felt* through the effect of familiarity. After all, when the crime is committed, it is not for the sake of the crime, but for the sake of what we gain by the crime acting on us as a bribe; the bribe, however, does not prevail until our sense of repugnance to the crime has been blunted by *familiarity*. And here it is that the demoralizing influence of ill-regulated thought appears; for to acquire this familiarity it is not necessary that we should *do* anything, it is not necessary that we should stir a finger; it is only necessary that we should go over the mischief we are meditating in thought (which we are foolish enough to suppose can hurt nobody), and thus to rehearse, as I have said, again and again, in imagination the part we are about to play in real life. Sometimes the novice in crime thinks himself ready to act when he is not; as appears from his hesitancy and reluctance when the moment for action arrives. If, however, this unexpected recoil of his nature does not induce him to change his purpose altogether, he knows but too well how to supply the defect in his training for sin. If we could look into his heart, we should find him at his accursed rehearsals again. A few more lessons, and the blush and the shudder will pass away, never to return.

Hence a third consideration which should impress us with the necessity of governing our thoughts is, that unless the restraint is laid there it is not likely to be effectual.

Because we maintain the sinfulness of bad thoughts, it does not follow that we must push this doctrine to the extent of asserting that the thought of sin is as bad as the deed. Unquestionably it is *not*. The actual perpetrator of a crime is guilty of a double offence, that of desiring to do it, and that of not restraining the desire. Nay, more; if the evil thought is suggested *from without*, and immediately disowned and rejected *from within*, it will depart and leave no stain. Accordingly there is no occasion for the morbid conscientiousness of those overscrupulous persons who live in constant terror of falling into mortal sin from the mere passage of evil thoughts through their minds against their will. The guilt of evil thoughts does not consist in our *having* them, but in our *indulging* them, accepting them as our own, making them our own, and allowing them to remain, or to return. If, therefore, instead of doing this, we repress the thought as soon as its true character is known, we not only do not fall from our innocence, but we stand higher, or at least more firmly, than we did before, because we have been tried, and stood the trial. Let the check be put upon the thought, and we not only prevent the sin from coming to maturity, but we take the character of sin from its first beginnings; that is to say, we turn what would otherwise have been a temptation yielded to, which is sin, into a temptation overcome, which is virtue.

Those, on the contrary, who indulge the thought, and yet rely on their power and resolution to prevent it from ever passing into act, do miserably miscalculate their strength. As has been said, "There can be no doubt with any reflecting mind but that the propensities of our nature must be subject to regulation; but the question is, *where* the check ought to be placed,—upon the thought, or only upon the action?" Paley finds an argument for the truth of Christianity in the decisive judgment which our Saviour pronounces in favor of the former course, indicating thereby his superior wisdom.* In proof of this point he adduces the testimony, not of theorists, nor even of moralists or theologians, but of practical men and men of the world, as being well qualified by their experience and observation to form a true opinion on the subject. They all concur in the view here given, being wont to say, that, in this respect at least, if in no other, " our Saviour knew mankind better than Socrates." It is commonly objected to evil thoughts,

---

* *Evidences of Christianity*, Part II. Chap. II.

that they inflame our desires and passions, and so make them more and more difficult of control: and this is true; but I find a still more serious objection in their influence on the principle of virtue itself. They corrupt, weaken, and destroy all power, all disposition, to control the conduct on *moral* grounds, the only restraint left being a regard for appearances, or mere worldly interest. Need I say, he who puts his virtues under the keeping of this principle makes a shepherd of the wolf, who may indeed be vigilant and active to keep off other depredators from the flock, but only to devour them all himself.

After all, the weightiest consideration which should lead us to govern our thoughts is that which religion suggests; they are known unto God, who will call them into judgment at the last day.

Something, doubtless, would be gained, as regards the duty in question, if we would merely give heed to that apothegm of Pagan wisdom, " Reverence *thyself*." For he who knowingly tolerates in himself what he would be ashamed to have others know, shows that he has less respect for his own good opinion than for that of the world. But this is a small matter compared with indifference or disregard for the good opinion of our Maker and Eternal Judge. We believe that he is everywhere present, that his eye penetrates the darkest chambers of the soul, yet still indulge in thoughts and imaginations which we are careful to hide from our fellow-men, from dread of their rebuke or scorn. Is man more than God? Is it in mockery that we come before him and say, "Search me, O God, and know my heart; try me, and know my thoughts, and see if there be any evil way in me, and lead me in the way everlasting." Consider, too, that all the consequences of evil thoughts are not revealed in the present life. We have reason to hope that some of our guilty *actions*, and some of the temptations to our guilty *actions*, will cease with the body which is their necessary occasion and instrument; but the body is not necessary to our evil thoughts. The mind, the soul, will go on *thinking* still, even in its disembodied state, and thinking as it did here, and take its place according to the spirit and tendency of its thoughts. Is not this what the Scriptures mean when they say, "Therefore, judge nothing before the time, until the Lord come, who both will bring to light the hidden things of darkness, and will make manifest the counsels of the hearts: and then shall every man have praise of God."

Shall I be told that throughout this discourse I have been insisting on a strictness and purity of conduct which is beyond the reach of mortals? Perfection here, as elsewhere, is so, I suppose; but this does not absolve us from the duty of making perfection itself an object of our aspirations, and of earnest and unremitting pursuit. And, besides, I am not speaking of what man can do by his unassisted strength; I suppose him to be sustained by faith in Christ, and the aids of the Holy Spirit. I suppose all heaven to be on his side. Because we find ourselves unequal to a duty, not being Christians, it does not follow that we should still be unequal to it if we were to become Christians, or better Christians. At any rate, we have no right to fall back on the plea of our weakness and insufficiency, until we have done what we *can*, — the condition not only of God's justice, but also of his mercy. And who can say that he has done all that he can? If, then, we wish to preserve peace of mind, if we wish to keep the sanctuary of the soul unprofaned, if we wish to prevent our virtues from being contaminated in their very source and to their very core, if we wish to plant a double guard round the heart, out of which are the issues of life, — let us maintain inviolate the purity of our thoughts, without which there can be no innocence, no security, no entrance into heaven, and no heaven to enter. "Seek ye the Lord while he may be found; call ye upon him while he is near. Let the wicked forsake his way and the unrighteous man his thoughts, and let him return unto the Lord, and he will have mercy upon him, and to our God, for he will abundantly pardon."

# DIFFICULTY, STRUGGLE, PROGRESS.

THOU, THEREFORE, ENDURE HARDNESS, AS A GOOD SOLDIER OF JESUS CHRIST. — 2 Timothy ii. 3.

MEN would be less likely to complain of life as it is, if they knew, or would consider, what are its great objects. "Nothing," they say, "which is worth having can be obtained without difficulty and effort. We must labor for it, we must struggle for it, or else not have it." And this is true; and what is more, it was meant to be so. It is not an oversight or an accident: God never meant that things should come easily; he always meant that they should come hard; and they do not come any harder, in point of fact, than he meant they should. Difficulties, struggles, and hardships, toilings, strivings, and buffetings,— these are not strewed through human life any more thickly than God intended they should be. And yet, I repeat it, in view of all this, men would be much less apt, than they now are, to complain of life, if they understood, or would consider, the great ends for which life is given. The multitude, practically at least, mistake the means for the end, and then wonder that the end should be what it is; and hence no small portion of the uneasiness and discontent to be met with everywhere in the world, and the consequent decay of faith and zeal.

To guard against this error, we must consider well two important distinctions, which, in the eagerness and distractions of human pursuits, are very apt to be overlooked or neglected. In the first place, though we very properly labor and strive for this object and that, the great end of life does not consist in our obtaining these particular objects, but in the self-improvement realized in the process of obtaining them, or of making the attempt. And, secondly, while happiness is one legitimate object of our existence, progress is another: so that the great end of our being is not answered in our becoming happy *as we are;* our very *capacities* of happiness must be enlarged and elevated; and in this way we are to be fitted for a higher life.

These are unalterable conditions of the accomplishment of the soul's destiny. We may shut our eyes upon them, if we see fit, but they will not on that account cease to be unalterable conditions of the accomplishment of the soul's destiny. On the other hand, if we take care to study them out, and reflect on them, often and seriously, it can hardly fail to do something to reconcile us to the world as it is, to the unavoidable difficulties with which we have to contend, and dispose us to "endure" the "hardness" thus incurred in a better and more resolved spirit, or, in the words of the text, "as a good soldier of Jesus Christ."

Let us consider, in the first place, that, though we very properly labor and strive for this object and that, the great end of life does not consist in our obtaining these particular objects, but in the self-improvement realized in the process of obtaining them, or in making the attempt.

If we exert our faculties for the accomplishment of a particular object, and succeed, we do not accomplish one object only, we accomplish two objects, a particular object and a general object, — the particular object at which we aim, and the general object of improving ourselves. This is true whatever the particular object may be, provided only that it is a legitimate object. It may be the simplest mechanical process, still if we go through it successfully, we not only go through the process in that particular instance, but we *improve ourselves*, inasmuch as we acquire a greater facility in going through the same or a similar process on any future occasion. And this secondary advantage is still more apparent when the exertion called for is of a nature to put in requisition the higher endowments of judgment and intellect. If an architect builds a house or a ship, he not only builds that particular house or ship, but he improves himself generally as an architect; that is, he is better able afterwards to build other houses or other ships. So likewise if a scholar acquires a language, or masters a science, he not only acquires that particular language, or masters that particular science, but improves his own mind generally, that is, increases his ability to acquire other languages, or to master other sciences.

So far all is plain. But these premises being conceded, it follows necessarily that it is not to the ease, but to the *difficulty*, with which particular objects are effected, that we must look for the furtherance of the general object of self-improvement. If a merchant could gain a fortune by asking for it, or by writing half a dozen letters or bills of credit, he might gain a fortune, but that would be all. He would not improve his knowledge or capacity for business; he would not be a better merchant than he was before. And this is the reason why inherited property and money got by gambling, lotteries, or speculation proves a curse as often as a blessing. It is because men come by it so easily. If they came by it with difficulty, if they were obliged to put all their faculties to the task in order to obtain it, their faculties themselves would be sharpened and invigorated, their minds generally would be strengthened and enlarged, and their heads, of course, would be less likely to be turned by success.

Or take another example. Suppose a mathematician to be able to solve the hardest problems at a glance, and without any labor or application of mind. This, I allow, would make it possible for him to solve a greater number of problems in a given time; but let him solve ever so many, it would not help him to acquire what is infinitely more valuable, the power and the habit of close and intense thought. It would help him to *fill* his mind, but it would not help him to *improve* or *strengthen* his mind. On the contrary, he would be in a fair way of becoming what is called " a learned fool "; that is, one who has the information of a man, but the faculties of a child, or one who has a great deal of knowledge without the capacity to apply it to any useful purpose.

Hence the radical objection to those modern devices in education, the ostensible object of which is to make education easy. Happily they never do what they promise; but suppose them to do it, suppose them to turn study into a pastime, it would only be so much the worse. The essential good of study consists in its being hard work; for it is on that condition only that it will put the faculties to the stretch, and so bring them out more fully. Who has yet to learn that education, properly so called, does not consist in putting things *into* the mind, but, as the name implies, in bringing things *out*, — in the development of the power and habit of self-activity, self-reliance, and self-government; and to effect this object, the faculties on which these traits of character depend must be stimulated, exercised, and put to the stretch. In this case, though all the information should be lost, the discipline will remain.

Thus it appears that the very difficulties of life, of which we are so apt to complain, are converted into the means of that discipline, that self-culture and self-improvement, which is the great end of life. The particular and immediate objects of our pursuit, which are so apt to engross our attention, such as knowledge and wealth, pleasure and fame, are not ends, but means, — means to the attainment of the one great end of our being, the development of the latent energies of the soul; and this end they are adapted to promote just in proportion to the difficulty of compassing them; that is to say, just in proportion to the mental activity they call forth.

One word now on the second proposition before stated. While happiness is one legitimate object of our existence, progress is another: so that the great end of our being is not answered in our becoming happy *as we are;* our very *capacities* of happiness must be enlarged and elevated.

To illustrate what I mean, take the case of a child

whose capacities of happiness, as at present developed, are exceedingly few and narrow. You would not be content with a constitution of things looking no further than to a gratification of the desires that child has already begun to feel. With reason you expect that other and higher desires will be awakened in him as his nature is more and more unfolded, and you count on the hard discipline of life as being likely to bring about this result. Could he gratify his first and lowest desires without pain, effort, or delay, there would be danger of his becoming satisfied with himself as he is. But let these be thwarted in many respects, or embarrassed with difficulty and opposition, and he is compelled, as it were, to fall back on other resources, which reveal to him, for the first time, the deeper and more essential wants of the soul. Thus are his very capacities of happiness enlarged and elevated.

And what is true of childhood in respect to maturer years is true also of every period of man's progress in respect to the further progress of which he is capable. Let all his present desires be met and satisfied without any exertion on his part, let all his present capacities of happiness be filled to overflowing without any mixture of bitterness or mortification, and he would be content to remain as he is; he would be content to stand still. Progress is the child of struggle, and struggle is the child of difficulty.

Hence in those countries where the soil and climate are so propitious as to leave hardly anything to be done by human endeavor, society is found to advance to a certain point, and there stop. Everything stagnates, merely because man, under such circumstances, is not compelled to labor by the hard necessities of his condition, by what we still persist in calling his hard lot. On the contrary, in those countries where the difficulties of life are the greatest, supposing them not to be of a nature to overwhelm and crush the very thought of success, we find that our nature is invariably developed to the best advantage, and becomes capable of the highest degrees not only of virtue, but of happiness.

Whence, then, this disposition to repine at a constitution of things which demands strenuous effort; which makes it necessary for us to put forth our utmost strength. For what else were we created? It is not, as I have said, an oversight or an accident that we are encompassed with difficulty, that obstacles meet us in every path, that we are constrained to "endure hardness." God meant it should be so; and he meant it not in anger, but in mercy. Difficulty, struggle, progress, — such is the law. In the operation of it many particular gratifications may be intercepted, but our happiness, on the whole, will be infinitely enhanced; many of our particular purposes will be frustrated, but the great end of our being will be secured; our circumstances may not be so well, but we ourselves shall be better.

"Thou, therefore, endure hardness, as a good soldier of Jesus Christ." If I have succeeded in making myself understood, there is good reason for obeying this injunction independently of the divine command. "In the sweat of thy face thou shalt eat bread" was the primal curse under which man fell by his disobedience; and we are still born under the same necessity. But the paternal care and love of God are evinced more, perhaps, in the nature of his curses, as they are called, than in anything else: when met, on our part, in a spirit at once just, resolved, and resigned, these curses are converted into blessings. We owe everything that is good and great and joyous in our destiny to the difficulties which have evoked the qualities on which all progress depends, and all self-reliance, and all self-activity.

You remember that one of the richest mines of the world was accidently discovered by a peasant, as he was climbing slowly up a difficult steep. He caught at a bush to save himself, and steady his steps; the bush gave way, but disclosed at the same time the exhaustless treasure which lay concealed underneath. And so it is in toiling up the difficult steeps of human life: we shall probably catch at many things for support or security which the slightest straining will uproot. As they give way, however, they constrain us to fall back on other resources, lay bare the unfailing energies of the inner man, and make the soul conscious of itself.

Difficulty, struggle, progress, — this, I repeat it, is the law. By this we conquer; by this it is that the spirit gradually obtains ascendency over the flesh; by this it is that the creatures of earth and dust gradually begin a heaven for themselves here; by this it is that the slaves of ignorance and fear and sin throw off the spirit of bondage, and aspire to be children of God; "and if children, then heirs, heirs of God, and joint heirs with Christ; if so be that we suffer with him that we may be glorified together."

# SINS OF OMISSION.

FOR THE GOOD THAT I WOULD, I DO NOT.—Romans vii. 19.

I DO not believe that mankind, as a general rule, think so well of themselves as is commonly supposed. They often put on the appearance of thinking well of themselves, presuming that it is only on this condition they can expect to be thought well of by others; and all wish to be thought well of by others. But, after all, I do not think it would be easy to find a man, unless of the lightest and most frivolous character, who is not humbled and oppressed at times by a sense of his unworthiness, by a sense of his ill-desert before conscience and before God.

Still, in estimating this unworthiness, this ill-desert, there is one class of sins, of which few, if any, make sufficient account. I mean, sins of omission. I do not mean that men in general are disposed to deny they are guilty of such sins. Almost every one, the best men among us, are willing to confess, with the Apostle, that, oftentimes, the good which they would, they do not; that they have left undone many things which they ought to have done. But they do not feel that mere omissions of duty are to be put on the same footing with transgressions of duty. They are willing to confess these omissions, nay, perhaps they sincerely regret them; but it is with but little of the compunction or concern with which they would regret a positive crime. They probably know and feel that they have *lost* more or less by such neglects; but they are slow to believe that they have also incurred thereby a heavy amount of guilt, and, it may be, a terrible retribution.

For this reason, I wish to speak at some length of sins of omission; first, of their nature as sins, and then of their punishment.

And first, of their nature *as sins*. Sin is often defined as consisting in a known opposition to the will of God; but if so, it follows of course that the sin is the same, whether it consists in doing what we know is forbidden, or in not doing what we know is required, for in either case we knowingly oppose God's will. Hence, also, there is an inconsistency in saying that sins of omission are either more or less sinful than positive transgressions; strictly speaking, they *are* positive transgressions. The form of the sin is negative, that is, it consists in *not* doing; but the transgression is positive and open; the law is actually and knowingly and positively broken. If I violate the commandment, "Honor thy father and thy mother," I am guilty of what is called a sin of omission; but it is just as much an open and positive transgression of the law, as if I should violate the commandment, "Thou shalt not steal," or "Thou shalt not kill."

It is true, and this perhaps has given some countenance to the alleged distinction, almost the only sins punished as crimes by *human* laws are sins of commission; but the reason of this is twofold. In the first place, the paramount object of human laws is, not to enforce morality, as such, but to secure social order; which is done, for the most part, merely by prohibiting such actions as subvert or disturb social order. And, in the second place, *the virtues* required of us are seldom capable of being so defined that they can be made to take the form of positive law. Thus the virtue of benevolence makes it to be the duty of every one to relieve the distressed according to his ability; but what human law can prescribe beforehand to whom, and precisely how much, you or I must give in order to fulfil this duty. Besides, our virtues depend, in no small measure, on the inward part of the action, — on *the motive* or *intention;* and motives and intentions are, for the most part, beyond the reach of human jurisdiction. *They* must be left to be rewarded or punished by conscience, and by Him who looketh on the heart.

For these reasons, human laws are content, for the most part, if they can only restrain men from the commission of crime: but not so, morality; above all, not so, Christian morality. In the Parable of the Talents it was no excuse in the case of "the *unprofitable* servant," that he had not wasted or misused his talent; he was "cast into outer darkness" because he had not *added* to his talent, because he had not used it aright, because he had buried it in the earth. A Christian is not made up of negative qualities; it is not enough that he abstains from evil, he must do good: "Therefore, to him that knoweth to do good, and doeth it not, to him it is sin." Even if a man were to keep the Ten Commandments ever so strictly, it would not make him a good Christian; at best, it would only make him a good Jew. The reason is that that ancient summary of the moral law relates, for the most part, to what is forbidden. A man may keep all the Commandments, yet not fulfil one of the Beatitudes; and in this case, without undertaking to say what he *would* be, it is certain what he would *not* be: he would not be a Christian. A man is not a good man, merely because he is not a bad man; at any rate, he is not a Christian. A Christian, I cannot repeat it too often, is not made up of negative qualities; he is not a Christian by virtue of what he has *not* done, but by virtue of what he *has* done, not by virtue of what he is *not*, but by virtue of what he *is*. The whole drift of the Sermon on the Mount is, to show that the external and negative morality which satisfied "them of old time" would no longer satisfy. Under the Gospel, it is not enough that we do not hate our enemy, which is negative morality: we must love him; it is not enough that we do not return evil for evil, which, again, is negative morality: we must "overcome evil with good." The Christian must *aim* "to fulfil all righteousness." I do not mean that he is likely to succeed in this; human infirmity makes it certain he will not: still his hope that his frequent failures will be forgiven is founded on the honesty and thoroughness of his purpose to leave nothing unattempted that may help to make him as perfect as possible in the sight of God.

Looking, therefore, at the essential morality of men's conduct, it is not for any one, certainly it is not for Christians, to make a distinction in favor of sins of omission, as if they were venial offences, as if they merely lessened a man's title to reward, without exposing him to blame or punishment. Whoever starts in life with the notion that nothing is absolutely required of him but to abstain from wrong-doing, forgets that he has to answer for life itself, which was not given to be filled up with wicked, or even with indifferent or unprofitable, but with worthy deeds.

Thus much of the sins of omission, considered as sins. I am next to speak of *the punishment* incurred thereby; that is to say, of the evils they bring on ourselves and on others.

And first, *on ourselves*. If we compare sins of omission with sins of commission, I do not deny that the latter inflict the most *direct* and the most *palpable* harm. A single sin of commission, a single crime of passion, will sometimes blast, in an hour, the prospects of a whole life. The same is also true of the crimes of intemperance, of inordinate ambition, of dishonesty; — their victims are everywhere; so much so, that when we hear of a man's having ruined himself, we always presume that it has been by something which he has *done*, and not by something which he has left *undone*.

But, after all, I suspect there is generally more or less of fallacy or illusion in such judgments. It may be true, as just intimated, that the self-injury caused by overt crime is more immediate and more conspicuous than that caused by culpable neglect; but it does not follow that it is greater or more certain in the long run. Who will say that the aggregate of loss, failure, and suffering occasioned by anger or revenge is greater than that occasioned by indolence; yet indolence is a vice which consists in not doing: it is a sin of omission. A French writer of great note has observed: "It is a mistake to believe that none but the violent passions, such as ambition and love, are able to triumph over the other active principles. Laziness, as languid as it is, often gets the mastery of them all; overrules all the designs and actions of life, and insensibly consumes and destroys both passions and virtues." * Besides, why is it that men are *so apt to fall* into sins of commission? Is it not mainly owing to neglect on their part to fortify themselves beforehand against temptation, as they might have done, and ought to have done? Take, for example, the sins of anger and self-indulgence, which do so much to swell the catalogue of human crimes; who does not know that they happen, in most cases, from neglect to cultivate habits of self-control? But all such neglects are sins of omission. Hence to this class of sins are to be referred not merely the loss and suffering which they directly produce, but also a large proportion of our other sins, together with the evils which follow in their train, including often ignominy and death. The last man that was hung for murder, became a murderer, probably, because he had neglected to cultivate habits of self-control and a proper horror for the shedding of blood; so that the radical wrong, even in his case, was a sin of omission.

There is also another general view to be taken of sins of omission, which will lead us — at least it

---

* One of La Rochefoucauld's *Maxims.*

ought to lead us — to attach more importance than we commonly do to the evils they bring on ourselves. The highest duty of man, and that which underlies all his other duties, is the duty of self-improvement, or *moral progress*. We are born neither virtuous nor vicious, neither righteous nor wicked, but with capacities to become either one or the other to an unlimited degree, according as we use or abuse, cultivate or neglect, the powers and opportunities put into our hands. As *persons*, and not *things*, we are to be what we become in consequence of what *we chose to do or to leave undone*. What we were originally made by the Creator, and what is done for us, day by day, under the forms of human or Divine assistance, are all necessary; nevertheless they result in no good to us personally, except in so far as they result in our actually making intellectual and moral progress. Moreover, in the existing constitution of things, the symbol of this progress is not that of a man floating passively on the stream, but of one struggling against it, and struggling for his life. Let him give over struggling, and he will infallibly be carried down; nay, let him intermit struggling for any considerable time, and his progress will be not only arrested, but reversed.

This being the law of man's moral life, it follows, as some of the best ethical writers have said, that the surest gauge of the gravity of a transgression is found in *the influence it has on our moral progress*. And here, again, I do not mean to deny that the effect of sins of *commission*, under this point of view, is always disastrous, and sometimes fatal. The crimes of injustice, of sensuality, of revenge, especially if deliberate and habitual, are sure to weaken, if they do not destroy, our faith and our moral and religious sensibility; and so are utterly subversive of "growth in grace." Still it may well be doubted whether these crimes, in their worst forms, are more likely to hinder or obstruct moral progress, than *a neglect to cultivate* those principles and dispositions, on which all progress depends.

It is a great mistake to suppose that *character* is spontaneous. I do not mean to call in question the existence of what are sometimes termed moral and religious instincts, as being natural to all men; but these instincts do not become character until moulded into habits. A man may have good or bad impulses; but it does not follow that he has a good or bad character, or *any* character, except perhaps that of fickleness and instability, which properly means *want* of character. There is doubtless a sense in which it is spontaneous and natural for men to tell the truth; nevertheless we do not call a man "a man of truth," until, by self-discipline, he has acquired so confirmed a habit of strict adherence to the truth, that his word can be relied on in all cases. For the same reason, though there is doubtless a sense in which it is spontaneous and natural for men to pray, we do not call a man "a man of prayer," until by constant practice prayer has become a habit with him; until he is not only surprised into it on extraordinary emergencies, but makes it a part of the daily food of his soul. Indeed, all the higher developments of character — integrity, piety, self-devotion — are so far from being spontaneous, that they can only be expected as the fruit of earnest discipline, of assiduous and long-continued self-culture. Accordingly, if this discipline, this self-culture, is neglected (which, however, is but a sin of omission), these virtues become *impossible*. Sins of commission interrupt us, and throw us back, in our progress; but sins of omission make it impossible that the progress should be carried on, or even so much as *begun*.

Again, in order to estimate aright the self-injury which sins of omission inflict, it is also necessary to take into account the bearing of these sins on our moral ability, and on our moral pleasures and satisfactions.

It is common to say, that every one can do what is right if he will; so that his failures are to be ascribed, in every particular instance, not to want of power, but to want of intention or purpose; any other doctrine, as many think, would make God an unrighteous Governor and Judge. And this is true, if nothing more is meant than merely to affirm, that all men are originally endowed with faculties equal to their work, provided only that these faculties are unfolded, trained, and applied as they might be, and ought to be, from the beginning. If, however, these faculties have been perverted, stifled, dwarfed, by any cause, — no matter whether by neglect or abuse, no matter whether by sins of omission or sins of commission, — it is plain that in every such instance the individual must lack *the power*, even if he should have the will, to enter *at once* on the highest acts or the highest enjoyments of the Christian life. Why shut our eyes on the fact, that the world is filled with the morally infirm and impotent of this description? At the same time, such infirmity or impotence is not of the nature of an excuse, because those who suffer from it have brought it on themselves, either by what they have done, or by what they have left undone. When it is said, that no one should be blamed for not doing what is beyond his strength, we are to understand by his strength, in this connection, not something which he possesses, whether he will or no, nor yet something which is given to him to be accepted passively, but something which is given to him *to be acquired*. Accordingly, every man's duty is to be measured, not by what he has actually made himself capable of doing, for he may have abused or neglected his powers, but by what he might have made himself capable of doing.

Thus we see, under another aspect, the wrong which a man does to his own soul by merely neglecting his duty; that is, by what are called "sins of omission." Sins of omission, as was said before, account for our falling so frequently into sins of commission; but this is not all; they absolutely *incapacitate* us, at least for the time, for many, and especially for the higher virtues. Take, for example, a merely *unspiritual* man, meaning thereby one who has merely neglected to excite and develop his spiritual capacities and aspirations, who has merely failed, from any cause, *to cultivate* the habit of faith and of prayer. Now we say of such a person that he is not only guilty of a sin, and that he has failed to surround himself with the sacred guards of religion as a defence against other sins, but also that he has left himself absolutely incapable, for the present, of the crowning graces and joys of the Christian life. He has not taken the preliminary steps. He has not educated himself up to the possibility of the best satisfactions of a religious experience. I do not say that such a man is incapable of believing in Christianity, if nothing more is meant by this than what is called an historical faith; but he is incapable, in the existing state of his mind, of that practical and saving faith which makes the spiritual world present to the imagination and consciousness through a living sympathy with divine things. Again, I do not say of such a man, that he cannot pray, or that he never prays; but this I say: he cannot pray as those do with whom prayer has become by habit as the breath of life, and who feel and know that they are heard in heaven.

You will observe that I have qualified my statements of this incapacity by the words, " for the present," and " in the existing state of his mind ;" but, in a practical view of the subject, these qualifications are hardly necessary. There is a considerable portion of every one's life, during which he can hardly be said to have any character, good or bad; that is, his habits of thought and feeling and action are not as yet determined and fixed. While the character is thus in process of formation, slight causes may essentially modify what it is to be; but after it has been formed, the basis of it, and the pervading spirit of it, are seldom changed. Hence, whoever neglects to do justice to the spiritual elements in his nature, *while his character is forming*, will be almost sure, after his character is formed, to go on as he has begun. With infrequent exceptions, the more noticed because rare, we may say of men of formed characters, " Once unspiritual, always unspiritual." And, besides, even when an unspiritual man in after life, from fear or interest, turns to religion, the service is almost always a constrained service, mingled with regrets and self-upbraidings; so much so, that should God forgive him in view of his sincere though late repentance, he will hardly be able to forgive himself. The only secret of a *happy* religious life, is a life religious from the beginning.

So true it is that a mere neglect, a sin of omission merely, in our early days when the character is taking a determinate shape, may, and often in fact does, seal our fate for time and for eternity.

One word, in conclusion, on the injury which our own sins of omission inflict directly *on others*. It is not pretended that they can be compared, in this respect, with many sins of commission; those, for example, of injustice and cruelty, where the injury, real or intended, which is done to others, measures the enormity of the offence. Even here, however, we should remember, according to what has been said, that injustice and cruelty are seldom committed except in consequence of some neglect,— of neglect to cultivate a spirit of moderation and self-control, and, above all, of that spirit which the Gospel makes to be the foundation and rule of social duty, loving our neighbor as ourselves. Hence it follows that a large proportion of the positive wrong done to others, as well as of that done to ourselves, may be traced, indirectly and remotely, to sins of omission, to early neglects.

Moreover, in estimating what others lose through our sins of omission, it is not enough to take into account their absolute loss. We are to consider that they lose, in this way, all that they *would have gained*, if we had been faithful. To apply this remark to a single case; that of giving faithful counsel and warning to a friend in danger of falling into sin. I have no doubt, that persons in early life are often in that critical condition, in which a word, a look of encouragement or expostulation is sufficient to determine the question of their whole lives. Not to give this word, this look, is a sin of omission merely; thousands are guilty of it without feeling much, if any, compunction; and, in consequence, thousands are lost.

There is also another injury which our sins of omission do to others, and one which is the more to be deprecated, because it falls, for the most part, on those whom we should be most unwilling to harm; I mean, our best friends. It is of the nature of all sin to involve the friends of the sinner, more or less, in the shame and suffering which he brings on himself. Thus in sins of commission, the drunkard, though he violates one of those duties which he is said to owe especially to himself, violates at the same time the duty which he owes to others, involving in his own disgrace and ruin all who cling to him in love, or lean on him for support. The same is also true of sins of omission. Our friends are not satisfied with knowing that we are not drunkards, with knowing that we are not addicted to gross vice of any kind. Their just pride, their affection, their partiality, often their own plans and prospects in life, are bound up with the hope that we shall distinguish ourselves, that we shall possess positive excellences of mind and character, that we shall so improve our opportunities as to fit ourselves for honorable if not distinguished places in society. Whoever wantonly disappoints this hope, fondly cherished by so many loving and anxious hearts, whoever disappoints it, though merely by indolence or remissness on his own part, that is, by sins of omission, by not doing what he knows he can do and ought to do, betrays an unkindness, an ingratitude, a baseness, which it is hard to overstate.

Let us learn, then, to regard mere neglects, sins of omission, in a more serious light. And it is the more necessary that this should be impressed on all, because the sins of which I now speak are those to which good men, as well as bad men, are continually liable. They are also sins which shock no natural sentiment, which attract no considerable attention at the time, which awaken no public indignation. Yet these sins prepare the way for all other sins. The world is full of folly and wickedness; but the fountain-head of all folly and wickedness is found in an indolent, neglectful, thoughtless spirit. "For the good that I would, I do not."

Let me remind you, once more, of the Parable of the Talents. It is not necessary that you should misapply or waste your talent; if you only bury it in the earth, you must expect the doom, "Cast ye the unprofitable servant into outer darkness; there shall be weeping and gnashing of teeth."

# NO HIDING-PLACE FOR THE WICKED.

**BE SURE YOUR SIN WILL FIND YOU OUT.** — Numbers xxxii. 23.

Less is done towards repressing crime by merely increasing the penalty than might, at first thought, be supposed. The reason is, that penalties are for the detected alone; but most persons in deliberating on crime count on escaping detection. Hence the importance of exposing the vanity of this expectation. I think to be able to show that the wicked in no case have a right to count upon concealment as an ultimate ground of security and peace. "Be sure your sin will find you out."

In cases of heinous crimes this, I suppose, will be generally admitted. When the deed is of such a nature as to outrage human feeling, and incense the community as one man, it is hardly possible that the perpetrator should escape. His guilt may come to light by what seems to be the merest accident, and hence it is sometimes thought, that his being detected *at all* is a mere accident: but this is a mistake. In such a case there are innumerable accidents, as they are called, any one of which may betray the culprit; and where, in a highly excited state of the public mind, there are innumerable accidents, any one of which *may* betray the culprit, it is not a mere accident, but amounts to moral certainty, that some one of them actually *will*. Thus, if a man has committed murder, or highway robbery, you may say it is a mere chance, that he was overheard plotting the crime, or that he was betrayed by an accomplice, or that he was seen lurking about the spot, or that anything was afterwards found about his person, or his residence, leading to his conviction: and so of any one of the thousand possible ways of detection. But that he should actually be detected in some one of these thousand possible ways is not a matter of chance, but of moral certainty.

With regard to minor offences, which create no public alarm, and lead to no special investigations, the offender, it is true, may often go, for a time, not only unconvicted, but unsuspected. Mark, however, the issue. The secrecy and impunity with which the deed is done will infallibly encourage and embolden him to repeat it under other circumstances, and with greater and greater aggravations, multiplying at every step the chances of discovery, until discovery, as in the case before mentioned, becomes morally certain. Felons have confessed on the scaffold, that they stood there in consequence of the misfortune of not having been detected in their first and slightest deviations from rectitude. The delay operated only as a decoy of the Evil One. It was the patient waiting of the Tempter, that his victim might become more entirely and hopelessly involved, before the snare was sprung.

But enough respecting crimes of which the laws take cognizance. Let us pass to the consideration of those offences which are punished, for the most part, by loss of reputation or loss of confidence.

And here, again, we do not suppose that every particular act will be detected or suspected: if it were so, it would do more harm than good. Men are sometimes surprised, over-persuaded, or betrayed into single acts which have little or nothing to do with their real character; that is to say, with their *habits* of thought and feeling and conduct. Thus, from momentary inadvertence, or misinformation, or mere physical depression, a man may be guilty of a single act of meanness, though in his nature and disposition the reverse of mean. And the same is also true of *single acts* of servility, rudeness, injustice, cruelty, excess. Now we do not say that every such act will be reported and believed; for the public, at least the best part of the public, is slow to credit rumors which are contradicted, or seem to be contradicted, by the whole tenor of a man's life. And this is well. No good would come from the occasional lapses of worthy men being in everybody's mouth. It is not necessary as a warning to beware of their society, for there is no danger in the society of such men; and, besides, it would lead to substantial injustice, because it would lead to charges or suspicions implicating the whole character of men whose character is in the main sound.

No doubt one of the consequences is, that while bad men often pass for being worse than they really are, good men quite as often pass for being better, or at any rate for being more faultless or immaculate than they really are; — a remark which is especially applicable to the great names of history, where only the leading and characteristic traits are given. But this, too, is wisely ordered, as it helps to keep up the standard of virtue; — not only of that virtue which has been, but also of that which is to be. Hence the repugnance so generally and so properly felt at the officiousness of those who seek to bring to light the infirmities and inconsistencies of really great and good men, now no more; especially when the reputation and memory of these men have come to be regarded as part of the moral wealth, as well as of the just pride, of their country.

Let it be, then, that single acts often are, and of right ought to be, buried in oblivion, especially when they do not represent the real character: but not so, with the character itself;—if that be bad, "be sure your sin will find you out." The scoffer, the intriguer, the sharper, the libertine,—are they not known? I do not mean, every particular offence they have committed, but what sort of men they are. Of course, the usages of what is called good society will not allow us to tell them so to their faces: nay more, these usages often lead us, far beyond what is necessary or right, to pay an outward respect to persons for whom no inward respect is felt. But listen to men's speeches in their places of business, or in social intercourse, or in the family circle, and you will find that they are not quite so regardless of moral distinctions, that they are not quite so much the dupes of hollow pretension, even when upheld by wealth and influence and show, as might at first sight appear.

Instances in which individuals have succeeded *for any length of time* in hiding their true character from the world are much more rare than is commonly thought. Take, for example, the vices of dissipation and excess,—how almost invariably do they betray themselves in the looks, the gait, and the decaying health, as well as in the wasted fortunes, of their victim! The mark is upon him, beyond the power of cosmetics, or grace of manners, or social position, to conceal. And even in respect to the vices of craft and dissimulation, — who does not know that it is of the nature of the plausibility and address which these imply to awaken distrust? so that, though a mist may thus be thrown around the character which will prevent anything from being distinctly seen, it will only be that everything may be suspected. I do not say, you will observe, that every bad action of such a man will come to light, but only that his leading propensities will; and after this, that is, after his neighbors have begun to look upon him as addicted to craft and dissimulation, depend upon it, for one bad action which he commits without being suspected, he will be suspected of twenty of which he is wholly innocent.

It will be objected, perhaps, that I have not allowed enough for the wonderful abilities of bad men, by which they are able to elude or baffle discovery. Let me begin my reply to this remark by protesting generally against that senseless cant, which would make every knave a man of talents, and talk about there being more ingenuity and mother wit in prisons than in colleges. Undoubtedly here and there an individual may be found, among the self-abandoned, of more than ordinary native power, who, in different circumstances, and under a different training, might have made himself a useful, and perhaps a distinguished member of society. But, even in such cases, it is of the nature of conscious guilt to contract and cow the most gifted mind; under the influence of which native sagacity degenerates into a vile cunning, that is proverbial for taking narrow views, and miscalculating remote consequences, and so, in the end, circumventing itself.

Of a piece with this cant about the wonderful abilities of bad men is the cant about their honor,— the honor, which, according to the proverb, is found among thieves, enabling them to trust each other with safety. Formerly, I suppose, there was more of this than there is now, or is likely to be again. Formerly superstition, though it did not keep bad men true to morality in general, often had the effect to keep them true to dark and mysterious pledges entered into among themselves. But superstition, among such persons, is now everywhere giving place to total infidelity, to a blank atheism, and this is destroying the last hold which the bad have on each other.

Under these circumstances, I might ask again for evidence of the caution or sagacity of bad men, of which so much is said, seeing that they are so ready to confide in others whom they must know to be as bad as themselves. Nay, on any principle, it would be difficult to account for such recklessness, if we did not know that daring outrages generally suppose and require an extended conspiracy; that there are few vices which a man can commit absolutely alone; and that, even in respect to these, there is a dreariness in crime which craves companionship at any risk. Explain the fact, however, as you will, or leave it unexplained, it cannot fail to multiply at every step the chances, that is to say, the antecedent probabilities, of exposure and public shame. "Be sure your sin will find you out."

"Curse not the king," says the Preacher, "no, not in thy thought; and curse not the rich in thy bed-chamber; for a bird of the air shall carry the voice, and that which hath wings shall tell the matter." The ways in which crime has been brought to light have been so mysterious, so inexplicable, as to afford to the popular mind, in all ages, the most convincing proof that an overruling Providence occasionally interposes in the affairs of men. This is true not only of the crimes which are punished judicially, but also of those which are punished by the loss of confidence, the loss of friendship, or the more terrible reprisals of public scorn and indignation. Everybody is known. The professed thieves and rogues of England make it matter of banter that, by a mathematical calculation of chances, they can tell beforehand, within the fraction of a year, how long they are likely to elude the vigilance of the police. Sooner or later everybody is known, — not only the thief, the robber, the murderer, but the rogue in a small way, the hypocritical pretender to religion, the charlatan in science, the gamester, the libertine, the swindler in genteel life, — sooner or later all are known. Indeed, so various and subtile are the means of self-delusion and self-mystification, I do not think I go too far when I say, that in many cases, perhaps in most cases, a man is sooner found out by his neighbors than by himself. This remark applies to the young especially, who, from want of experience, do not know how far they can go in vicious indulgences before a character is formed, and who therefore think but lightly of what they have done thus far, as implying nothing worse than levity or indiscretion on their part, while their friends, who understand human nature better, are mourning over them as wellnigh lost.

But I have insisted on the notoriety of crime further than my text requires : " Be sure your *sin* will find you out," *even if the world does not*. Suppose the sin locked up in the sinner's breast, and suppose, moreover, that he feels no proper compunction for it, it does not follow that he feels no inquietude, no anxiety. The freedom, the confidence, the peace, the self-respect of conscious integrity are gone when the integrity itself is gone. Mere reputation, whether well or ill-founded, may win applause, it is true ; but applause is not likely to give much inward satisfaction to one who is conscious that it is bestowed through ignorance or mistake, and that it would be changed into scorn if the truth were known. And then there is the unceasing apprehension that the truth will be known, — a nervous uneasiness about the future, an anxious looking into men's faces to see whether they have not begun to suspect us, an ingenuity of self-torture which construes the slightest coincidence into evidence that the secret is out. So keenly is this sometimes felt, even in matters involving only the loss of property and social position, that persons who have contrived to conceal their failing circumstances from the world for years, have afterwards confessed that they never had a moment's peace until their real condition was known; in other words, that the dreaded discovery was a means of relieving their minds of a burden which had become intolerable. And so, of crime. Felons have borne about the secret of their guilt, until they could bear it no longer, and then have informed against themselves, and surrendered themselves up to justice, under the maddening conviction that the hell of reality could not be worse than the hell of suspense.

I will now go one step further, and suppose the sin not only unknown to the public, but unacknowledged and ususpected by the sinner himself. This may sometimes happen from the influence of custom or fashion or a bad education in making men insensible to moral distinctions; especially where the sin consists not so much in what we have done, as in what we have left undone. Even in this case, however, "be sure your sin will find you out"; for its effects on your progress and happiness, and its consequences generally in the present life and the life to come, will still follow, whether you trace them or not to their true cause. Thousands, for example, lament the want of a devout spirit, ascribing it to constitutional defects, or the necessities of their condition, when, in fact, it is mostly, if not wholly, the just penalty of an habitual and voluntary neglect of the means of religion. Others, again, are cursed, they know not why, with a sceptical turn of mind, or with a misanthropic disposition, or with sordid or depraved tastes, which make them incapable, for the time, of seeing or enjoying the highest truth and the highest good. If they would look a little more closely and faithfully into their own conduct, and into the laws of the human constitution, they would find, at least as a general rule, that they are but abiding the penalty, the just and inevitable doom which follows, whether they know it or not, the indulgence of a cavilling spirit, or low desires, or the mere neglect to cultivate and cherish the social virtues. Their sin has found them out, though they have not found out their sin.

Those, therefore, who do not find out the sin from itself, will be likely to find it out sooner or later from its consequences, and see its connection with these consequences, and awake at length to their true moral condition. Remorse does not depend on the fact of our degradation, nor on our sense of this fact, but on our sense of the manner in which it has been incurred. We feel that we have brought it on ourselves. We feel that we might have done differently. We feel that we have taken the sovereign gifts of reason and freedom, and made one the pander, and the other the slave of our passions and lusts. Hence our abasement and anguish under the impending decree of Eternal Justice. And this remorse, — exult not in the thought that you can stifle or dissipate it for a while. It is the madness of one who would drug himself with opiates in the first stages of a fever; it is allowing the fire to burn on, which is burning into the very heart of your life and peace. And all such efforts must fail at last. History abounds with instances of bold bad men, whom a self-accusing spirit has overtaken at last, even in this world, and smitten them with sudden and unimaginable terrors. But suppose them to die, untouched and unreclaimed, it will not be through any incapacity or insensibility of the soul itself; but through the power of worldly objects and pursuits to blind, distract, or lull the soul. At death all these will pass away, and the soul will be left as it is, naked and defenceless in the hands of an avenging conscience and an avenging God.

This, then, is the conclusion of the whole matter.

Let no one count upon concealment as an ultimate ground of security and peace. If addicted to sin, by no cunning or address can we hope to elude the eye even of man for any length of time; much less that of God, or the scourges of a self-upbraiding mind, or those dark and shapeless forms of woe which menace us from the eternal world, and await us there. How truly and solemnly do the Scriptures say of a wicked man, that he "walketh upon a snare." "He that walketh uprightly walketh surely: but he that perverteth his ways shall be known."

# THOU SHALT SAY, NO.

THOU SHALT SAY, NO. — Judges iv. 20.

HERE is one of the shortest words in our language; yet there is none which persons of an easy and yielding disposition find it so difficult to pronounce. To say it, however, is one of the first lessons which we have occasion to learn, and one of the most frequent we are called upon to practise. You can hardly mention a cause which has done more to lead men into embarrassment, distress, and crime, than disregard of this caution. And what makes it worse is, that men of the best understandings and finest natural dispositions are quite as liable as any to fall into the snare. It is not generally our judgment which is at fault in such cases. We know that the solicitation is an improper one, and ought to be resisted; still we cannot muster resolution enough to do it.

A young man just entering into life is solicited by his gay companions to take part in their dissipations. He feels that it would be wrong; that it can lead to nothing but evil; that it ought to be resisted. And yet he cannot muster resolution enough to say, No. He consents, goes on from step to step, and in the end is ruined. An affectionate mother is besought by her children to grant them some improper indulgence. She feels that it would be an improper indulgence; that it can only do them harm, and therefore that she ought not to grant it. And yet she cannot find it in her heart to say, No. She consents, and her children are materially injured, perhaps ruined. A person is importuned by his family, or his friends, to go into habits of living more expensive than he can afford. He knows that his resources are not equal to it. He feels that this will soon appear, and therefore that it is folly and madness in him to do it. And yet he cannot muster resolution enough to say, No. He consents, and is ruined. A man in business is importuned to be bound for another. He feels that it would be the height of imprudence; that it would be to risk not his own property only, but that of his creditors, and this too, perhaps, without any real benefit to the person he would befriend. He feels that he has no right to do it. And yet he cannot find it in his heart to say, No. He consents, and it turns out just as he expected, — he is ruined.

All this comes from a man's not having resolution enough to say, No, when he feels and knows that this is the proper word. You must admit, therefore, I think, that the subject is of sufficient importance to engage your attention, while a few considerations are offered which should induce us all to act with more firmness and consistency in this respect.

In the first place, then, let us learn to respect our own judgment in what we do. If, on a view of all the circumstances, we think we ought to say, No, let us have the *courage and firmness and independence* to say it.

As we have before observed, it is not often that our judgment is at fault in such cases. We think right, but we have not courage and independence enough to act as we think; for fear that after all we may be mistaken; or for fear of the construction other people may put on our motives; or for fear of losing the favor or incurring the enmity of the persons we may disoblige by our refusal. We should remember, however, that there is a degree of courage, firmness, and independence necessary, not only to a wise, but even to a virtuous conduct. A man who dares not act according to his own convictions of what is right, for fear that after all he may be mistaken,—I will not say that he has no regard for conscience, but this I will say: he has no confidence in conscience, which in practice amounts to nearly the same thing. Besides, with respect to the construction which other people may put on our motives, if we only take care that our motives are what they should be, and that our whole conduct is in keeping, we need not entertain any apprehensions but that in the long run ample justice will be done them by all whose approbation is worth having. Nay, a person who is understood to pursue this independent course, — who is understood to act in all cases from his own convictions of what is proper and right, derives a peculiar credit from this very circumstance; so that though in his conduct he may sometimes fall into manifest error, his motives will never be called in question. Things will not be blamed in him which would hardly be tolerated in anybody else. And even the person whom you disoblige by your refusal, you will not lose his regard if he is convinced, by the firmness and consistency of your general conduct, that you refuse him on principle. Nay, he will feel, and in spite of himself he cannot but feel, a thousand times more respect for you who thus refuse his request, than for those who grant it, under circumstances, however, which convince him, that it is only because they have not, like you, sufficient firmness and independence to say, No.

I have shown that it is but the part of a manly independence to have the courage and firmness to say, No, when we are convinced that this is the proper word. I shall proceed to show, in the second place, that it is no less a dictate of *prudence, and practical wisdom.*

You can hardly step your foot on the threshold of life without encountering seduction in every possible shape; and unless you are prepared to resist it firmly, you are a doomed man. What makes it still more dangerous is, that the first solicitations of vice often come under such disguised forms, and relate to things seemingly so trivial, as to give hardly any warning of the fatal consequences, to which by slow and insensible gradations they are almost sure to lead. As you value, then, your health and reputation, your peace of mind and personal independence, learn to say, No. You that are just entering into life, do not wait to learn it from your own bitter experience; learn it from the example and fate of others; learn it from the Word of God. Remember, it was for not doing this that our first parents fell; and after them all their children, in like manner. "The serpent beguiled me, and I did eat," has been the history of sin, from its first commencement in the Garden of Eden. Inquire into the sources of human misery, study the first beginnings of crime, and, meet with it where you may, by tracing it back to its first cause you will find it to have been, in almost every instance, merely because they could not say, No, to the

Tempter. Put the question to one who has wasted his substance in riotous living, put it to him who has staked his last shilling and lost it at the gaming-table, put it to the first miserable object who asks alms of you in the streets, or go into your prisons and put it to the felon there; and they will all answer you to the same effect, and almost in the same words. The burden of their confession will be, that they owe every calamity which has befallen them to their not having had firmness enough, at some turning-point of their destiny, to say, No.

As you would avoid their fate, let me then conjure you to avoid its cause. I am not now appealing to your sense of right, or the obligations you are under to society or your Maker. I am appealing to the strongest, or at least the most universal instinct in the human mind, — a desire to escape evil in your own persons; and if there were no other topic of which I could avail myself, this alone I should consider as sufficient, so clearly is the maxim which I am recommending a dictate of an enlightened and well-regulated self-love. To be sure it is easy enough to conceive of cases in which to say, No, even though we ought to say it, may give us some pain at the time. But what of that? How much better, how much more prudent to meet this evil at once, rather than suffer it to grow upon us by concession and delay, and this, too, with a moral certainty that it must be met sooner or later, and under circumstances of continually increasing pain and difficulty. If we could say, Yes, to everything, and that were the last of it, we might be inclined, very naturally and very reasonably, to a course apparently so amiable and so accommodating. But when we know that it is only to involve ourselves and our friends in the ruinous consequences of a mistake which will certainly injure, and very possibly may ruin both,—who does not perceive that it is to violate every principle of practical wisdom?

The same conduct which I have shown to be necessary to a manly independence and to a prudent regard to our own interest, I shall next prove to be *in no sense inconsistent with a benevolent and truly generous disposition.*

One of the most common mistakes on this subject is to confound an *easy* disposition with a *benevolent* disposition: two things which in fact are as wide asunder as the East from the West. A man of an easy disposition is so commonly merely because he will not make the effort a more firm and steady conduct requires. And why will he not make this effort? Because he will not take the trouble of making it. He yields to importunity in almost every instance from the same motive with the unjust judge mentioned in Scripture: "Lest by her continual coming she weary me." But is this benevolence? Is it so much as an abuse of benevolence? Is it not sheer selfishness?

I know that another plea is often set up. It is remarkable of most of our weaknesses, as of our vices, that all are for claiming kindred with virtue, pretending to be the offspring of some good disposition, — carried a little too far perhaps, but still a good disposition. This propensity is strikingly exemplified in the weakness which it is our present object to expose. We choose to believe and to have others believe, that our unwillingness to say, No, arises wholly, or chiefly, from our unwillingness to give anybody the pain of a refusal; that it springs from benevolence, because it hurts our feelings to hurt the feelings of other people: so that, after all, the worst that can be said of it is, that it is an excess of benevolence.

But let us examine this plea a little more closely. It is, you will observe, because it hurts *our* feelings to hurt the feelings of other people that we are thus unwilling to say, No. It might hurt the feelings of other people just as much as it now does, and still if this did not, by a law of our nature, have the effect to hurt *our* feelings too, it is not pretended that we should experience any of this reluctance. To give a case in point. A weak mother cannot make up her mind to refuse anything to a darling child, even though she knows it will be to the child's serious injury, and all, forsooth, because it will hurt her feelings so much to give the child the pain of a refusal. Suppose it will hurt *her* feelings; it is certainly a strange mark of benevolence to the child to be willing to do him an essential injury, rather than to hurt her own feelings. After all, you perceive that it is *her own* feelings she is thinking of, and not the good of the child; nay, that she is willing to sacrifice the good of the child to her own feelings. And pray, is not this selfishness, — a little disguised perhaps, a little refined perhaps, but still at bottom a real selfishness?

A timid acquiescence in what we feel to be wrong is often the result of mere selfishness; and where it is not the result of selfishness, it is the result of weakness. Indeed, we can hardly give to any one so strong a proof of genuine friendship, as to resist his importunities to the last, when convinced that it would be to his injury, were we to consent. For it shows that we are thinking of his good, and that we have more regard for that than for our own feelings, or even for his good opinion.

Having shown that independence, prudence, and benevolence alike require the conduct I have been recommending, it only remains for me, in the fourth and last place, to urge it upon you as a matter of *moral and religious duty*.

It is a great error, though a common one, not to

suppose that the principle of duty extends to almost all our actions; requiring them or forbidding them, as being either right or wrong. We talk of actions as being honorable or dishonorable, as being prudent or imprudent, as being benevolent or otherwise, but what is honorable or prudent or benevolent is also right. Everything, therefore, which has already been said to prove the conduct in question a dictate of benevolence, prudence, and manly independence, goes also to the same extent to prove it to be our duty, — our imperative duty.

Besides, take the words as they stand. If, considering all the circumstances, we *ought* to say, No, then it is our duty to say it, let the consequences be what they may. It is nothing, that the customs of the country authorize and even expect a different conduct; it is nothing, that the world may put a false construction on our motives; it is nothing that it may hurt our own feelings or the feelings of others. There are many other duties which we are called upon to practise at all these hazards; but in no case do these hazards, or can these hazards, procure for us a dispensation. If it is our duty, it is our duty. If it can only be practised at great sacrifices, this is our misfortune; but it does not annul the laws of God; it does not destroy our obligations or make them any less binding, or the consequences of violating them any the less certain or fearful.

It is then our duty, our imperative duty to say, No, to all improper solicitations. Let us do it, therefore, *because it is our duty.* Let this be our motive; for but little reliance can be placed on the other motives if this be not also felt; nay, if this be not the predominant motive. Some men can never say, No, unless they are in a passion, and are therefore driven to the mortifying necessity of working themselves up into a passion before they can find the courage to do it. Again there are others, who will trust themselves to say, No, only as a matter of policy; and with whom, therefore, the question is not, What ought I to say? but, What will it be for my interest to say? There is also a third class that will say, No, — and say it often enough too, if that were all, — from mere churlishness and ill-humor; but I need not observe that this is very far from being the conduct I am here recommending. Putting aside all such considerations, let us learn to resist improper solicitations from a sense of duty. It should be enough to know that it is our duty. Let us act on this principle, and we shall never refuse except when duty requires it; but at such times our refusal will be much more decided and effectual, while it will be made under circumstances of much greater dignity on our part, and of much less irritation on the part of those whom it may disappoint.

Moreover, while we act from a sense of duty, we

should connect with this feeling a conviction that it is one of *religious* obligation. God has required us to pursue a course of undeviating rectitude. Whoever, therefore, would seduce us from this, sets himself against God, and we must deny one or the other. Whether in such a case we should deny God, rather than man, let conscience judge.

From what has been said we must perceive, that it is alike the dictate of independence, prudence, benevolence, and duty to resist all improper solicitations. Let us learn then to say, No; and let us mean what we say; and let us stand by what we mean.

Are you solicited to engage in any pursuits, or to enter into any engagements which your consciences reject, or which you foresee will bring a cloud on your prospects of honor and usefulness? "Thou shalt say, No." Are you pressed to grant favors or indulgences to persons who have no right to ask them, or who can only be injured by them, — favors or indulgences, too, which you are not in a condition to bestow consistently with your other engagements? "Thou shalt say, No." Are you importuned to join in any amusements, to consent in any customs or concur in any measures, which you believe will sully the purity of your character or lessen the weight of your good influences, or in any way exert a mischievous effect on society?

"Thou shalt say, No." Let the consequences be what they may, "Thou shalt say, No."

And for your reward you will have the approbation of your own consciences, the esteem and confidence of all whose favor is worth desiring, and an escape from all those embarrassing and perhaps fatal consequences in which a more compliant conduct would have entangled you. And what shall I say more? In a better world such a course of firm, consistent, and undeviating rectitude will be rewarded by the applause of angels, the welcome of the Saviour, — "glory, honor, and peace."

# THE HEART MORE THAN THE HEAD.

KEEP THY HEART WITH ALL DILIGENCE; FOR OUT OF IT ARE THE ISSUES OF LIFE. — Proverbs iv. 23.

It is quite obvious that most men practically underrate the influence of the *heart*, compared with that of the *head*, on success and happiness. It is also easy to account for the mistake, and, at the same time, to show that it *is* a mistake; and this is what I now propose to do. I propose to show that the Heart is more than the Head in all the great interests and issues of human life.

It is so, in the first place, if we look only at *human dignity*. We are apt, I know, to slide into a different opinion, from the habit of regarding *reason* as man's distinction and glory. As for the passions and affections, we are said to share *them* with the inferior animals; but reason belongs to man alone. Hence the natural conclusion, that reason, the intellect, the head and not the heart, is the principal thing.

But this conclusion, however natural, is unfounded. There can be no doubt that what constitutes the distinction and glory of man may be traced ultimately to his reason. Still his highest distinction and glory are not found in his reason as manifested in mere understanding, but in his reason as manifested in his active and moral powers; that is to say, in his sentiments, dispositions, affections, after they have been informed and transfigured by reason. When we are told, as above, that we share our passions and affections with the inferior animals, we are told one of those half-truths, which are often found to be among the most pernicious, certainly among the most seductive, of errors. I do not deny that animals have what may be called the shadows, or, if you please, the germs, the beginnings of *some* of the human passions and affections: such as gratitude and resentment, the love of society and the love of offspring. But in animals these springs of action always operate as blind instincts; they are never unfolded by thought, as in man, into intelligent and moral principles, and never can be; and therefore can never properly be represented as being the same in animals as in man, though called by the same name. Moreover, there are some passions and affections in man, which not only suppose reason, but are founded on it; such as the love of truth, the love of beauty, the love of virtue, and the love of God; of which animals do not have, and cannot have, even so much as the beginnings or germs. Accordingly we say, that the proper *human* passions and affections, some of which are founded on reason, and all of which are touched and illuminated by reason, are *not* shared by the inferior animals; that there is nothing among the animal instincts which answers to what is meant by *the human heart;* and furthermore, that it is in the distinctions of this heart, and not in those of mere understanding, sagacity, cunning, that the loftiest qualities of human nature are found.

Some may object with confidence, that compass and reach of intellect are certainly elements of *power*, and that power *exalts*, if it does not *bless*. But is it so clear that compass and reach of intellect, simply considered, are elements of power? Can you not conceive of persons, have you never met with persons, who are very *knowing*, yet very inefficient and weak where anything is to be *done?* I am afraid it may sound like affectation or pedantry to call in question the often repeated aphorism of Lord Bacon, that "Knowledge is power." Nevertheless, knowledge is *not* power, personal power, but only one of its instruments. The power is not in the knowledge, but in the moral qualities or the passions which accompany it, which lie behind it, constituting what is called *force of character*. Without this force of character, which resides in the impulsive part of our nature, all the knowledge in the world would not make a man personally powerful either for good or for evil. I do not deny that the highest order of greatness among civilized men supposes high intellectual endowments; but it supposes them just as the highest order of greatness among savages supposes gigantic strength and stature. It supposes them, not as the essence, but as the instrument of greatness: the essence of greatness, always and everywhere, is a *great spirit*. Where this exists in an eminent degree, that is to say, where there is a union of courage, self-devotion, and a lofty purpose, it is amazing how much a man can do, without extraordinary intellectual gifts, to make himself really great, to impress himself on the circle in which he moves, and even on his country and the age, and this, too, not merely as a man of affairs, but as a controlling mind in church or state.

Thus much of human *greatness*. But if, as befits the condition and prospects of most men, we do not aspire to be great, but only to be truly *happy*, here I hardly need say that the heart is not only the principal thing, but almost everything. What is happiness but the sum total of the gratifications of a man's affections and desires? Here, therefore, it is certain that the heart is more than the head. *Intellectual* superiority has been shown to be, and we have expressly allowed it to be, one of the instruments of greatness, though not any part of the essence of real greatness; but I am not sure that we have a right to set it down as being even so much as one of the means or *instruments* of happiness. You may urge that it often enlarges a man's sphere of usefulness: and so it does; but the *happiness* resulting from usefulness does not depend on the *amount* of good done; it depends on the *spirit* with which it is done, on its being done from the *love* of goodness. Still you may insist, that so far as happiness is made up of the pleasures of knowledge, it must certainly be greater in proportion to the extent of the knowledge. Even this, however, by no means follows. The pleasures of knowledge itself do not depend on the *extent* of the knowledge, or of the capacity of knowledge, but on the *love* of knowledge; which brings us back again to a quality of the heart.

But enough of greatness and happiness; it is time to speak of *character*. I observe, then, secondly, that the heart has more to do than the head in determining *the distinctions of character*.

We have just seen that men often mistake the relation which reason bears to human dignity. It is also true that they often mistake the relation which *principle* bears to character. There is an ambiguity in the meaning of this word, on the strength of which many will argue thus: Every man becomes what his *principles* make him; but a man's principles are what he *thinks* to be right. Now *to think* is obviously a function of the head, and not of the heart, of the intellect, and not of the feelings: whence they conclude that every man is what the use or abuse of his intellect makes him to be.

In order to set aside this conclusion it is not necessary to contradict, in terms, the proposition on which the argument is based. All must agree that a man's real character depends, not on his outward actions, but on the principles from which he acts. By *principles*, however, in this connection, we are not to understand *express*, but *operative* principles; not abstract rules assented to as true and right, but real *springs of action* existing in the individual himself; that is to say, his predominant appetites, desires, affections. We aim to judge men, as far as we are able, not according to what they *do*, nor yet according to what they *think;* but according to what they *incline to* or *love:* not according to what they think they *ought* to love, but according to what they show they *really* love. Thus we do not call a man a miser merely because he saves money; for he may save money to give it away: but we call a man a miser because he saves money from the *love* of money. Again, we call a man generous, not because he is lavish of his gifts; for he may be lavish of his gifts from ostentation, or from political motives: but we call him generous, because we believe him to give from a generous *disposition*. For the same reason, we call a man cheerful and resigned, not because we understand him to have come to the conclusion that cheerfulness and resignation are good things; but because we believe that he really has a cheerful and resigned *temper*.

But why multiply illustrations? In our judgments of character, and especially in our more solemn judgments of moral character, it is always so. Law, human law, deals with the outward act; morality, with the inward feeling, sentiment, or propensity which prompts the act. Morality, it is true, pronounces the *act* to be right or wrong; it approves or condemns the *outward act*, but it approves or condemns it as *exemplifying* some good or bad affection or disposition. At bottom, what is approved or condemned is some good or bad affection or disposition. To be convinced of this it is only necessary to reflect, how instantly our gratitude for a gift is changed into indifference or contempt, on ascertaining that it did not originate, as we at first supposed, in the kindness or generosity of the giver, but in some selfish or sinister purpose: for example, that it was intended to seduce or corrupt us.

Thus it appears that all the distinctions of character, as well as of happiness and dignity, resolve themselves at last into distinctions of disposition or temper, and not of intellect or understanding, showing incontestably, as it seems to me, that the heart, and not the head, is the principal thing.

So likewise the Gospel teaches. Here, I am aware, we have no right to construe the term *heart*, which is of so frequent recurrence in Scripture, as suggesting *of itself*, as it commonly does in modern speech, the antithesis between the affections and the understanding; or, in other words, *the heart* in contradistinction to *the head*. The reason is, that, in popular language, the ancients generally, and among the rest the Hebrews, did not, like us, make the head the seat of the understanding, and the heart the seat of the affections: they made the heart to be the seat of both. Still whenever the state of the heart is referred to in the New Testament as a condition of Divine favor, or of final salvation, I believe it can always be shown, either from the connection, or in some other way, to denote a state of the affections, — a state of the active and moral powers, — and not of the understanding merely, or of the speculative convictions, or of outward service. "For he is not a Jew, who is one outwardly; neither is that circumcision which is outward in the flesh: but he is a Jew, who is one *inwardly;* and circumcision is that of the heart, *in the spirit* and not in the letter, whose praise is not of men, but of God." The same doctrine is inculcated, and if possible still more explicitly and emphatically, in the two great commandments which sum up the whole of what is peculiar to Christian duty. "Jesus said unto him, 'Thou shalt *love* the Lord thy God with all thy heart, and with all thy soul, and with all thy mind. This is the first and great commandment. And the second is like unto it, Thou shalt *love* thy neighbor as thyself.'"

To this some may object, that the primary conception of Christianity is that of *a revelation*, a revelation of *truth*; so that the great and all-important act of accepting it must be an *intellectual* act; not something to be felt, but something to be understood and believed; something, in short, which the head is to do, and not the heart.

The objection, as here stated, is certainly not without force. If the Gospel were now set forth for the first time as a new revelation, and we were called upon to believe it, or not, according as the evidence should strike our minds, it would perhaps be true, that the *first* act in becoming a Christian, or rather, in putting ourselves into a condition to become a Christian, would be an intellectual act. First of all, we should have to decide the question, whether Jesus really was, what he claimed to be, "a Teacher come from God;" and this decision, right or wrong, would be an act of the understanding, — of the judgment, and not of the affections. To a certain extent this *was* the state of things in the primitive Church: the Gospel was preached to

Jews and pagans, who had to be convinced that the old religions were false or imperfect, and that the new religion was true, before they could be said to be in a condition to become Christians. Hence, I hardly need say, much of the stress which the New Testament lays on *knowing* and *believing*, and on distinguishing between the *true* and the *false*, as the first things to be attended to. Even under such circumstances, however, though the intellectual act must be admitted to be the first act in the order of time, it by no means follows that it would be the principal act. Thousands and tens of thousands have believed that " Jesus is the Christ," without even so much as trying, or seriously intending, to have his spirit, or walk in his steps; who were, therefore, " none of His." They have not even so much as begun *to be Christians:* they have only begun *to believe in Christianity.* " Yea, a man may say, Thou hast faith, and I have works: show me thy faith without thy works, and I will show thee my faith by my works. Thou believest that there is one God; thou doest well: *the devils also believe, and tremble.*"

And, besides, I have been referring to a state of things very different from that which prevails at present in the Christian world. We are now born into a community which is Christian, so far at least as this, that the truth of Christianity is taken for granted in most of the forms and institutions of society, in the current literature of the day, in the prayers and catechisms which are taught in the nursery. The consequence is, that we *begin with believing*. We do not begin with doubting, or even with inquiring; we begin with believing, and the multitude never know what it is *not to believe*. They are not called upon to choose their religion; they do not pass from a state of unbelief or misbelief into the true belief; they take Christianity for granted from the beginning. Though they may occasionally have their difficulties about it, the multitude never think of renouncing it as a fable. With respect to them, therefore, not merely the principal, but the first and sole change through which they pass in becoming practical Christians, is a change from believing Christianity to be true to *feeling* it to be true, and *acting* accordingly. In other words, it is a change, not of the intellect, but of the affections and life; not of the head, but, as the Scriptures continually teach, of the heart.

But the objection may be made to assume another form. It may be said, that the Christian life must certainly have its peculiar principles, by which it is distinguished as the Christian life; and these principles must be understood by the believer, in order that he may act them out. A man is not a Christian, not at least in a practical sense of that word, merely because he believes that Christianity is true, or merely because he feels it to be all-important, necessary indeed to salvation; but because he knows what it teaches, and endeavors to live up to it, as nearly as human infirmity will permit. Hence it would seem, that we can have Christian affections only on the conditions of first having a Christian understanding or intellect.

Here, again, there is no occasion to urge extreme views. I have not undertaken to prove that the heart is everything, and the head nothing; but only, that the heart is more than the head. Accordingly, in my reply to that form of the objection which is now before us, it is not necessary, neither would it be wise on general grounds, to undervalue the importance of learning in its place, or of right opinions in religion, or of a sound judgment in religious matters. Right religious views are of great moment, and they are becoming more and more so in proportion as the community is becoming more and more generally educated. Nothing but right religious views will be likely to satisfy such a community for any length of time; nothing else will bear the criticism to which it will be exposed under such circumstances; nothing else can be put in harmony with the advanced state and free character of thought on other subjects; nothing else, when reduced to practice, will become in all respects the practice which Christianity requires. All this is freely conceded; nevertheless, even here, right religious views are not *the principal* thing. Right religious views of themselves do not make a man to be a Christian in a practical sense of that word (that is, in the only sense in which it is of much importance whether a man is a Christian or not), but *right religious dispositions*. Right religious views are not the *end*, but the *means;* right religious dispositions are the end, and right religious views are only *one* of the probable or possible means to that end.

I say, *probable* or *possible* means; for, in the first place, because right religious views *may* lead to right religious dispositions, it does not follow that they *must*, or that they *will* in any particular case, or that they *generally do*. It belongs to minds more sanguine than wise to fancy that they have found at last a doctrinal system, or theory of religion which, if it were generally understood and adopted, would regenerate the world. A little more experience and observation would convince such persons, at least it *ought* to convince them, that the conduct of mankind is determined much less by their theories than by the customs of the society in which they live, by sympathy with their neighbors and associates, and by constitutional tendencies and prevailing tastes. Even in the matter of health or worldly prosperity, where we might naturally presume that selfishness alone would lead every one to turn his knowledge to immediate account, I do not believe that one man in ten thousand takes that course which he, *in theory*, is convinced is the wisest and best course. And for this reason ; — it does not happen to be the common course, or an agreeable course. Because a man believes a thing to be true or right or expedient, it does not follow that he will like to do it, or that he means to do it, or that he will do it. No doubt something is gained to Christianity by disabusing men of their ignorance and their prejudices in respect to it, and setting the whole subject before them in a true and strong light; but not so much as theorists and dogmatists are apt to suppose. Where the Bible is so generally read, and early religious instruction is so generally attended to, as among us, the great difficulty in the way of a Christian life is not want of knowledge, but want of heart. Men have their worldly and selfish nature, and their bad passions; and these they will continue to gratify, though they know it to be wrong, and contrary to God's word, *until their hearts are changed.*

Here and there an individual may be met with who first forms a theory of what life should be, and then lives it out. Under some circumstances, as in the springing up of a new religion, or of a new sect, instances of this sort are more frequent than under others; still they constitute the exceptions and not the general rule. The general rule is, that men participate in the sentiments and character of the community to which they belong; and this, too, not so much by instruction, as by imitation and sympathy, through the heart, and not through the head. Speaking generally, men do not live according to theory or system of any kind, but according to example and sympathy. In morals, a man does not begin by forming a conception of what he ought to be, and then set himself to work to turn that conception into reality. He is won to virtue partly by virtuous impulses awakened in his own nature, partly by his worldly interests pointing the same way, and partly by the example of the good men around him; the fact of his becoming virtuous not depending on his having the right theory of virtue, or any theory. And so in religion. As a general rule, a man becomes religious, not from any theory of religion, true or false; but partly from the religious instincts of his nature, and partly from intercourse with religious men, and the many impressive experiences of life, all of which have the effect to awaken and call out his religious instincts. Take away his religious instincts, and all the teaching in the world would not make him religious; and even the peculiar form under which his religious instincts manifest themselves will be determined, for the most part, not by teaching, but by imitation and sympathy.

Do you ask again, How can a man be a Christian unless he acts from Christian principles? and how can he act from Christian principles, unless he knows what Christian principles are? I answer, that whatever apparent force or pertinency these questions may have is wholly owing to a fallacy which underlies them, and which, under another connection, has already been exposed in this discourse. You would build an argument on an ambiguity in the meaning of the term *principle*. The Christian principles which are necessary to Christian obedience, are not theoretical principles, dogmas, articles of creeds, but practical principles, Christian *springs of action;* that is to say, Christian affections and dispositions. When it is said, and said truly, that a man cannot be a Christian without acting from Christian principles, it is meant that he cannot be a Christian without acting from Christian affections and dispositions: but affections and dispositions are not *taught*: they are awakened, unfolded, developed. They do not depend on the state of the head, but on the state of the heart. "With the heart man believeth unto righteousness, and with the mouth confession is made unto salvation."

This, then, is the conclusion, to which I am brought. In everything pertaining to human greatness and human happiness, to moral and Christian character and to final salvation, the heart is more than the head. The heart is the principal thing. Out of that, and out of that alone, "are the issues of life."

To some, indeed, the doctrine here laid down may be so obvious and incontestable, that my pains to establish it will seem a waste of words. But with the bulk of mankind it is not so. What young man starts in life, believing, as he should, that his success as well as his happiness will depend more on the *spirit* which he brings to his work, than on his genius, his ability, his industry, or his acquirements? And the popular notion of education — does it not fall in with and confirm the common mistake? Talk about giving to a young man the advantages of the best education, and the thoughts immediately run on what is taught in schools and colleges; as if what is taught in schools and colleges were able, of itself, to make a man either good or great or happy? And what shall I say of the Church? For eighteen centuries its best energies have been consumed, its best blood has been poured out like water, in the vain hope of bringing about a unity of Christian principles, meaning thereby a unity of opinion and belief; which cannot be, and, even if it could be, would only lead to evil. Meanwhile who has set a right value on "the hidden man of the heart"? who has remembered that "the end of the commandment is charity out of a pure heart"?

The public mind is everywhere troubled by the thought that neither civilization nor Christianity has accomplished anything like the good which was expected from it, and which it seemed to promise. So it will continue to be until men learn that mere refinement and intellectual culture, progress in science and progress in the arts, are utterly incompetent to exalt a people, or to make them capable of self-government, or to convert them from nominal Christianity to real Christianity. What is wanted, is the education of the conscience; and this, too, not on the side of intelligence, but of sensibility, — "a new heart and a new spirit." The text has said it: "Keep thy heart with all diligence; for out of it are the issues of life."

# COMPROMISES.

I AM MADE ALL THINGS TO ALL MEN, THAT I MIGHT BY ALL MEANS SAVE SOME.—1 Corinthians ix. 22.

St. Paul speaks here of his readiness to make concessions in order to conciliate. He is willing to conform, as far as he innocently can, to prevailing customs, institutions, and modes of thought, in the hope of being able in this way to gain over more to his views. In one word, he shows himself prepared to give up something by way of compromise.

Taking the example of this apostle for my authority and my point of departure, I propose to offer a few suggestions on *the morality of compromises*.

My first remark is one in which all, I suppose, will concur. As a general rule, compromises of every description are to be regarded with distrust, and rejected when they can be without serious loss or inconvenience. Taken at the best they are of the nature of sacrifices, as each party is supposed to give up something which he considers of more or less importance. And this is not all. A plan or policy which is the result of a compromise is not a single plan or policy, but a mixture of plans, a mixture of policies. Now it can hardly be expected of such a medley, that it will have either unity or consistency; the several parts, instead of aiding and sustaining each other, will be very likely to interfere with and obstruct each other. Take any one of the plans originally proposed, in its simplicity and integrity, and you would probably have a good plan *on the principles assumed;* but mix them together, and the chance is that you will have a plan which is not a good one on *any* principles. Add to this, what is of great moment in a practical view of the matter, it will be a plan for the successful working of which no one will feel himself to be personally responsible. After all, it will not be *his* plan, though he adopts it for the sake of peace.

Accordingly, if a compromise is called for, the first question which we should ask ourselves is, whether the occasion for making it may not be avoided altogether. If we conclude *to act together*, we must expect to be called upon to give up more or less to each other; for it is not to be presumed that several persons will accord exactly in their tastes, their interests, or their notions of right. But it is often a matter of comparative indifference whether we act together or not. Many of our associations are entirely voluntary. A joint-stock company, a mercantile firm, a literary or scientific society,—it is entirely optional with us whether we enter into such an association or not; or, if we belong to it already, whether we continue in it or not. If we find, therefore, that we cannot enter into or retain such a connection without being called upon to make important sacrifices by way of compromise, it would be better for us, as it seems to me, to decline the connection, or to renounce it if already formed. If the association involves the compromise, and if the association is at the same time entirely voluntary, it would be better for us, as it seems to me, certainly it would be better for us as a general rule, to have nothing to do with the association.

But all our associations are not *voluntary*, in the sense here intended. The family, for example, is not a voluntary, but a necessary association; and so likewise, in a certain sense and to a certain extent, is the neighborhood, the church, the state. I do not mean that a man is not at liberty to quit the neighborhood in which he lives, the church to which he belongs, and even the country in which he was born; nay, it is easy to conceive of a state of things in which this would be not only a possible, but the only proper course. Suppose this course taken, however, and what would be the consequence. Simply that he would live in *another* neighborhood, worship in *another* church, be subject to *another* jurisdiction.

I say it must be so, because the only other alternative would be absolute solitude; it would be to refuse to worship with anybody, or to recognize any government, or any one as his neighbor; and this, manifestly, he has no right to do, because virtues and duties are enjoined upon him, as a Christian and a man, which can neither be acquired nor practised except in society. We are not at liberty to run away from society. A man has no more right to run away from society, even if the thing were practicable or easy, than to run away from his family. He has virtues and duties to acquire and practise there which are necessary to his own character and final acceptance. Every man must live in society;—I do not say, in *this* or *that* society, but in *some* society. We must live and act together; and this being the case, one of the first and most obvious of our duties is the duty of mutual concession in the shape of compromise.

Concessions, then, we must make; but *what* concessions? Neither you nor I can expect to have everything in our own way. We must give up more or less to others, in order that they may be disposed to give up more or less to us. But *what* are we to give up? and *how much* are we to give up?

Some may think it enough to refer to the example of Paul as set forth in the text; simply affirming that, whenever it is necessary to a benevolent or moral purpose, we should, like him, become "all things to all men." But what did the Apostle mean when he used these words? when he spake of being "made all things to all men"? Certainly it will not do to interpret this language to the letter. It must not be so construed as to intimate that he was ready to conform to the opinions and practices of the world whatever they might be, or any further than he innocently could. The question, therefore, returns: How far can we carry the spirit of compromise without trenching at the same time on the laws of Christian truth and righteousness?

To this question I reply, in the first place, by observing that we are in no danger of trenching on the laws of Christian truth and righteousness so long as our compromises do not involve anything more than the giving up of our own tastes, our own convenience, our own innocent pleasures, our own interests, even our own rights, out of regard to others, and in the spirit of Christian concession and self-sacrifice. Here, as it seems to me, there is no room for doubt, or difference of opinion. Whoever is willing, on proper occasions and in a proper spirit, to forego his own tastes and pleasures, or waive his own acknowledged rights and privileges, for the sake of peace and for the public good, is not only justified in so doing, but universally applauded. Even those who maintain that *duty* does not require this at our hands, must mean, not that it is *less*, but *more*, than duty requires. Indeed, I do not see how it can be regarded as *more* than our duty, if we are to pay any respect whatever to the example of Paul, who was " made all things to all men," who exhorts his disciples to abstain from so asserting their acknowledged liberty as to make it a stumbling-block to the weak, and who generously exclaims, on one occasion, " If meat make my brother to offend, I will eat no flesh while the world standeth, lest I make my brother to offend." Above all, I do not see how it can be regarded as *more* than our duty, if we would be followers of Him, who, though he was rich, yet for our sakes became poor, that we, through his poverty, might be rich, and who gave his life a ransom for all.

If by possibility any difference of opinion should arise respecting the principles here laid down, it must be as to our right to give up even our own *rights*. To say that we have a right to give up our rights, may sound to some like a contradiction; but it is a contradiction in sound, in appearance, only. If a debt is due me, I have a right to immediate payment; but most assuredly, at least in a majority of cases, I have also a right to postpone the payment, if I see fit, or to remit the debt altogether. Indeed, not to give up our rights, is to give up nothing; for why talk about giving up what we have no right to retain if we would?

At the same time it is proper to add what has doubtless done something to countenance, and perhaps to introduce, the mistake just exposed. Our right to give up our rights depends on their being *ours exclusively.* We have no right to give up our neighbors' rights without their consent, express or implied. It may be right for them to give up the rights in question, but it is not right for us to do it for them, unless in their name, and with their consent. Thus, a lawyer must insist on the rights of his clients, and, unless otherwise instructed, on *all* their rights, this being not merely his right, but his duty, as their agent. It is not for him to give up what belongs to others, though he might be disposed, and though it might be very proper for him to give it up if it were his own. Moreover, the rights of others are often so involved and complicated with ours, that to give up ours is to give up, or seriously to compromise theirs. Here, again, a good man will hesitate. A parent, for example, might be willing to give up one or more of his own rights, if he were sure that the loss would fall on him alone; but if, on the contrary, he knows that, directly or indirectly, it will fall on the whole family, on all whom he represents, he will feel that they also ought to have a voice in the matter.

Again, a right may be held *in common*, and require to be maintained *in common*, and all therefore may be in some sense pledged to its defence *in common*, as in the case of civil or religious liberty. Here, as before, no individual can honestly act as if he alone were interested in the event. It is not only the right, but the duty of all to stand by each other, and this, too, though many, if left to act out their individual preferences, would be willing, and would choose to yield. I say, it is not only their *right*, but their *duty;* and the distinction here indicated between a right and a duty is of great moment in this connection; for though it may be true, as I have attempted to show, that it is right, in some cases, to give up *a right* in order to conciliate, or by way of compromise, for the good of others, it by no means follows that it would be right, in any such case, to give up *a duty*.

And this brings me to what may be called the pinch of the question. Have we a right, under any circumstances whatever, to go contrary to *our duty* for the sake of peace, or to meet those we must act with half-way, or on the plea that in a choice of evils we should take the least, or in the hope that in the end virtue and humanity will be gainers by such a course? In one word, for it comes to this at last, have we a right, under any circumstances whatever, to " do evil that good may come " ?

Thus stated, it seems to me that the question answers itself. We have no such right. The New Testament says emphatically of persons guilty of the conduct here described, that their "damnation is just." I can easily conceive that the circumstances will have more or less to do in determining what a man's duty *is* in the exigency in which he is called to act. But supposing this point settled, as is the case in the form of the question as stated above, — supposing it to be determined what a man's duty in the circumstances *is*, it is as clear as day that he has no right to swerve one hair's breadth from the direction in which that duty points, *come what may.*

But we must not think that the annunciation of a moral truism like this will go far to clear up the great practical difficulty we are considering. The question disappears in one form, it is true, but only to come up in another. In a sharp collision of opinions and interests, of rights and duties, of reciprocal benefits and mutual obligations, may not *my duty itself become changed?* In such an emergency, and in order to meet and satisfy the new responsibilities growing out of it, may it not be proper for me to deviate from the ordinary rules of human conduct, on the ground, not that it is a deviation from duty, but that duty requires the deviation? May I not in certain circumstances become a party to a compromise, even as regards great moral issues, on the ground, not that the compromise will justify me in giving up my duty, but that duty calls upon me to make the compromise?

Let me suppose a case. A community, bound together by a multitude of reciprocal affections, interests, and obligations, fall into irreconcilable difference respecting a single question, and that a moral one. What are they to do?

Some may think to cut the matter short by insisting that *the party which is right* ought not to give up, ought not to meet the other half-way, ought not to make the smallest concessions. And this is true, supposing it to be known and conceded which party *is* right; but unhappily this is not a conceded point; it is the very point in dispute. The question is not, what the party shall do which *is* right, but what the party shall do which *thinks* itself right. And if you still answer, "Not concede one jot nor tittle," then you have no ground of complaint against your opponents for not conceding one jot nor tittle to you, for they also *think* themselves right. If it should be objected that this is assuming too much; that we have no right to take it for granted that both parties are equally sincere in their pretensions, I reply: Perhaps not. But which party are you going to set down as insincere, or as less sincere. If, as usually happens, both parties claim to be right, and give the same evidence of sincerity, is it not plain that we must regard both as sincere, or neither?

Still there are those who will recur to the argument that our duty is determined by what we think, and not by what others think, and therefore that, in a moral view, there is no substantial distinction between what we *think* to be our duty and what *is* our duty. What we think to be our duty is duty *for us;* what we think to be the right course is the right course *for us.*

But here, again, the conclusion is broader, or, at any rate, more unqualified, than the premises will warrant. I do not deny that mistake extenuates, and sometimes, perhaps, excuses wrong-doing; but it does this only on one condition; namely, that we have not wilfully shut our eyes on important and obvious facts in the case. Now in the case under consideration two of the most important and most obvious facts are these: first, that we ourselves are fallible; and, secondly, that others, no more fallible than we are, have come to a different conclusion. So far all must be agreed. If, therefore, we persist in shutting our eyes on these important and obvious and admitted facts, that is to say, pay no regard to the judgment and the consciences of others, but proceed to act on our own as if we were infallible, when we know we are not, the mistake, if we fall into one, does not make wrong to be right even *for us;* nay, is no excuse for the wrong. It is not mistake, properly so called, but obstinacy; and whatever may be said of mistake, all, I presume, will agree that *obstinacy* is no excuse for moral delinquency of any kind.

Another ground sometimes taken is, that where two parties are at variance, only *one* can be right; and consequently that a compromise supposes a departure from the right course *on one side or the other*. This, however, does not follow. I admit that where two parties are at variance, *both* cannot be right; but it does not follow that *either* is so, that is, *wholly* right. Both parties cannot be right, but both parties may be wrong; at least more or less so. Indeed, where the question at issue is a large and complicated one, having a multitude of connections and bearings, as is commonly the case in civil and religious dissensions, it is much more reasonable to suppose that each party is partly right and partly wrong. And if so, it would seem that each party has something of *wrong* to give up, and the compromise that should consist of mutual concessions of this sort would evidently result, not in a departure from right on either side, but in an approximation to right on both sides.

I have now glanced at some of the abstract and speculative objections to all moral compromises, as such. Others are disposed to take a more practical view of the subject. They will tell you that party differences are not to be settled by compromise, but by vote. The party which can command the largest number of votes has a right to have its own way in everything, on the ground that the majority have a right to govern. On this ground, some would seem to argue that the majority have a right to impose on the whole country their peculiar system not only of political expediency, but of political morals, to which the minority must submit as they best can.

But is not this the essence of tyranny, and not the less so because it is in the hands of many, and not of one or a few? What signifies it to the oppressed minority, the oppression being the same, that the name of the oppressor is Legion? Not that I mean to call in question the doctrine that the majority have a right to govern, — that is, to govern *justly*. But to govern justly the majority must consider the just claims of the minority, and, above all, those claims which are founded on a difference of moral conviction, and make concessions to them; as is actually done by our own and other governments in the case of the Quakers. Yet these concessions are of the nature of a compromise. Accordingly the right of the majority to govern does not exclude the necessity of compromise. The utmost extent of that right consists in the right to fix for the time being the *terms* of the compromise; and this they have no right to do capriciously, or with a single view to their own party maxims and preferences, but as they honestly think an impartial umpire would approve, in view of all the circumstances. If you say that nothing is due to the dissenting consciences of the minority, you have no right to find fault with the Spanish Inquisition. Often, also, the practical question is, not what either party would have things be as a finality, or if they were to begin anew, but what, on the whole, ought to be done "in the present distress."

The consideration in this connection which probably has the greatest weight with tender consciences is, that by compromising with what we think to be evil, we make ourselves, to a certain extent, parties to it. What we insist upon doing, at any rate, is simply to wash our own hands from all responsibility in the matter. But is this all that is required? Our responsibility does not consist in *freeing* ourselves from the responsibility, but in *fulfilling* the responsibility by adopting such measures as we honestly believe will be most likely to abate the evil, and in the right way. A mere solicitude to save *ourselves* from responsibility would indicate but too clearly, that the motive which in fact determines us is not the philanthropy of which we boast, nor yet the justice to which we appeal, but a selfish desire to escape suffering in our own persons, here or hereafter. When men talk about "washing their hands" from all participation in a supposed wrong, without doing anything, or attempting to do anything, to remove or remedy or lessen the wrong, it always reminds me of Pilate's conduct at the trial of Jesus.

I have spoken of compromises in general; not of any particular compromise. I have endeavored to treat the question dispassionately as a purely abstract one, coming up in the study of Christian ethics. I am aware that there is often less difficulty in laying down general principles than in applying them with the limitations and qualifications which the circumstances of the case require. Still something is gained by clearly apprehending the principles, — the applications *must be* left to the occasion as it arises; and let me add, that a right application of the principles in the most perplexing circumstances will mainly depend, not on a morbid sensitiveness to the question at issue, nor yet on casuistical subtlety, but on downright honesty of purpose, a sound understanding, and a truly generous and magnanimous spirit. It is easy to conceive of compromises from which we should turn away, as from a compact with the Evil One. Nevertheless, without a *spirit* of mutual concession in constant exercise it is plain that no family, no neighborhood, no community, can subsist for a single day in tolerable comfort and quiet.

Undoubtedly there is danger that our compromises will lose all moral significance by originating in low, selfish, and worldly inducements. Undoubtedly there is danger that we may be ready to concede truth and justice and humanity, in order to save our interests and our pleasures; on the ground that truth and justice and humanity are mere sentiments, mere prejudices, while interest and pleasure are real and substantial things. Undoubtedly there is danger that, while we talk about exercising mutual forbearance, and becoming "all things to all men," as the Gospel requires, we may all the time be acting from motives which the Gospel disowns and condemns. The existence and prevalence among us of compromises of this description would be one of the most alarming symptoms of national decay and ruin: which may God avert! At the same time, the *spirit of compromise*, righteously carried out, as it gave birth to our Union, is absolutely indispensable to its continuance. Let not the eye say unto the hand, "I have no need of thee;" nor again, the head to the feet, "I have no need of you;" but let the whole body, fitly joined together, and compacted by that which every joint supplieth, according to effectual working in the measure of every part, make increase of the body unto the edification of the whole in love.

# CONDITIONS OF SUCCESS IN LIFE.*

I RETURNED, AND SAW UNDER THE SUN THAT THE RACE IS NOT TO THE SWIFT, NOR THE BATTLE TO THE STRONG, NEITHER YET BREAD TO THE WISE, NOR YET RICHES TO MEN OF UNDERSTANDING, NOR YET FAVOR TO MEN OF SKILL; BUT TIME AND CHANCE HAPPENETH TO THEM ALL. — Ecclesiastes ix. 11.

THIS is one of those gloomy and despondent views of human life in which Ecclesiastes abounds. At first sight it would seem to inculcate the extreme doctrine, that success is wholly dependent on circumstances, and even on accidental circumstances, and not at all on ourselves. Thus understood, I need not say, it shocks our sense of justice, and contradicts our general experience. Moreover, we feel that if received in this sense, especially by those just entering into life, its only effect must be to discourage effort, to lower men's aims, and to subvert the foundations of a just self-reliance. What the writer meant to inculcate was probably this: as it is not for man to

---

* It is customary to deliver a Farewell Discourse in the College Chapel to the Senior Class, on the Sunday before they leave. This and the two following sermons were preached on those occasions.

read the future, or direct his steps, he must be content with doing as well as he can, and leave the rest to that Providence which shapes and determines all events.

Understand the text, however, as we may, it very naturally introduces the question how far a man's success in life, including his character as well as his outward condition, is to be regarded as *his own work?*

This is not a subject on which to advance hasty or extreme opinions. I am willing to start with the concession, that there is a large pre-ordained element in the life of every individual, and a still larger one in the life of every community. It certainly does not depend on the man himself in what place or condition he is *born*,— whether in savage or civilized life, whether in a Christian or pagan country, whether in the midst of abundance, or in the midst of want, whether in a virtuous and happy home, or in the haunts of vice; and we must be beside ourselves not to see that these things have much to do in making a man what he becomes. Everybody ascribes a great deal, and the older we grow I believe we generally ascribe more and more, to differences of race, to hereditary or constitutional aptitudes and tendencies, to the power of education, example, custom, and even to what the world calls good or bad fortune. So Lord Bacon: "I did ever hold it for an insolent and unlucky saying, 'Every man maketh his own fortune,' except it be uttered only as an hortative or spur to correct sloth. For otherwise, if it be believed as it soundeth, and that a man entereth into an high imagination, that he can compass and fathom all accidents, and ascribeth all successes to his drifts and reaches, and the contrary to his errors and slippings, it is commonly seen that the evening fortune of that man is not so prosperous, as of him that, without slackening of his industry, attributeth much to felicity and providence above him."\*

Many are tempted to go further. "We talk," they will say, "about what we are going to do, or be; after all, however, it does not depend on ourselves. We are, to a great extent at least, the creatures of circumstances, — predetermined, inexorable. The key-note to almost every man's life is pitched, long before he can properly be said to have had anything to do with it. We do not *make* ourselves, we *find* ourselves: we have to take ourselves as we are, and make the best of it. We think it of great moment to be Christians; but if a man is born in Constantinople, or Pekin, or Timbuctoo, what likelihood, we had almost said what possibility, is there that he will become one? Take the inmates of a penitentiary, — if you

---

\* *A Discourse touching Helps for the Intellectual Powers.* Works (Montagu's Ed.), Vol. I. p. 339.

could know all their antecedents, you would not wonder, in respect to many of them, that they are there. You may say, that a *strong will* sometimes triumphs over the most formidable obstacles of education and physical condition. And so it does; but what is a man to do, who is so unfortunate as not to have a strong will? we do not deny that the mind has great influence over the body; we only say, in reply, that the body has great influence over the mind, and that the influence begins on this side. A single drop of blood in the wrong place makes all the difference between a philosopher and a maniac."

But enough of this. Very little practical wisdom is ever gathered from the consideration of supposed and extreme cases. It is not because the statements themselves are untrue, but because they are inapplicable, at least in an unqualified form, to our own condition and prospects, or to what may be termed the average of human life. A larger survey and juster appreciation of things will convince us that there is nothing in "the doctrine of circumstances," rightly understood, to discourage effort or destroy a proper degree of self-reliance, especially where this self-reliance recognizes a Divine support, holding that, in some mysterious way, it is "God which worketh in us both to will and to do."

For, in the first place, if you say, it is the circumstances which make the man, you must also admit at the same time, that it is the man who often *makes*, and can always *modify*, the circumstances. There would seem to be no room for a real difference of opinion here. All agree that some of the circumstances materially affecting our condition and progress are determined *for* us, and not *by* us. It is so, for example, as regards the place of our birth, the form of society, government, or religion under which we are brought up, whether we are born with a strong and healthy constitution, or with a feeble and sickly one, what are our natural abilities, and what our natural temperament. Even in regard to such circumstances, however, it would be idle to pretend that we cannot *alter* or *modify* them in any manner or degree. In point of fact men are doing this very thing every day, and every hour. Look where you will, and you cannot help seeing that the bulk of mankind are doing more or less to improve their natural advantages, and to correct or guard against their natural disadvantages, and with more or less success.

These remarks apply especially to those circumstances which have most to do in making the differences existing between *individuals belonging to the same class*, living under the same laws, professing the same creed, and sharing in the same measure of general civilization. And this, let me say in passing, is the only aspect of the subject under which it is of much practical moment to you or me. With us the question is not, whether we shall be civilized men, or savages, for that point is already settled, — we *are* civilized men, — but what sort of civilized men we shall be. So likewise as regards religion, the great question, with us at least, is not, whether we shall be Christians or Mohammedans, for that again is a settled point: we *are* Christians, at least in the sense of belonging to Christendom; the only question still at issue being, what sort of Christians we shall become. Granting, therefore, that we are Christians and not Mohammedans merely because we were born and brought up in a Christian country, how happens it, I still ask, that one is a better and happier Christian than another? Is it not, in great measure, because he takes more pains to inform his mind, to subdue his passions, to regulate his habits? because he selects better companions and chooses to follow better counsels? because he takes care to surround himself with better means, and seeks out better opportunities, of self-improvement, and a better field of labor and usefulness?

I know how slow men are to give up their theories. Probably many will still insist that the whole is nevertheless resolvable into the effect of circumstances. If a man is any better or happier than the multitude immediately around him, it must be because, though his *general* circumstances have been the same with theirs, he has somehow or other come under the influence of better *special* circumstances. Be it so. I only ask you to consider to how great an extent these better *special* circumstances are of his own choosing, of his own moulding, and often of his own creating. The general circumstances determining the class or order to which we shall belong may, and often do, originate in what others have done for us; but the special circumstances, determining our relative character and condition *as individuals* of that class or order, are almost always our own work. For instance, that we belong to the educated class is probably owing, in a majority of cases, to our parents; but whether we, as individuals, are to be a credit or a disgrace to that class, is left to depend almost wholly on ourselves.

There is also another train of thought, which, if followed out, leads to the same general conclusion. The influence of circumstances, however important and indispensable must not be regarded as annihilating, nor even as necessarily limiting or abridging, human power. On the contrary, this very influence is continually resorted to as an instrument of human power, and used as a means of extending it. True, a portion of our circumstances are pre-determined, imposed, inevitable; but it is also true that another portion of them are variable, subject more or less to our control, to be shaped, rearranged, and directed as we see fit. In this way we can, if we see fit, take one set of circumstances and play them off against another, so as to neutralize, or essentially to modify, the *effects* even of those circumstances which can neither be prevented nor altered in themselves. To say that we *can* do this is not enough; we *are* doing it continually. Every time the agriculturist changes his mode of tillage, every time the physician sits down to write a prescription, every time the statesman proposes the enactment of a new law, every time the philanthropist founds a new institution of mercy or beneficence, — what is it but playing off one set of circumstances against another, that the whole may be brought under human control? What, indeed, is civilization itself but the result of a succession of triumphs effected by such means, — triumphs of mind over matter, of man over nature! The best interests of a savage tribe, and sometimes its very existence, are put in jeopardy by the ill success of a single hunting party, by the accidental failure of a single natural production, by the unwonted rigor of a single winter, — contingencies which it has neither the skill to foresee nor the means to provide against. But in civilized communities it is not so. Every step in science and the arts, every step in education and civil government, is a step in the direction of rescuing life and society from the dominion of nature and chance, and bringing the whole under human calculation and control, and this, too, by making *a wise use* of circumstances.

It would do something to save theorists from confusion and mistake in speaking of the power of circumstances, if they would only bear in mind how much is included under that familiar term. If you say that man is the creature of circumstances, it must be with the understanding, that the greatest and most effective of these circumstances is *the man himself*. And by the man himself I here mean not merely his physical constitution, including his brain and nervous temperament, and his innate aptitudes and predispositions, but also the habits he has contracted, the acquisitions he has made, even his humors and caprices, — in short, whatever he is, or has become, at any given moment. This, I hardly need say, is one of the circumstances, under the influence of which he is called to act, and beyond all question the greatest and most effective of them all in its bearings on his present conduct and his future prospects. Now will any one seriously pretend that men have nothing to do in determining what their habits and acquisitions and tempers shall be? Is there no such thing as self-culture? If not, why are we *here?* Why this vast, complicated, and expensive apparatus of churches and schools and colleges, of libraries, museums, and laboratories? And do not think that in thus referring to the means of education I have forgotten my argument, which is to show, not what can be done *for* men, but what men can do *for themselves*. It is a superficial view of things which leads to the distinction between education and self-education. In point of fact, all education is self-education, the only difference being, that education in churches and schools and colleges, and amidst libraries, museums, and laboratories, is self-education under the best advantages.

In making so much to depend on ourselves, notwithstanding the important part which accident and external necessity play in human life, I trust I shall not be suspected of meaning to involve myself or you in the perplexities of the old metaphysical puzzle about free-agency, the liberty of indifference and absolute self-determination. Let those who have nothing better to do continue to sharpen their speculative faculties on that insoluble problem; my aim in this discourse is wholly practical. No sensible person denies or questions the power of circumstances. It is not pretended that you or I can do substantial and lasting good to ourselves or others, simply by *willing* it, or by merely saying the word. Change of character is a vital process; we have grown into our present set of habits, and in order to change them, we must grow into another set of habits, and growth is not *an act of the will;* — it is the slow result of influences, as well from without as from within. We must avail ourselves of the proper occasions, instrumentalities, circumstances. To argue, however, that what we do by such means we cannot be said to do at all, because we do it through them, is a mere abuse of language, an affront to the practical understanding of mankind.

The doctrine of circumstances here laid down extends, with some obvious qualifications, to heavenly things and the spiritual life. That we have the means of "the great salvation" is wholly owing to the Divine condescension and mercy, and not to any merits or any exertions on our own part; but we *do* have them. They are not *to be* given; they *have been* given. The Scriptures, the Church, the sacraments, faith, prayer, the example of holy men, doing good in the name of Christ, — these are the acts and influences by which men are trained for heaven. And they are open to all. They are not *forced* on this one or that one, on you or me, but they are *open* to all. Who will say, that it does not depend on himself whether he avails himself of them or not, and in what spirit he avails himself of them, and therefore to what effect? I am recommending no way of salvation but that which the Gospel points out: "And the Spirit and the Bride say, Come. And let him that heareth say, Come. And let him that is athirst come: *whosoever will*, let him take of the water of life freely."

"Whosoever will"! In what better terms could the Gospel confirm and sanction every word that has here been spoken? Let us not go about to imagine cases of moral and spiritual destitution and despair. There may be such cases, but it is not so with us. We must also make a distinction between worldly success and acceptance with God. Whether you are to be rich or poor depends on others, as well as you; but if rich, whether you are to be a good rich man, or a bad rich man, and if poor, whether you are to be a good poor man, or a bad poor man, depends, under God, on yourself alone. Even with each one of us, I do not mean to deny that there is still a fearful uncertainty as to what he is to be in the sight of God; but I insist that this uncertainty does not come in between the will and the act, between the will and the success: it lies *behind the will*. The uncertainty consists in this, whether we shall will, and persevere in that will, or not. Where there is a will, there is a way.

Away, then, with that fatalism which makes man the creature and sport of circumstances he has had no voice nor influence in determining. Never for a moment believe that we are in the hands and at the mercy of the blind forces of nature. It is not religion, it is atheism, which makes nature everything, and man nothing. "And the Lord God formed man of the dust of the ground, and breathed into his nostrils the breath of life; and *man became a living soul.*" That "living soul" is not a product of nature, nor yet one of the many forces of nature: it is a force distinct from nature, confronting nature face to face, and often in direct conflict and struggle with nature. In this conflict and struggle the secret of the soul's strength consists in believing, in feeling, that its strength is not from nature, but from itself and from God. Where this faith, this feeling, is intense, even error and sin cannot cripple the soul's invincible energy; their only effect will be, as in the case of the conquerors and scourges of mankind, to convert what would otherwise have been a Divine into a Satanic power, — terrible even in its apostasy and perversion. The body, as it is formed "of the dust of the ground," belongs to nature, and is subject to the laws of nature, acting as it is acted on; but the soul, the inspiration of the Almighty, vindicates its relationship to a higher order of existences by being essentially self-active and free. Self-activity and freedom, however, are no protection against abuse and ruin. To be able to look forward into a dark and untried future without presumption and without fear, we must feel and know that "greater is He that is in us, than he that is in the world;" —

without presumption, because always ready to exclaim, with the Apostle, "Yet not I, but the grace of God which was with me;" and without fear, because always prepared to take up the testimony of the same Apostle, "Not that I speak in respect to want; for I have learned, in whatsoever state I am, therewith to be content. I know both how to be abased, and I know how to abound: everywhere, and in all things I am instructed, both to be full and to be hungry, both to abound and to suffer need. I can do all things through Christ which strengtheneth me."

Though my subject is a general one, it is directly and specially applicable to those who, having completed their College course, are now full of the thought as to what their future condition shall be. Life is before them. Is that life a lottery, a game of chance? Is it something which they are to accept or submit to as a fatality. Or is it something which they are to achieve? My young friends, it is neither one nor the other exclusively; it is all three, strangely blended together.

It is to no purpose to shut your eyes on the uncertainty and vicissitude which are impressed on all earthly things. How many have won the highest university distinctions, like Kirke White, merely to die? How many, after graduating with the fairest promise, have lived merely to disappoint it, and this, too, without any fault of their own, but through the fault of others, or some infelicity of manner, or temper, or intellect, which did not interfere with their success here, but was fatal to it in the world? It is certain that "the race is not *always* to the swift, nor the battle to the strong, neither yet riches to men of understanding, nor yet favor to men of skill, but time and chance happeneth to them all." I do not say this to damp a generous enthusiasm, or to dispel, if I could, the dreams of life in which the young are apt to indulge. I honor, I revere those dreams, as often leading to their own fulfilment, nay, as coming much nearer to the truth of what life ought to be, and might be, than the vulgar experience. But this I say: I would not give much for a young man's chance of eminence whose pillow is never wet with tears at the thought of the difficulties to be overcome. And besides, to minds of the highest order, there is a strange fascination in the prospect of hardship and difficulty; they like life the better for its struggles and its perils.

My friends, whether you look to public or private life, my last words to you shall be words of encouragement and benediction. The final cause of the chances and changes of this mortal life is to evoke and strengthen that principle in your nature, which is superior to them all. Take counsel of your humility; take counsel of your caution; but never take counsel of your fears. More than half of the obstacles in your path are like a rotten stump in the woods, which a timid man takes for a ghost, and runs away. A brave man walks up to it, and finds it to be what it is. Never be appalled and unmanned by what is said about risks, and difficulties and competitions. Never retreat into a narrow and obscure walk, with its only one chance of success and usefulness, as if it were the safer for that. Push forward, if you have the common consciousness of ability, into the great thoroughfares, where, though a hundred chances of success and usefulness should fail, a hundred chances are left. And take with you our best wishes and our best prayers that you may succeed in the best things. I will not commend you to the favor of the world, or to the promise of your own genius and activity, for all these may prove vain; but "I commend you to God, and the word of his grace," who alone "is able to keep you from falling, and to present you faultless before the presence of his glory with exceeding joy."

# ON THE CHOICE OF A PROFESSION.

LET EVERY MAN ABIDE IN THE SAME CALLING WHEREIN HE WAS CALLED. — 1 Corinthians vii. 20.

In seasons of unusual religious excitement and earnestness men are tempted to regard all political and social distinctions, and all ordinary secular employments, as abolished or suspended. So it was in some parts of Germany at the breaking out of the Protestant Reformation. So it was in the Corinthian Church at the first planting of Christianity. The Apostolic injunction addressed to that church, and recorded in the text, may be considered as directed generally and in principle against a twofold form of error especially prevalent at such times.

In the first place, it is directed against the error of making religion a business or profession *by itself*, leaving us no time or thought for anything else. Of course, I do not mean that anything whatever should be allowed to come into competition with religion; or that there is any extravagance in the doctrine which teaches that religion is everything or nothing. Still its genius and office are entirely misapprehended, if we suppose it requires us to desert our post in society; if we fancy it expects us, or calls upon us, to withdraw from the world, and give ourselves wholly up to ascetic practices and devout contemplation. No such thing. Religion is the sovereign rule of life; its spirit should pervade and transfigure the whole of life, even its humblest offices; but it was never intended to be a life by itself, or something patched upon life. If you ask, Who is the best Christian? I answer: Not he who makes the loudest professions of Christianity, nor he who gives the most time to thinking about it, nor yet he who best understands its principles; but he who best succeeds in applying these principles to his daily cares and duties, and in filling his place in society, whatever it may be, in a Christ-like spirit.

Again, the injunction in the text is directed generally, and in principle, against the kindred error of supposing, that there are many lawful callings or professions, in which it is impossible to lead a Christian life. More difficult it may be, but not impossible, the difficulty only enhancing the virtue which has strength and resolution enough to overcome it. The military profession, a life in camps, is not likely to be recommended as particularly favorable to moral and religious culture; yet this profession has contributed not a few illustrious examples, not only of patriotism, but also of integrity and honor, and even of reverence for religion, and of a Christian detestation of war, except as a dire necessity of nations. On the other hand, the clerical profession, to those who are fit for it, is generally thought, in a moral and religious point of view, to promise best of all; because the special business and object of the calling coincide so entirely with what ought to be the highest business and object of us all. But here also there is difficulty and drawback, showing that the difference in the eligibility of the various professions on moral grounds is not so great as is often supposed. Where the profession is religious, the danger is that the religion will become professional. Undoubtedly it is our duty to feel and express devout emotions; but the trouble with the clergyman is, that he is sometimes called upon to express devout emotions whether he feels them or not. Hence his danger of allowing his very earnestness to become mechanical; of sacrificing the life and freshness, and sometimes even the entire sincerity, of his religious experiences to professional repetition and routine. Then, too, looking merely at the effect of his labors, I believe it is often possible for a layman to do more for religion than a clergyman, from the very fact that he cannot be suspected of a professional bias or bribe.

We arrive, then, at the conclusion that all the great professions are open to choice, and that there is nothing in any one of them, in itself considered, to hinder a good man in certain cases from choosing it. But it by no means follows that all professions are equally eligible in themselves; much less, that all are equally eligible to every person, and under all circumstances. All are open to choice; but this does not exclude occasion for choice, or necessity for choice, or the duty of making a wise choice, as being that on which, more perhaps than on any other one thing, a man's usefulness and happiness will depend. Every day is adding to the importance of this step, by multiplying the number of the professions; by making it more and more indispensable that each individual should confine himself to a single profession; and also on account of the essential changes which some of the professions have undergone. For these reasons many of the old commonplaces no longer apply, making it necessary that every young man, on reaching the period when the choice can no longer be deferred, should give his own thoughts to the subject in view of the new demands of learning, society, and the times, as well as of his own capabilities and peculiar aptitudes.

Accordingly, I can think of no subject more proper, or more likely, to engage your attention at this time, than the principles and considerations which should influence and determine young men in the choice of a profession at the present day. A considerable portion of our society will not worship with us again: they have completed their general education, and must now make up their minds, if they have not made them up already, as to their special calling in life. Even in the case of those who have made up their minds definitively as to what they are to do, being determined perhaps for the most part by prudential considerations, or by personal preference, or by natural bias, it will still be well that the whole subject should be reconsidered under its moral and religious aspects.

Let me begin by observing, that if the time for choosing a profession has come, it is not well, as a general rule, to postpone it by unnecessary delays. If you say, your mind is unsettled; I reply, in the first place, that in practical matters the *will* has more to do in settling the mind than arguments; and, secondly, that the probable effect of another year spent without an object will only be to unsettle your minds still more. Perhaps, however, you are bent on devoting a year or two to general reading, or foreign travel, as a means of enlarging and expanding your minds. This sounds well; but, in point of fact, general reading and foreign travel, under such circumstances, are much more likely to dissipate the mind than to enlarge or expand it.

Indeed, what considerable advantage can there be, and I may even add, what practical interest, in reading or travelling without any particular object in view, without any reason why we should consider one thing rather than another, without being able to turn anything to immediate account by seeing how it bears on our own special pursuits? But you may have another motive for the delay: you may think to avoid in this way the error, so common in this country, of hurrying into active life without due preparation. To enter on the practice of any profession without being duly prepared for it is, I admit, a great error; but this is a reason for beginning the preparation as soon as may be; certainly it is no reason for unnecessary delays. So much impressed was Dr. Johnson with the mischiefs of hesitancy and fickleness on this subject, that he is half inclined to recommend that every one's calling should be determined by his parents or guardian; at any rate, he does not hesitate to conclude, "that of two states of life equally consistent with religion and virtue, he who chooses earliest chooses best."

Another preliminary suggestion is, that in choosing a profession we should take care not to allow too much weight to local and temporary considerations; — considerations which will have no bearing on our future progress, except perhaps to narrow and limit it. I suppose there are those who can give no better reason for being in one profession rather than another than this; that they found it easier to get into it. But certainly our success and happiness are to depend, not on our *getting into* a profession, but on our *getting on* in it; that is to say, on our being able to fill it honorably and well. I know the common excuse. It will be said, that we are often placed in circumstances where we must do, not as we *would*, but as we *can*. And this is true. But certainly, as regards so important and eventful a step as the choice of a profession, it is seldom necessary for a young man in this country, with health and strength in his limbs, and courage in his heart, and nobody dependent on him, to resort to such an excuse for not resolving to find his proper place, cost what it may. We talk about what we *can* do, and what we *cannot;* but, after all, this is, for the most part, an arbitrary distinction. What one man calls *impossible*, another man calls *merely difficult;* and, with minds which are made of the right sort of stuff, difficulties do not repel or dishearten; they only stimulate to new and greater efforts. Do you still object, "But we must *live* meanwhile"? I reply, in the first place, that this does not necessarily follow: there are many things which we had better *die* rather than do or suffer. And besides, suppose we must live, we can live on bread and water; as a multitude of poor scholars have done for years, and afterwards won for themselves a brilliant success, an imperishable renown. Better, a thousand times better, live on bread and water for a few days, or a few months, than sacrifice the prospects of a whole life.

Hence we conclude, that every young man owes it to himself, at any cost or sacrifice consistent with virtue and religion, to find, as soon as may be, his proper place and calling, meaning thereby the place and calling in which, with his education and abilities, he is most likely to become useful and happy.

But how is he to find it? that is the great question. I answer generally, By considering what he was made for, taking into view, at the same time, his intellectual aptitudes, and his moral needs and dangers.

As regards intellectual or mental aptitudes, or what is sometimes called the natural bent of one's genius, two extreme opinions have found supporters, which seem to me to be almost equally removed from practical wisdom. The first is that of those who contend that a strong tendency to one profession rather than to another is to be considered; but only, that it may be crossed and overruled. They argue thus: Our highest object should be, not professional success and eminence, but human perfection, which supposes and requires balance and harmony of character. Now when any one betrays a strong proclivity to a particular profession, it shows that some parts of his mind are unduly, or at least disproportionately developed, while others are kept back; and, therefore, in choosing a profession, his object should be to find one which will tend to bring out the latter, so that he may become a complete and perfect *man*. Thus, if a person early manifests extraordinary talents for business and affairs, this is a reason why he should not be, by profession, a man of business and affairs, for he is enough of that already: he ought rather to go into the army or the Church, which will have the effect to call forth his *latent* qualities.

I hardly need say that this doctrine, plausible as it may seem to some minds, is theoretically false, and practically absurd. It is theoretically false; for, though balance and harmony of *character* enter into the theory of what a man ought to be, these have nothing to do with an equal, or even with a proportionate development of his *faculties*. His *occupations* may be wholly mechanical, for example; but it does not follow that his *character* will be either one-sided, or in any manner distorted. And besides, a man is not the whole of humanity; neither does he represent the whole of humanity; neither is he called upon, even in theory, to embody or personate the whole of this humanity, in all its ideal completeness and proportions. We are the many members which go to make up the one body; and it is enough if each member does its appropriate work, and does it well.

Moreover, to pursue the course recommended above would be practically absurd. Every man would do what he is least fitted to do; and the consequence would be, that the whole work of life would be done in the worst possible manner and under the greatest possible disadvantages.

Nor is this all; for the subject has its religious aspects. When we refer to a man's profession as being his *vocation*, or *calling*, we suppose him to be *called*. There is one profession, indeed, that of the divine, which it is generally, and, as I conceive, justly, thought to be presumptuous to enter without being distinctly and emphatically called, and called of God. But *how* called? The fancies and dreams of the enthusiast have nothing to do with a sober and practical matter of this kind. Every man is calmly and impartially to consider what he was made for, what by the constitution of his mind and character he is best fitted to become, and to look upon this as a call from God, — the voice of God speaking in his own nature, which, when distinct and emphatic, he has no right to disregard.

Often, however, and I suppose I may say, generally, the call is not distinct and emphatic, at least as regards most professions; and this leads me to notice the other of the two extreme opinions referred to above. It consists in supposing that every man has his place, and that everything depends on his finding that particular place, a mistake here being final and fatal. No such thing. We are not born with *adaptations*, but with *adaptabilities;* and these are such in most men that they can fit themselves as well, or nearly as well, for one as another of several professions. Leaving out of view eminence in the fine arts, which seems to require at the start a peculiar nervous organization, I do not believe there is one man in ten whom nature has endowed with aptitudes and predispositions so special and marked that he might not succeed perfectly well in any one out of several pursuits. In a large majority of cases the battle of life is won, not by natural, but by personal qualities; by those personal qualities which invite favor and inspire confidence and insure courage and persistency in whatever is undertaken. If any of you are perplexed and in trouble, not knowing what you were made for, this very doubt shows that, probably, you were not made for anything in particular. But what follows? Merely that your success in life will depend much less on mental aptitudes, or what is called bent of genius, than on what lies behind all this, — on strength of will, power of self-control, force of character. These will do more and better for you than incline you to a particular profession: they will make it as certain as anything human can be, that you will prosper, whatever may be your profession.

Even taste for a profession, or interest in it, is often

an aftergrowth; that is to say, not only acquired, but acquired after the profession is adopted and entered upon. The childish preference and longing for a particular profession, sometimes awakened in the young in consequence of hearing it continually talked about, or of hearing themselves continually designated for it, really signifies nothing, and generally ends in nothing. To play with a pursuit, to amuse one's self with it in the spirit of an amateur, is no evidence of a radical and effective bent of mind: a man must be ready for the hard work necessary to distinction in it, or that distinction is not for him.

A proper taste for a particular profession, or interest in it, depends, for the most part, on the direction which *curiosity* takes, or rather on the path into which it is turned. Now this curiosity, especially when it becomes earnest and intense, is not born, as some would seem to imagine, of ignorance, but of knowledge. Idiots and savages who know comparatively nothing, are also found to be equally deficient in *a desire to know*. It is because we know so much already, that we pine and yearn to know more: the problems we have raised haunt us, and give us no rest until they are solved. Thus it is, that in proportion as the great questions and uses of a noble profession break on the mind, the mind, if it is of the right sort, is seized with a passion to master them, and make them its own. And this love of one's profession, which is *generated* by the profession itself, is much more to be relied on than any antecedent and supposed natural leaning; for the latter makes us love a profession before we can be said to know what it is, and therefore may often turn out to be a love of what we fancy the profession to be, but not of what it is in reality, or, at any rate, a love of some things about a profession, but not of the profession itself.

Nay, more. The most genuine and thorough devotion to one's chosen work is sometimes not merely an *after*, but also a *slow* growth, beginning even in positive dislike. "I have heard it observed," says a writer of excellent judgment, "that those men who have risen to the greatest eminence in the profession of law have been in general such as had at first an aversion to the study. The reason probably is, that to a mind fond of general principles every study must be at first disgusting which presents to it a chaos of facts apparently unconnected with each other. . . . . A man destitute of genius may, with little effort, treasure up in his memory a number of particulars which he refers to no principle, and from which he deduces no conclusion; and from his facility in acquiring this stock of information, may flatter himself with the belief that he possesses *a natural taste* for this or that branch of knowledge. But they who are really destined to extend the boundaries of science, when they first enter on new pursuits, feel their attention distracted, and their memory overloaded with facts among which they can trace no relation, and are sometimes apt to despair entirely of their future progress."* In due time, however, their superiority appears, and arises in part from that very dissatisfaction which they at first experienced, as it will not cease to stimulate their inquiries until they penetrate to the foundations; until, underneath this confused mass of facts, they can discern those great laws of order and harmony which give meaning and unity to the whole, and which have such power to charm and hold the best minds.

I have dwelt longer than I intended on the regard which is to be paid to bent of genius and natural taste in the choice of a profession. Where these are distinctly pronounced they are generally decisive, and ought to be so: it would be folly, I had almost said impiety, to disregard them. On the other hand, where, as in a vast majority of cases, they are not distinctly pronounced, this is no ground of apprehension that a wrong choice will be made, for a wrong choice, under such circumstances, is hardly possible: the very occasion of the hesitancy as to what ought to be done is the fact that several things can be done almost equally well. Neither is it ground of discouragement as to final success. Any of the great professions, if entered into with

---

* Stewart's *Elements of the Philosophy of the Human Mind*, Ch. VI. § 9.

an honest and earnest purpose, and faithfully followed up, will soon generate, if it does not find, the spirit and mental aptitude it requires: so that every one may begin life with a reasonable assurance that his progress will be in proportion to his general ability, provided only that he is true to his calling, whatever it may be, and true to himself.

But, as intimated before, there is another consideration which every one should take into view in the choice of a profession: I mean, *his moral needs and dangers.*

Complaints, frequent and deep, come up from all quarters, that moral and religious education is more and more neglected; that young men are trained in letters and science, but not in Christianity, and then are sent forth into the world, to do as they may. These complaints are doubtless, to a certain extent, well founded; but there is no occasion for exaggerating existing evils, no wisdom in turning a sermon into a lampoon on the country or the age. After all, the best part of a Christian education does not result from the formal teaching of a catechism, or the formal observance of an outward ritual, but from participation in the life of a community acting, consciously or unconsciously, under the influence of Christian ideas. And in this respect I do not believe in the degeneracy of modern times. The thousand reformatory movements going on around us, although attended with not a little of folly and extravagance, prove incontestably one thing: they prove that men are beginning to feel, as they never did before, that religion is not merely to be professed, but *lived;* that it is to mould, not merely the faith and worship of individuals, but the manners and customs of society, the institutions and the laws; in short, that a community is Christian so far as it acts out Christian ideas, and no further. Now I say, that merely to grow up in such a community, and, as a necessary consequence, to partake more or less of the prevailing spirit, is a sort of Christian education, and, with all its drawbacks and shortcomings, a better Christian education, in my opinion, than was ever given in the conventual schools of the Middle Ages, where theology, and the means and forms of a mechanical devotion, were almost the only things taught.

Growing up amidst these movements, and partaking more or less of the common life, it is hardly to be expected that young men, in deliberately laying down a plan of life, will make it part of that plan to purchase success by the sacrifice of integrity and honor. But the danger is, that they will not take care, in the outset, effectually to guard against the possibility of such an event, though it does not enter into their plan. The danger is, that they will allow themselves to be drawn into connections, and under influences, which will slowly and unconsciously undermine their integrity and honor; that in selecting their worldly pursuits they will think only of worldly ends, not reflecting, that, without personal dignity and worth, distinction is an empty name, and wealth but a temptation, or at best a vulgar care.

It will not do to rank the choice of a profession among things indifferent, or things allowable, in a moral point of view, on the ground that there is no morality whatever in preferring the study of medicine to that of law, or the study of law to that of medicine. True, there is no morality in preferring one study to another, nor in the act of choice founded on that preference, simply considered; nevertheless, the consequences of the act may be of unspeakable moment in their bearing on a man's moral progress, as it determines the sphere and kind of his actions, and it is in the doing of these actions that his character will be formed. Again, it will not do to assume that it must be safe to adopt this or that profession, on the ground that good men have done so, without ceasing to be good men. The safety of such men may be owing to conditions in which they differ from you; — to a different temperament, to a different previous training, or perhaps to their very goodness itself, leading them to take a higher and more Christian view of the nature and ends of the profession, and of their duties to it. We know from Scripture that some can tread on serpents and scorpions without being hurt; but it is not so with all.

And besides, it is not enough to know that your profession will not *hurt* you: it should help you; it is to make you, for the most part, what you are to be. Much, I am aware, is said, at the present day, about extra-professional duties and activities, and many appear to look in that direction for their principal influence and distinction. In order to vindicate this course by a show of reasoning, they will tell you that a clergyman, for example, is more a citizen than he is a clergyman, and more a man than he is a citizen. Indeed! on this principle they might go one step further, and say that he is more an animal than either. The argument is fallacious at bottom; if it proved anything, it would prove too much. The mistake originates in overlooking or misapplying the logical paradox, that the less extensive a general term is, the more it includes. The clergyman is a man and a citizen, and something more. Speaking generally, the office indicates and defines the sphere in which the duties of the man and the citizen are to be fulfilled. In one word, he has an appropriate and specific care which he has no right to forsake, that he may look after another man's. See how such conduct would strike you in other and simpler relations. The helm is put into the pilot's hands, which he neglects that he may talk politics with the crew,—on the plea, forsooth, that he is more a citizen than a pilot,—and the vessel is lost. Would the owners be satisfied? Would anybody be satisfied? I think not. Among the ultraisms with which the age teems, there is none for which less can be said than for that unnatural and impracticable cosmopolitanism which makes our responsibilities begin with the duties farthest from us, and is chiefly anxious lest we should love our friends, our country, our profession, too well. Let not the cant of a so-called liberalism make you ashamed of a hearty devotion to your profession, after you have chosen it, seeking by your success in that, and not in digressions from it, to build up an honest independence and a good name. But for this very reason it becomes the more necessary that your profession should be one which will afford scope for your best affections and abilities, and tend to make the most, not only of your circumstances, but of yourselves.

Hence it may be thought that I have done nothing, after all, to lessen the embarrassment attendant on the choice of a profession, but only changed its issues, making it to turn on the question of moral fitness, and not, as a general rule, on that of mental aptitude, or bent of genius. This, however, is only partially true. The *moral* embarrassments almost entirely disappear, as soon as the subject is approached with an honest purpose to do what is right. In such a frame of mind it is hardly possible that a thought should be entertained of a pursuit involving great moral dangers or incongruities. A man's profession is no longer regarded as a field of selfish competition, but of a noble and generous emulation in the public service, the only, or the main solicitude being, that he may find a situation in which he can best fulfil all his duties to God and man. And even this solicitude need not trouble the upright in heart; for moral safety and moral progress seldom require that a man should change his profession, but only that he should take a different and a higher view of what belongs to the profession he has chosen. A profession, which to low and sordid men is as low and sordid as they, becomes transfigured in the new lights and relations under which it is regarded by the enlightened and devoted Christian. Meanwhile the lawyer does not cease to be a lawyer, merely because he becomes a Christian lawyer; neither does the physician cease to be a physician, merely because he becomes a Christian physician.

I have now set before you, my friends, what seems to me to be the duty of a young man in the choice of his profession, and I have endeavored to do it in such a manner, that no one may think to find in his perplexity as to what he ought to do an excuse for doing nothing. Neither your profession nor your circumstances, but the quick eye, and the strong arm, and the iron will must work out for you the great problem of life. These qualities, however, are little better than brute force, unless inspired and directed by a high moral purpose; and this high moral purpose little better than a breath of air, unless it rests on religious faith; and this religious faith "unstable as water," unless accepted as the revealed will of God. "For other foundation can no man lay than that is laid, which is Jesus Christ."

# THE END NOT YET.

NOT AS THOUGH I HAD ALREADY ATTAINED, EITHER WERE ALREADY PERFECT: BUT I FOLLOW AFTER. — Philippians iii. 12.

ONE of the strongest natural proofs or presumptions of man's immortality is found in the fact, that his entire destiny never seems to be accomplished in this life. He never becomes, in the present constitution of things, all that his nature, in itself considered, makes him capable of becoming. It is not so with the inferior animals. All mere animals, without a single exception, have their instincts with fixed boundaries, which are soon reached and never passed, and never would be passed if they were to live forever. But no such boundaries are set to the human faculties. Every new acquisition which a man makes is not only so much gained, but a new power of gaining more; and so on, without end. Now, why endow him with a nature capable of unlimited growth and progress, why introduce this into the plan of creation, and yet not provide scope in the same plan for the actual or possible development of such a nature? Can we believe that man, alone of all beings, should be clothed with a nature which is in contradiction to his destiny? that he is constituted and contrived for one issue, and doomed to another? that he, alone of all beings, is mocked with conscious powers and irrepressible aspirations, which were *intended* from the beginning to be disappointed? in fine, that the sentiments which most ennoble him, and the faith which most inspires and exalts him, should all have their foundation and root in a delusion and a lie?

No; though man can never attain to perfection, he will always be in a condition, if so disposed, to make continual advances towards it. And hence the distinguishing peculiarity of human life, *that it is never finished*, never completed, in the sense of all being done that ought to be done. Man's goal in the distance is not a stationary one; it is continually moving on before him: and this is provided for, in the mind of man, as well as in his circumstances, by making his powers of conception to transcend his powers of execution. By the very process of transmuting the *ideal* of yesterday into the *actual* of to-day, he is put into a condition to elevate and purify his former *ideal;* his notion or conception of what he ought to be is still in advance of what he is. His rule should be, always to do his best; but his *best* of to-day is a *better best* than that of yesterday, because his views have been enlarged and extended.

Hence it is, that, with every man in whom there is the slightest pretension to activity of thought, the ideal of life always keeps in advance of the actual, to beckon him on. Constituted as his nature is, there never will come a time, in this world or the next, when he will not have occasion to say, with the Apostle, "Not as though I had already attained, either were already perfect: but I follow after." The end is not yet.

From this constitution of human life two consequences flow; both of which will strike us at first sight as evil, but on further consideration will be approved as good.

In the first place, a foundation is thus laid in the human soul for a profound and ineradicable feeling of *discontent* and *unrest*. I do not here use the term "discontent" in the sense in which it is most frequently taken; I do not mean discontent with the past, or discontent with our condition and circumstances; but merely discontent with ourselves *as we are*, grounded on a conviction that we might be, and ought to be, continually growing better. If it should be objected, that all discontent supposes uneasiness, and all uneasiness pain, and that all pain is evil, I answer that this is reasoning according to sound, and not according to sense. All uneasiness does not suppose positive pain. That uneasiness with our present selves which puts us on self-improvement is not attended with pain, provided only that nothing exists within or without to hinder such self-improvement. It is nothing but the uneasiness of desire; and who would live with nothing to desire? It is not necessarily accompanied by a shade of remorse, or repentance, or even of regret; for the self-improvement desired may not be from bad to good, but from good to better; and this is a longing which may burn in the heart of an archangel, as well as in that of halting and fainting man. What, however, under this view, becomes of the peace and rest which the Gospel promises as the reward of faith and obedience? "Take my yoke upon you, and learn of me; for I am meek and lowly of heart; and ye shall find rest to your souls." I answer, again, that the "rest" here spoken of is rest from worldly uneasiness and discontent, rest from struggle and conflict with external or internal foes, — not rest from progress, not rest from self-improvement.

There is also, as I have intimated above, another consequence, and one of still greater practical moment, flowing from the fact, that the end of human life is not an attainment made once for all, but a continual unfolding, a continual advancing. This consequence is, that, as human life is never complete, *education*, which is the preparation for it in its different and successive degrees and stages, *is never complete*. You remember those noble words of Milton:

"I call, therefore, a complete and generous education that which fits a man to perform justly, skilfully, and magnanimously all the offices, both private and public, of peace and war."* But when, in the very next sentence, he proceeds to call attention to the manner in which "all this may be done between twelve and one and twenty," we feel that he has lost sight of his own conception of what education should be, and sunk down to the common and low view of the subject. Education, in its highest and best sense, does not consist wholly or mainly in mere teaching, but still more in the unfolding and training of the intellectual and moral faculties. It comprehends the sum total of the preparation for the life to follow; and, understood in this sense, it is obvious that no bounds are set to it, or can be set to it. Childhood is the education for youth; youth, for manhood; manhood, for old age; and the whole of this life for the life to come. Neither will it stop there. Hints abound in Scripture which confirm the expectation, founded on the analogies of nature, that progress will not end with the world that now is. The immortal spirit will still need to be fitted for higher and higher stages in the heavenly society and the heavenly occupations and enjoyments. Education will never stand still; its work will never be accomplished; the time will never come when it can-

---

* *Tractate on Education,* § 7.

not be said, with as much truth as now, "The end is not yet." The great Apostle to the Gentiles is probably repeating now, what he said or implied so often on earth, "Not as though I had already attained, either were already perfect: but I follow after."

This train of thought has been suggested by the condition and prospects of that portion of my audience who have just accomplished their collegiate course, and are worshipping with us for the last time.

To say, my young friends, that your education is not as yet complete, would be to say what you all feel and know. Many of you have already made arrangements to enter immediately on professional or more exclusively scientific studies, understanding it to be in continuation of the education which you have begun here. Under these circumstances it is of importance to apprehend as clearly as may be the precise place which an academic training holds in the life of a liberally educated man.

In the first place, there is the exercise and discipline of the intellectual faculties. Bishop Butler has told you, that "if we suppose a person brought into the world with all his powers of body and mind in maturity, as far as this is conceivable, he would plainly be at first as unqualified for the human life of mature age as an idiot."* And the

---

* *Analogy*, Part I. Chap. V.

reason is obvious. It is not enough that we have powers; we must know how to use them, have them under our command, be able to concentrate them on this subject or that, as we choose; which is the work of experience and discipline. Now I admit that any mode of life supposes some kind and some degree of experience and intellectual activity; and this is of the nature of education, and leads to more or less of self-culture. All life is exercise, and all exercise is education of some sort or other; but a collegiate education has this distinction and privilege: it is *systematic* education, — education systematically contrived with a view to bring out and cultivate in the best manner all the faculties, neither neglecting any nor exaggerating any. Provided it does this effectively, it accomplishes, as far as it goes, the great purpose of a general and preparatory education.

Here, then, is a sufficient answer to the shallow but popular objection, that many things studied in colleges have no direct bearing on after life. This is often doubtless the case with some particular studies, in themselves considered, but not with the general discipline they induce, which is the principal thing. It cannot be repeated too often, that the principal object aimed at in preliminary and general education is, not to teach one what he ought to think in after life, but to put him into a condition *to think for himself,* with judgment, discrimination, energy, and taste. For this reason the wisdom of ages has pronounced in favor of classical studies, as laying the best foundation of a liberal culture; no matter though the student should never have occasion in after life to open a Latin or Greek book, or, indeed, attain to such proficiency as would enable him to enjoy it, if he did. The same may also be said of the study of mathematics and metaphysics, at least in respect to minds having any natural aptitude for it. A great master of the last-mentioned science has said: "It is as the *best gymnastic of the mind*, — as a mean, principally, and almost exclusively conducive to the highest education of our noblest powers, that we would vindicate to these speculations the necessity which has too frequently been denied them. By no other intellectual application (and least of all by physical pursuits) is the soul thus reflected on itself, and its faculties concentred in such independent, vigorous, unwonted, and continued energy;—by none, therefore, are its best capacities so variously and intensely evolved. 'Where there is most life, there is the victory.'" *

Even, therefore, if all that is learned in colleges in the way of positive instruction were forgotten at

---

\* Sir William Hamilton's *Discussions on Philosophy and Literature,* p. 40.

the moment of leaving them, it does not follow that the time spent there is misspent. But all is not forgotten.

Accordingly I would mention, as the second advantage of a college course, the general information it imparts in almost every field of human inquiry; which general information, considered as the basis of a special scientific or professional education, makes the whole to be a truly *liberal* education. Who does not know that what are called the learned professions may be adopted and followed in a spirit as narrow and sordid as any of the handicrafts? This is the case, for the most part, with the lawyer who is nothing but a lawyer, and with the physician who is nothing but a physician; neither being bent on understanding his profession in its highest relations, or exalting it to its highest uses, but only on turning it to immediate profit. Some have thought that this might be prevented by resisting the tendency of modern times to a division and subdivision of intellectual labor. But not so. This tendency to a division and subdivision of intellectual labor is a necessary consequence of the advancement of the arts and sciences, making it indispensable to success, certainly to eminence, that a man should give himself mainly to a single department. Under these circumstances, if a professional man does not start with a mind stored with the fruits of good learning, or at least with an acquired taste for such things, it is hardly to be expected that he will ever have them. A lawyer or physician in full practice can find opportunity for liberal studies and a general self-culture, if he is so disposed; but the disposition itself is not likely to spring up amidst the fatigues and distractions of his daily and hourly cares. If you mean by a lawyer nothing more than a cunning and successful trier of cases, one who can browbeat a witness or mystify the jury, I do not suppose that a college education is necessary to such a person, or even that it would be useful. But if you mean by a lawyer, an accomplished advocate, one who can seize the principle which lies concealed under the precedent, and make the darkest subject plain to common minds, by throwing upon it the lights of an extended and various erudition, it is certain that mere legal culture will not do. It must be legal culture, founded on the highest general and learned culture which the age affords.

The third principal benefit resulting from a college training, considered as preliminary to the more special vocations in life, is not so much intellectual as moral and practical. A college, as we have been told again and again, is a little world, a microcosm, where almost every faculty, disposition, and passion is put to the proof which is ever called out in the great world. Here the student must exercise self-control, especially as regards the love of ease and the love of pleasure, or take the consequences. Here he must choose his amusements and his companions wisely, or take the consequences. Here also he must concentrate his attention on the work of the hour, and submit to earnest and continuous labor, or take the consequences. And these consequences, though not always the same in form, are the same in substance, and, as far as they go, the same in their bearing on success and happiness as in the great world. All this, however, may be said to hold true of early life, wherever passed; and so it does. What distinguishes a college life is, that it comes to a natural close; judgment is pronounced upon it; we say of one person, he has succeeded, and of another, he has failed. The same actors will reappear, indeed; but it will be on another stage, in other connections, and with other objects in view; hence it will not follow necessarily, because a man has failed here, that he will fail there. He may be said to have a second trial, while others, with a continuous, unbroken life, have but one.

Now I look on this as an obvious and great advantage. It is not uncommon for persons when near the close of their earthly existence to express a wish that they could live this life over again. With their present experience they are not unwilling to admit that they should do differently in many respects; that they should set a different estimate on many of the pursuits of ambition and pleasure, and know how to shun many a hidden pitfall. This cannot be; but a privilege resembling it to a certain extent is enjoyed by all those who, after having completed their college course, can carry the often dear-bought wisdom which they have gained there into new scenes. Thus college life is not merely a preparation for the life to follow,—a quality which it possesses in common with every form of novitiate or apprenticeship,—but also a life by itself, a rehearsal, so to speak, of the life to follow, a sort of trial-life, with its retributions carried out, leaving those who have just passed through it to enter upon another career with the singular benefit of such an experience.

This, my friends, is precisely your condition at this moment. With one foot on the threshold of the great world, you cannot help looking back; and you cannot help looking forward.

You cannot help *looking back*. And what do you see? Many things, I hope, which you can review with satisfaction. But are there not also many things which you now wish had not been? No writer has sufficiently explained that law of our nature by which an excited state of the passions is able to pervert our judgment as to what is right and safe. Explain it, however, as we may, one thing is certain; in the moment of action, with our desires raised and inflamed, we are seldom in a condition to form a just opinion of the true character and real tendency of what we do. Afterwards comes a season of sober reflection, when we can see things as they are; when we can pronounce as impartially on our own conduct as on that of others; when we can feel that we have been made fools of by sophistries which will not bear a moment's examination; that we have sought to reconcile ourselves to ourselves by excuses which we suspected at the time, and which we now know, were hollow and vain. This is generally the crisis in a young man's destiny. If he is of a dull or reckless mind, he will refuse to dwell on the subject, and go on as before. If he is of a sensitive and weak mind, he will be apt to indulge in unavailing regrets, and perhaps give up all as lost. But if he is of a sound and resolute mind, he will make his past mistakes and failures to be his teachers; the consciousness of his very sins will stir his moral nature to its depths, and sometimes have the effect to rouse him to a new activity. Thus students of good natural dispositions and gifts, who have spent their time in college to but little purpose, not unfrequently wake up at the close of it, and give themselves to their subsequent pursuits with an earnestness and devotion which redeem the evil days and surprise all. In this way they may be said, more perhaps than any other class of persons, to have a second chance to distinguish themselves, a second chance to satisfy their friends and put themselves right before the world and before God; but it is commonly their last chance.

Again, you cannot help *looking forward*. And what do you see? You see, in the first place, that success is to depend, much more than it has done hitherto, on yourselves. Up to this hour fond and anxious eyes have watched over you; your wants have been anticipated, and provided for, day by day; other hands have assisted yours in removing the obstacles in your path; you have pursued your studies under a routine, which, however irksome to you in other respects, has had this effect at least: it has helped to supply the defects in your own self-direction and self-control. But all this is now over. In the pursuit of your professional studies the restraints of discipline will no longer be felt. The momentous, the terrible gift of freedom is put into your hands, and you will be left to make yourselves as wise and virtuous and happy as you please, or as foolish and vicious and miserable as you please. This, more perhaps than anything else, must have the effect to induce you to pause, and ponder your steps. But the doctrine is one which has its bright as well as its dark side. Many young men are troubled by the apprehension that their success in life will depend on their choosing the right profession, or on finding their proper place in society. But no such thing. If your tastes and aptitudes are strongly marked, you can hardly help choosing the right profession, and falling into the proper place; and if your tastes and aptitudes are not strongly marked, it is plain that you would do about as well in one profession or place as in another. In any event, success will not depend on profession or place; it will depend *on yourselves*. Under God it will depend on yourselves whether you become something or nothing; and even the help you are to expect from God is to come through your own choice and your own exertions. "Work out your own salvation with fear and trembling; for it is God that worketh *in you* both to will and to do of his good pleasure."

Again; you see, you can hardly help seeing, that in the life before you everything will depend, in the last resort, on moral worth sustained by Christian faith. In early life we have to content ourselves with good dispositions and generous impulses, for these have not had time to take the form of habit. But good dispositions and generous impulses are motives merely; they do not constitute a solid foundation of character, on which alone a truly happy and prosperous life can be built. I do not deny that knowledge, talent, genius, may procure a certain measure of renown, a certain sort of power; but there is one thing which is absolutely indispensable to a happy and prosperous life, and which they never did and never can procure; I mean, *public confidence*. This depends on moral worth; and moral worth must find its support in religious principle; and the religious principle must be, in your case, enlightened religious principle. A merely practical man may accept the religion which prevails around him, and in such unthinking acquiescence find all the support he needs. But the scholar, whose business it is to inquire and investigate, must see with his own eyes; he must see that the religion he professes is consistent with itself and with all known truth, otherwise it will not be likely to do much to give either stability to his character or peace to his soul.

Remember, you have but begun your education, an education which is never to come to an end; but you have begun it well, if you have laid the foundation of a broad and generous culture of the whole mind. Hereafter you are to pursue a narrower walk; but let not your eagerness for professional advancement narrow your thoughts or your affections, or lead you to neglect what is necessary to moral and religious progress. "For what shall it profit a man, if he gain the whole world and lose his own soul?" As professional men, as scholars, as Christians, let me beseech you to take up the noble declaration of the Apostle, "I count not myself to have apprehended: but this one thing I do; forgetting those things which are behind, and reaching forth unto those things which are before, I press toward the mark for the prize of the high calling of God in Christ Jesus."

# FAITH AND WORKS.

YE SEE THEN HOW THAT BY WORKS A MAN IS JUSTIFIED, AND NOT BY FAITH ONLY. — James ii. 24.

LUTHER, unable to reconcile this and other passages in the Epistle of James with his favorite doctrine of justification by faith alone, did not hesitate to stigmatize the whole as "an epistle of straw." Others, also, have presumed to speak in terms almost equally disparaging and contemptuous of this Apostle, not only on account of the supposed contradiction between him and Paul respecting justification, but also because the name of Christ is scarcely mentioned by him above once or twice, and then coldly; and because he is silent respecting the mysteries of the incarnation and redemption, morality being the principal theme.

But this is not the way, as it seems to me, in which to show our respect for the Scriptures. Instead of setting up one writer above another, one book above another, or one passage above another, it certainly would be more becoming to inquire whether some statement of the Christian doctrine cannot be found in which all will be seen to harmonize.

Take, for example, this long-contested question respecting Faith and Works. Some, relying on one set of texts, maintain that mankind are justified and saved by faith " without works ; " others, relying on another set of texts, maintain that " faith without works is dead." How are these apparently contradictory doctrines to be reconciled ?

It seems to me that the origin and continuance of this controversy in the Church, as well as of many others, are mainly, if not entirely, owing to the imperfection and ambiguity of language. When we are said to be saved by *faith alone*, faith is understood to include all that is essential to obedience in a moral point of view ; that is to say, a *disposition and purpose to obey*, an effective principle of obedience, an inward act of self-surrender and trust. On the other hand, when we are said to be saved by *works*, works are understood to include the *internal* as well as the external part of the virtuous act ; not merely the outward form of obedience, but also its spring and soul ; that is to say, the conviction, the faith, which the works express, and which must really exist or the works are a vain show.

Accordingly, both the doctrines, when rightly understood, agree in making obedience, " righteousness and true holiness," to be the ultimate ground of salvation; the only difference being, that one regards this obedience in the inward principle from which it starts, and the other in the outward act in which it is consummated. Thus, if we cannot say that these two doctrines are one and identical, we can say, nevertheless, that they do but represent different sides of one and the same truth, and indeed that each supposes or involves the other. The only faith which saves, is the faith which leads to good works, as occasion offers; and the only works which save, are the works which spring from faith, — from faith in some moral or religious principle, as their living root in the soul; and the only reason why either of them saves is, that both alike denote a life brought inwardly and outwardly into harmony with the Divine Will.

Let us now inquire whether this view of faith and works, and their connection with salvation, is not confirmed by Scripture, and whether it does not afford the means of reconciling what have been thought the discordant teachings of the two Apostles on this subject.

We begin with an example from the Old Testament, often cited in this discussion. "Abraham," it is said, "believed God, and it was counted unto him for righteousness." Now it will not be pretended that the faith here spoken of was a mere assenting to propositions, or the holding of a creed, or an intellectual act of any kind. It was not a speculative, but a practical faith. The patriarch "believed God;" that is to say, confided in him, was willing to be led by him, was ready to *do* whatever God required. It was not a mere conviction, but a *disposition;* one which he evinced pre-eminently in the first recorded act of his life, when he went out from his own country, in implicit obedience to a Divine intimation, "not knowing whither he went"; and again, on a still more memorable occasion, when, in implicit obedience to a like intimation, he "stretched forth his hand, and took the knife to slay his son." True, in the last-mentioned case his hand was stayed; but this made no *moral* difference, no difference in his disposition to obey, no difference in his deserts. No matter whether his faith was acted out or not; he was ready to act it out, being hindered by extraneous causes alone. The *will* was there, and the will was taken for the deed, as having all the moral character the deed itself could have, under any circumstances.

To be convinced that there was nothing unreasonable or strange in all this, it is only necessary to reverse the conditions of the case. Suppose that Abraham had made up his mind to *disobey*, but had been frustrated in the attempt by some unforeseen accident; every one would have said that, in the eye of conscience, he was guilty. If, then, a disposition to disobey would of itself have been counted unto him for unrighteousness, why wonder that *faith*, which stands in this connection for a disposition to obey, was counted unto him for righteousness? Above all, why appeal to such texts to prove that righteousness is unnecessary, when from these very texts it appears that it was only in so far as his faith "was counted unto him *for righteousness*" that it was of any avail?

Before considering more particularly the language used in the New Testament in speaking of faith as a condition of salvation, it will be proper to say a few words of the relation which the New Testament, taken as a whole, bears to the Old, in the education of the great human family.

A wise parent, in bringing up his children, accommodates his modes of training to their years; that is, to the degree of development which their moral and intellectual faculties have attained. He does not begin by inculcating general principles and dispositions, which his children are not as yet in a condition to comprehend, and then tell them to go and apply these principles and dispositions, as occasion offers, in the multiplied and complicated relations of human life. This would be to treat children as if they were men. He begins by commanding or forbidding easily intelligible actions. Why these particular actions are to be done or avoided it is not necessary that the child should know: it is enough if the parent knows that the habits thus formed are likely to generate the inward spirit required and unfold the character aright. And so with the Universal Father. Judaism was not a dispensation of inward principles, of moral and spiritual truth, for which the world was as yet unprepared, but a dispensation of outward routine, of specific regulations and ordinances. Even the morality inculcated by Moses was inculcated, for the most part, under the form of specific outward acts to be done or avoided, and not of inward principles or dispositions to be believed in, cherished, and carried out.

We do not mention this in order to find fault with it. We do not complain that an all-wise Providence has adapted his special modes of human training to the successive stages of human progress. Considered with reference to the age and people for which it was designed, Judaism was undoubtedly better fitted to accomplish its purpose, than if it had been conceived on the same plan with Christianity: we only say that it was not conceived on the same plan. Its ultimate object, indeed, was the same, — human progress; but it aimed to accomplish this object in another and, for the time, a better way. The Jews were to be carried forward in their moral and religious culture by the reflex influence on their minds and hearts of an imposing ritual, which meant much more than they were as yet in a condition to comprehend, if stated in the form of principles. Children in spiritual understanding, they were treated as children; that is, subjected to an outward discipline, which, whether they could enter at first into its profound spiritual import or not, was of such a nature that it could hardly fail, however blindly and mechanically gone through with, to react powerfully on their feelings and imagination, and so keep alive among them a sense of religion, and gradually form them to a capacity for a higher and more spiritual revelation.

Mark, then, the radical distinction between the Jewish peculiarity and the Christian peculiarity,— a distinction which holds as well in respect to the moral as the ceremonial law. The Jew was expected to conform his life and worship to certain externally imposed rules; the Christian is expected to accept and carry out certain internal principles. With the Jew, the reforming power of his religion acted from without inwardly; with the Christian, the reforming power of his religion acts from within outwardly. The great question with the Jew was, Have I done what is required? The great question with the Christian is, Are my moral convictions, my inward purposes and dispositions, my spirit and my trust, what they ought to be? In one word, the former was a dispensation of "works," the latter, a dispensation of "faith," but both, equally and alike, dispensations of obedience and of progress.

This being premised, it is easy to see why the New Testament lays so much stress on *faith*, often representing it as the one thing needful, the sole, indispensable condition of acceptance with God.

Sometimes it is stated thus: "Believe on the Lord Jesus Christ, and thou shalt be saved, and thine house." That is to say, "Put your trust in him; commit yourself wholly to his guidance; renounce all confidence in other teachers and leaders; and confide in him, and follow him." Obviously, therefore, faith in this case is not meant to exclude obedience, or to supersede its necessity: on the contrary, it involves or supposes obedience, or at least a disposition to obey in all things. To make this clear, take a parallel case. A man in attempting to traverse an unfrequented forest is bewildered and lost; he does not know which way to turn. You procure for him a trusty and experienced guide, and say: "Have faith in this guide; confide in him; do as he advises, and go as he directs, and you are safe." Here salvation is made to depend, you will observe, on *faith*, on faith in a guide; but, I repeat, so far is this from excluding obedience, or dispensing with its necessity, that it is understood by all to involve or suppose it, or to lead to it; so that without a purpose at least of obedience it cannot exist even *as faith*. What if the traveller should say, "I have entire faith in the guide;" but still should refuse or neglect to follow him? Would not all exclaim that this is not the faith which saves? Merely to believe that the guide is able and willing to lead you to a place of safety is nothing: you must *actually follow him*, or you will never reach that place of safety.

Again, not the person, but the teachings of our Lord, are sometimes made the objects of a saving faith. Thus we are told: "For I am not ashamed of the Gospel of Christ; for it is the power of God unto salvation to every one that believeth." That is to say, it is the power of God unto salvation to every one who *confides* in it; who *gives himself up to it;* who accepts its revelations as realities, and therefore is affected by them as realities; who takes the view which the Gospel gives of the spiritual life and the spiritual world into his inmost consciousness, and governs himself accordingly in his inmost purposes and thoughts. But faith in Christianity, thus understood, supposes something more than a mere conviction that the system is trustworthy: it supposes the practical exercise of this trust on our part, an act of self-surrender, giving ourselves up to it; just as a merchant is said to have faith in a ship when he embarks in it, or puts his property on board of it;

or a sick man in a new method of cure, when he abandons all others, and trusts himself to that. The sick man, however, *takes the medicine*. Nobody expects to be healed merely by believing in the efficacy of a medicine, if he does not take it. For the same reason the impotent in virtue must not expect advantage from faith in the remedies which the Gospel proposes, if they do not also take these remedies; but to do this is to obey.

One word, now, on the apparent discrepancy between Paul and James on this subject. "Therefore we conclude," says the former, "that a man is justified by faith without the works of the law." By "works of the law" we are not to understand, in this place, what is commonly meant in discourses on practical religion by "good works," that is, the acting out of Christian principles, but a mere external conformity to a prescribed rule of conduct. The doctrine is, that under the Christian dispensation men are not justified and saved by a mere external conformity, however exact, to any externally imposed law, however righteous and good. "Works," overt actions, have no proper moral or religious worth, unless they have their root in faith and love. It is not enough that the hand obeys; the will, the heart, must also obey; and this supposes an act of self-surrender; and this, again, supposes faith. What a man is inwardly, that is, in himself, and not what he is outwardly (except as it is the evidence, the expression, the carrying out of what he is inwardly), has weight with God. The heart to obey, the spirit of obedience, that confidence and trust which begets a willingness to be led, and which is all comprehended under the single term *faith*, is the great thing. "Man looketh on the outward appearance," for it is by that only that he can judge his fellow-man; "but the Lord looketh on the heart," so that if the heart, the disposition, be right, even though no opportunity for manifesting it in outward action should occur, the disposition alone will be accepted. In one word, as in the case of Abraham before mentioned, the will is taken for the deed; the spirit of obedience for actual obedience; a meek and trustful self-surrender to Christian guidance, or faith alone, for the works to which it leads.

Nay, more; even when our faith is manifested by our works, we are not saved, according to the Gospel, by our outward works, but by the inward principle from which they spring, by our faith: so that here again we are saved, not by works, but by faith. Without faith in Christian principles a man may do many things which those principles sanction or require. Thus, he may give largely to the poor, or endow hospitals or colleges, which are certainly liberal acts, and yet be a stranger to the Christian principle of liberality; but you would hardly say, in such cases, that he acts out a Christian principle. You would hardly say that a man can act out a principle which he does not feel; or, again, that he can truly feel a principle in which he does not believe. Accordingly, the Gospel is conceived on the plan of inducing faith in a higher set of principles than that which the world acknowledges as the necessary condition and prerequisite of a higher form of character. Everything, therefore, has its root in this faith. While this faith is alive, all is alive; when this faith is dead, all is dead; and hence the whole dispensation is not inaptly denominated by the Apostle "the Law of Faith."

This is the doctrine of Paul. When rightly and clearly apprehended, it will be seen not to conflict with the prevailing opinion, that Christianity is almost wholly a practical thing, and that the Christian salvation depends on "righteousness and true holiness," on conformity of heart and will with the Divine law. But it is a doctrine, which, in certain states of the public mind, is peculiarly liable to perversion, and this perversion began to manifest itself in the Apostolic Age, calling forth the earnest expostulations of James in the chapter from which my text is taken. "Ye see, then, how that *by works* a man is justified, and not by faith only." Here it is plain, from the examples adduced, that by "works" we are to understand really good works, by which I mean, the acting out of Christian principles; and the object of the Apostle is to warn men against forsaking this ground of hope, and building on a merely speculative faith, or a dreamy, sentimental, sterile admiration of our Lord's character and words. Still, the only difference between the two Apostles is this: one regards obedience in the inward principle from which it starts, and the other in the outward act in which it is consummated; — both, however, making obedience, "righteousness and true holiness," the ultimate ground of salvation, the breath of eternal life.

Let me impress upon you the great practical lesson to be gathered from the twofold aspect of the Apostolic doctrine respecting faith and works. There are times when, on account of the hollowness and superficialness of the public morals, we ought to insist, with Paul, that works, apart from the living principle of faith in the soul, are vain; and, again, there are times when, on account of the prevalent sentimentalism, mysticism, and morbid introversion of spirit, we ought to insist, with James, "that faith without works is dead."

# SALVATION BY HOPE.

FOR WE ARE SAVED BY HOPE. — Romans viii. 24.

THE Gospel, as the term denotes, is glad tidings; — glad tidings to all, not excepting the chiefest of sinners. No matter what may have been a man's past life, if he is *now* sincerely disposed to turn unto God, it holds out to him the promise of sympathy, pardon, and help. It is a Divine dispensation of encouragement. Its salvation is a salvation "by hope."

To understand this doctrine, it will be necessary to begin by considering generally what mankind stand most in need of as a motive and means to that change of heart and life on which salvation depends.

And, first, in case of hardened and abandoned sinners. With respect to such men, at least, I believe the impression is almost universal, that what they stand most in need of is, to be thoroughly alarmed. The preacher, it is said, must arouse them to a proper sense of their danger, by an honest dealing with the terrors of the law, by vivid pictures of the judgment to come if they die impenitent. Undoubtedly this is among the means which are appointed for reclaiming bad men; but that it is the only means, or the means most likely to be effectual, or the means most needed, is not so clear. The usual argument for resorting to it, in preference to all others, is far from being satisfactory. This argument is, that as bad men, through the indurating effects of sin, have become insensible to higher and better motives, they must be moved, if moved at all, by a fear of God's indignation and wrath. But those who insist thus on the indurating effects of sin should remember that these effects are nowhere more apparent than in respect to the very motive in question. Sin hardens men, I admit, against a sense of duty and a sense of shame; but it hardens them, if possible, still more against a sense of any dangers dependent on what religion threatens; that is to say, against their spiritual dangers.

For this reason, I am not surprised to find that the two Christian sects which have distinguished themselves above all others for their successful dealing with hardened and abandoned sinners, I mean the Moravians and the Methodists, are remarkable for founding religion, not on selfish fear, or on calculations of interest or danger of any kind, but on hearts melted by a sense of the unutterable love of God. It is also in obedience to the same instinct of spiritual wisdom that

Howard and Elizabeth Fry, with the men and women who have followed them in their mission to carry the Gospel into prisons, and among convicted felons, are found to have trusted almost exclusively to the power of Christian sympathy, aided by a gentle and kind manner, as a means of subduing those who feared neither God nor man, neither death nor hell. Let me add, that not more than forty years ago a confirmed drunkard was generally regarded as incorrigible. At last it occurred to a few reformers that the supposed incorrigibleness of the drunkard might be owing, not to insensibility to his degradation, but to distrust of his competency to escape from it; in other words, that he did not stand in need of menace, or even of rebuke or warning, so much as of sympathy and encouragement. Here was a great moral discovery, and hence, in no small measure, the new life in the Temperance cause, and the marvellous success which has attended it.

But if this is true of hardened and abandoned sinners, how much more so of all such as still have their misgivings and relentings, whose sin consists, for the most part, in halting between two opinions, not having made up their minds what course to take, or having made them up only so far as this, that they will become religious at some future day, but not yet. Speaking generally, such persons do not need to be convinced that religion is the best and only safe course. When they read the life of an enlightened and consistent Christian, or meet with one in their intercourse with society, they cannot help wishing that they were just such a man; that they had his faith and his works and his prospects. But there are obstacles, discouragements in the way. They think it would be harder work for them to be Christians than for most men; that it is beyond their reach, at least for the present; that it would be vanity or presumption in them to make the attempt. Now, I ask, how are these obstacles, all consisting radically in a want of confidence, most likely to be removed or overcome? Clearly and incontestably as the Gospel aims to do it; — by inspiring new confidence, by holding out the promise of sympathy and help; by a divinely authenticated dispensation of encouragement. "We are saved by hope."

But if I were to stop here, half of my purpose would be left unaccomplished. All will agree, I doubt not, that life without hope from any quarter would be insupportable. Still, some may ask, why look to religion, why look to Christianity for this hope? Why not hope each one in the strength of his own right arm, or in what the world has to promise, or simply in the righteousness of his claim?

To answer these questions intelligibly and satisfactorily, it will be necessary to speak of the nature and excellence of the Christian hope.

In the first place, the Christian hope is not limited and bounded, like all worldly, irreligious, infidel hopes, by what *man can do*. In a storm at sea we naturally and properly look to the pilot; if dangerously sick ourselves, or if our friends are dangerously sick, we naturally and properly look to the physician; in civil troubles we naturally and properly look to the experienced and trustworthy statesman. But we know beforehand that the pilot, the physician, the statesman can do so much and no more; and when this point is reached, to whom are we to look? There are situations, and they too of not infrequent occurrence, in which the offer of human aid, however kindly intended, seems almost like mockery. This may not be my situation, or yours, at the present moment; but it will be sooner or later,—before many years, perhaps before many days; and what shall we look to then? If our hope is in man alone, it is plainly one which is crumbling, day by day, into dust. Unless we recognize the being, and trust in the presence and agency of a Higher Power, the hour is coming, every setting sun is bringing us one day nearer to it, when the soul will be without hope. Despair will take the place of hope. Here also it is of importance to observe, that, with persons of reflection and forethought, whatever is seen to *end* in despair, *begins* in despair.

Another distinction of the Christian hope consists in its not being limited and bounded, as all worldly, irreligious, and infidel hopes must be, by *the present life*. Hope, to be hope, must not be liable to be swept away by the very vicissitudes under which it is to sustain and cheer us. The first Christians shared but the common fate of earnest and devoted men in difficult times; yet one of them could say: "If in this life only we have hope in Christ, we are of all men most miserable." The hope "in this life only" is one which plays along the pathways of youth and wealth and power, but leaves the wronged and the forsaken to weep and die. Go with this hope into the abodes of extreme penury and want; go with it to the bedside of one who is suffering under an incurable malady. It may answer well enough for the house of feasting and merriment, where hope is not wanted; but go with it where hope is most wanted, go with it to the house of mourning, where death has just stricken down the joy or the stay of that now desolate home. What can it do? Almost the entire language of condolence under grief, hardship, and oppression is borrowed from the Bible, and owes its significance and force to the Christian doctrine that "the sufferings of this present time are not worthy to be compared with the glory which shall be revealed in us." Even those who do not profess to be religious themselves, participate more or less in the benefits of the common hope,— through a common sympathy, if not through a common conviction. The soothing effects of the prayer or the hymn reach every heart.

A third circumstance distinguishing the Christian hope is, that, unlike all worldly, irreligious, infidel hopes, it does not profess to measure itself by the real or supposed *deserts of the individual*, but by the *boundless goodness and mercy of the Supreme Disposer*. Some preachers are accustomed to speak of human nature in the most disparaging terms, representing man's best services as no better than a hollow pretence, an outside show, a false glitter. If they speak thus from conviction of its truth, not a word is to be said; every one must preach what he believes. But if they think by rhetorical exaggerations of human depravity to inculcate humility and self-abasement, it would be well for them to consider whether language of this kind is as likely to *humble* men as it is to *degrade* and *discourage* them; whether it as likely to rouse them to exertion, as it is to suggest a good, or at least a plausible excuse for not so much as making the attempt. For this reason, I have no wish to join in any sweeping and indiscriminate repudiation of human virtue. Still I think all must agree that this virtue is too imperfect even in the best men, and that in most men it is alloyed and offset by too many vices or failings, to authorize them to expect much on the score of absolute merit. Hope, therefore, that is founded on merit alone is not suited to the actual condition of mankind. Accordingly the Gospel is conceived on the plan of providing, not only recompense for the righteous, but also encouragement and hope for sinners. It begins with us as sinners; it addresses us as sinners, and sinners we are; and the excellency of "the hope set before us" is, that there is nothing in our sins to exclude us from it, if we repent and turn to God. Under the Christian dispensation it is impiety to despair of God's mercy on account of our past sins; for this would be to suppose these sins to be greater than His mercy. Of course, when we compare what we are and what we can do, with what we hope to receive, we cannot fail to be struck with the infinite disparity; but neither is this just ground for misgivings. What is promised is to be regarded, not as being of the nature of wages for work done, but as being of the nature of a gift on condition of obedience; and in this character, *as a gift*, it takes its proportions, not from our poor earnings, but from the munificence of the Giver.

These, then, are the characteristics by which the Christian hope is distinguished from all worldly, irreligious, infidel hopes. It is not bounded and limited by human weakness, by the narrow scope of this life, or the poor deserts of the individual, but measures itself by the possible succors of the Almighty, by the range of eternity, and by the infinite benignity and clemency of our heavenly Father.

Who, it may be asked in conclusion, does not feel his *need* of this hope? I speak to many who are not unhappy now; but I speak to none who are not unhappy at times. This thought should chasten our feelings of confidence and security even when we happen to be free from pain and sorrow; and reconcile us to them when they come, as the common and inevitable lot. Above all, it should lead us to put ourselves into a condition to meet the disastrous vicissitudes of human life with composure and dignity. There is, I know, a kind of *philosophy*, which is sometimes set forward as a substitute for religion in such cases. This philosophy will tell you, that everything is determined and fixed by an inexorable fate; that it is mere weakness and folly, therefore, to tremble and shrink at what is inevitable,—to give way to regrets and apprehensions which can be of no avail. As if men shrank from evil because they expected to gain by such conduct; as if it were a voluntary thing with them whether to feel dread, or not. Discipline, habit, this philosophy, if you please, may help them to conceal their dread, and make it consistent with presence of mind, and a manly composure; it may make them still, but the stillness is that of despair, and not of hope. The groans are not there, but the torment is there, and not the less because the usual signs of it are suppressed. In one respect religion, I admit, resembles this philosophy; it teaches us, like this philosophy, that everything is determined and fixed; but here the resemblance ends. Religion teaches us that everything is determined and fixed, not by a blind and inexorable fate, but *by an infinitely wise and good Being;* and here is ground for confidence and implicit trust,—a *reason* why we should put away our fears;—not, indeed, because everything is determined and fixed, so that our fears can be of no avail, but because everything is *so* determined and fixed that all will come right at last, leaving us no occasion for fear. Hence it is the believer alone who is able to say, "Why art thou cast down, O my soul? and why art thou disquieted within me? Hope thou in God; for I shall yet praise him, who is the health of my countenance, and my God."

Again, who would not *cultivate* this hope? As religious dispositions are not of this world, they are not likely to spring up spontaneously under worldly appliances, amidst worldly avocations. Religion, religion at least in its highest forms, is a delicate exotic, which must not be expected to grow wild in the fields; it must be nurtured with effort and care; it must be sheltered from all ungenial influences, and surrounded, as far as may be, with the atmosphere, so to speak, of its native heaven. Why wonder that our affections are not set on things above, while almost everything we are saying and doing tends to set them on things on the earth? Why wonder that we do not find the pleasure and satisfaction in religion of which others tell, if accustomed to think of it only at remote intervals, and then chiefly as a law to curb our passions, or as an avenger to punish our misdeeds? We must *cultivate*, we must *assiduously* cultivate a temper of cheerful, grateful, childlike trust in our heavenly Father, by acts of duty and humanity, by prayer and all holy exercises, and, above all, by making ourselves familiar with the pure, meek, loving spirit of Jesus, which will generate in us not only righteousness, but that peculiar form of righteousness whereby the Christian is known. In this way Christ will be formed in us the hope of glory; " for the law made nothing perfect, but the bringing in of a better hope did, by the which we draw nigh unto God." It may be said, that to be without this hope, is to fail in happiness; not in duty. But we should consider, that if it is not to fail in duty, it is to fail in the *motives* to duty, which in effect will amount to the same thing. Hence, as Jeremy Taylor has said, " a man may be damned for despairing to be saved."

Finally, who would knowingly and willingly *disappoint* or *frustrate* this hope? Because a man has hope in Christ it does not follow that this hope is well founded in his case. Our very hope may perish; nay, it will do so, unless we establish it in righteousness, and unless "we show the same diligence, to the full assurance of hope, unto the end."

# THE DIFFERENCES AMONG CHRISTIANS NO OBJECTION TO CHRISTIANITY.

IS CHRIST DIVIDED? — 1 Corinthians i. 13.

THE differences among Christians are frequently referred to at the present day. To some they are a reason for scepticism; to some, an excuse for indifference; to some, an occasion for cynical and contemptuous reflections on truth and human nature.

To understand this subject aright, it will be necessary to begin by considering, how it is that men come to differ in morals and religion.

Almost every action, character, or doctrine, on which we are called upon to make up an opinion, is more or less complex; that is to say, has more than one side or aspect. This being the case, if one man regards it on one side, under one aspect, and another regards it on another side, and under another aspect, their impressions will be different, at least they ought to be. It does not follow that one is true, and the other false: both may be true; that is, just and faithful representations of the same reality, only under different aspects.

You know how it is with views of a church, or palace, or mountain, taken from different positions. The views themselves are different; nevertheless they are views of the same thing, and all of them faithful representations of the reality, though not of the same side of it. Very probably, if a man has always been accustomed to regard the object from one position alone, he will hardly recognize it in any of the views except in those taken from the same, or a near position. For this reason one man may recognize the object in one of the views, and not in the rest; another man may recognize the object in another of the views, and not in the rest; and so on. It is not that the rest are not as faithful and true representations of the object; only they are not representations of that aspect of the object, of which alone the individual in question is cognizant.

This illustration will help us to account for the origin of those differences in morals, which have been thought by some to throw everything into doubt. Thus it has been said, that not a vice can be named which has not been practised in some ages, and in some countries, as a virtue. For example, assassination, infanticide, robbery, have all been committed, in certain states of society, without apparent compunction, — nay, sometimes with the countenance and support of public opinion, as being necessary, useful, or heroic acts. Ethical writers, in order to account for these anomalies, have been in the habit of ascribing them to differences of culture, and differences of physical and social circumstances; and these, doubtless, are among the principal *remote* causes which conspire to bring about the results in question. But *how* do they bring them about? Simply and solely by leading men to regard the action to be pronounced upon under a particular point of view, and under that alone. In this way retaliation for wrong, under the form of assassination and revenge, in a rude state of society, or in very unsettled times, may come to be regarded as a kind of *wild justice*, and the only justice accessible, and so be approved; for this certainly is *one* of the aspects of such actions at such times, and it may be the only one which strikes minds thus situated. And so of the other cases. I am not aware of a single vicious action which was ever held as right, unless, in the circumstances, it really had a good or plausible side, on which alone, from some cause, it was contemplated, the whole action being judged by this one side.

The same account is also to be given of the origin of most of our differences in religious doctrine when sincerely entertained. Take, for instance, what is perhaps the most fundamental difference of all, the different opinions which have prevailed respecting human nature. Who does not know that man *actually appears* under all these various aspects? — sometimes but little lower than the angels, and sometimes but little better than a fiend. Hence the most extreme and contradictory views on this subject are so far well founded as this, that they are faithful and true representations of real phases of human nature, the error consisting not in misconceiving or misrepresenting some single phase, but in judging our whole nature by that alone.

We arrive, then, at this conclusion: real and sincere differences in morals and religion originate for the most part in the fact, that men regard the matter in question from different positions, and of course under different aspects, each one judging the whole matter by that particular aspect of it which happens to be turned towards him. And if so, then it follows, that what we call errors are not so much *false* as *partial* views of the reality. A celebrated French writer has said, "that, if we except the common maxims of morality, there is no one *truth* which can boast of having been so generally adopted, or through such a succession of ages, as certain ridiculous and pernicious *errors.*" * The statement has been objected to as an exaggeration; but even if it were not, to what would it amount? Simply to this, that thus far *partial* views, espe-

---

* Condorcet in his *Eloge* of Euler.

cially of large and complicated subjects, have prevailed more generally, and more extensively, than *complete* and *perfect* views.

Such being the origin and nature of most religious differences, it will next be in order to inquire on what grounds they can be regarded as a reason or occasion for sceptical, or cynical, or desponding thoughts.

In the first place, do they afford us any reason or pretext for denying the trustworthiness or competency of the human faculties? Certainly not. If, indeed, as the language sometimes used on this subject would seem to imply, we actually *saw* differently, one man from another, and the same man from himself at different times, there would be some ground for despair of the human faculties. But we do not see differently. From what has been said it appears, that, though we receive different impressions from the same object, it is not because we see differently, but because we look at different sides of the object, and regard it under different lights, or from different positions. Could we be induced to regard the object under precisely the same lights and aspects, we should doubtless see it alike; and better still, could we be induced to regard the object under all lights and aspects, we should doubtless not only see it alike, but see it as it is.

Accordingly, the differences among Christians are

not to be construed into evidence of the incompetency of the human faculties in themselves considered, but only of their partial application. This, however, it may be argued, is merely to give another explanation of the evil, without removing or lessening it; the partial application always existing will render the conflicting views of the different sects alike unsatisfactory and worthless, and mutually destructive of each other.

But why assume that the partial application will always exist? When we begin our inquiries respecting any subject, we must begin, of course, by looking at it on one side: our views must be partial at first; but it does not follow that they must always continue so. What, indeed, is progress in any inquiry but the gradual enlargement of our views, which supposes them to become less and less partial? And hence the generally acknowledged fact, that thought and study, a wider observation and a more generous culture, tend to dissolve differences and bring men together.

To this some may object the permanent existence of religious sects, retaining all their jealousies and antipathies against each other. But it should be remembered that these sects exist in a twofold character, as parties striving for power, and as schools of theology seeking the truth; and that it is only in the latter capacity that we are concerned with them here. Now, the rise and progress of sects, considered as schools of theology, would seem to be as follows: A number of persons are led by various causes — some historical, some local, some personal — to *concur* in regarding Christianity from a particular position, — on one of its sides, and therefore under one of its various aspects. The consequence is, that, though the view is a partial one, it is one in which the whole sect agree; differing, at the same time, from all other sects, who, in a similar way, have been led to adopt and agree in some other partial view. Now, we say, that, as knowledge advances, there is nothing to hinder these sects, any more than so many individuals, from making their views less and less partial, which will have the effect to bring them nearer and nearer together; for though partial views of truth are many and various, truth comprehended in its entireness is one. Nay, more; what we thus see *might* take place, *is* taking place continually; in some cases, complete amalgamations of sects; in others, unions and alliances for certain purposes; and even where, for political reasons, the old names and organizations are strenuously maintained, and with them some of the old jealousies and antipathies, it is seldom without some abatement of the rigor of the old doctrine. The Calvinism of to-day is a very different thing from Calvin's Calvinism.

To those, therefore, who think to find arguments for scepticism or despair in the differences and divisions of Christians, and who are ready to pronounce the partial views which prevail as unsatisfactory, worthless, and mutually destructive of each other, the answer is plain and conclusive. In the first place, even the most partial of these views are worth a great deal; for they are partial views of an all-important truth, and as such contain much that is enduring and eternal. Again, as the error of these views grows mainly out of their being partial, it is one which must be expected to pertain to the first stages of every inquiry, but gradually disappear as the inquiry goes on. And, finally, though it is too much to hope that the time will ever come on earth when all religious differences will be healed, or, in other words, when the multitude of partial views will be swallowed up and lost in a single all-comprehensive view, still we are to consider that this knowing "in part," and prophesying "in part," and the trials and responsibilities which pertain to such a condition, may be of advantage while it lasts, — may be essential to the discipline which is to fit us for that world, where "that which is in part shall be done away."

Admitting all this, however, it may still be contended that I have not touched, as yet, the real "stone of stumbling and rock of offence;" which is not these differences and divisions, simply considered, but the controversies to which they have given birth. I ask, then, what there is in these *controversies*, — I do not say to condemn, for, considering how they are often conducted, there is enough in them, Heaven knows, to condemn, — but to authorize, or invite, or excuse, in lookers on, either indifference or unbelief?

Certainly of themselves they do not argue indifference or unbelief; but the contrary. An age of controversy is pre-eminently an age of faith; a man is not likely to dispute earnestly unless he believes in something, and attaches importance to it. Luther was the greatest disputant of his day; but he did not speak or write or act like one who looked on religion as a sham or a dream or a shifting cloud. These controversies, by the manner in which they are carried on, may sometimes show the distemper of the times; they are symptomatic, it may be, of moral disorders, but they prove, at any rate, that men are not spiritually dead.

Besides, how is it in other things? Name, if you can, a single interesting and important subject of inquiry which has not given occasion to controversy, and led, in the language of the Apostle, to "envying, and strife, and divisions." At this moment the world is about as much divided, and, may I not add? about as much estranged, on scientific and political and philanthropic questions as on religious questions. But do men hence infer that there is no such thing as truth in any of these matters, or that we have no faculties to discover it? God forbid! It is often in the sharp collision of many minds that the sacred spark is struck out. Controversy, with all its objectionable liabilities, is nevertheless the great stimulant and purifier of thought, the appointed means by which the mind struggles on in every pursuit, and communicates and establishes the progress it has made.

Obviously, therefore, it cannot be controversy, *as such*, that is objected to in this connection, but something peculiar to *religious* controversy.

In the first place, it is said that controversy is well enough where it really has the effect to help forward the truth, or to diffuse and establish it; but in religion it does neither, leaving every question just where it found it. I reply, that even if this were so, it would not be to the purpose: it would follow, indeed, that controversy is of no use in religion, and ought to be avoided; but it would not follow, that religion itself is of no use, or that controversy has made it of less use or less certain. But the whole statement is erroneous. There are those, who, from extreme distaste for speculation, or for want of what is called speculative power, are fond of admitting the advances made by the experimental sciences, but still contend that the speculative sciences are just where they were when men first began to think. But this doctrine, an extravagance at best, when applied to the understanding of Christianity, becomes manifestly absurd; for here we have to do, not only with speculation, but with history and criticism. Who has yet to learn the invaluable services of discussion and controversy in settling the laws of evidence on which the genuineness and authenticity of the Sacred Books depend, and the laws of interpretation by which their import is determined? To discussion and controversy we also owe it, that the Christian doctrines generally have been unfolded, cleared up, and re-stated. Even where the old terms are to a certain extent retained, discussion and controversy have compelled the resort to new explications more in accordance with the advanced state of society and human intelligence.

Again; religious controversy is objected to because of its asperities, and spirit of denunciation, which on such a subject are peculiarly odious, creating in some minds an invincible disgust for religion itself. That religious controversy, even among Christians, sometimes assumes the character here given to it, I am sorry to be obliged to confess; but it is easy to see that it is not because Christians are Christians, but because Christians are *men*, having the weaknesses and imperfections of men. Besides, the very intemperance of the controversy proves thus much at least, that there is something in the subject by which men are powerfully moved. Does party spirit run highest when there is nothing at stake? When the question is one of life and death, — of eternal life and eternal death, — we can hardly expect that well-disposed persons will always stop to measure and exactly balance their words. Nay, this spirit of denunciation, for which so much disgust is felt or affected, — I trust, after what has been said, I shall not be suspected of going too far, when I say, that it admits of an explanation less dishonorable to society and human nature, than the opposite vice of indifferentism. As we have shown, men take different sides in religion, because they view it on different sides. What they see, they really see; and by gazing on it intently they come at length to see it so plainly as to conclude, that those who do not see it as they do must be *wilfully blind*. They denounce them, therefore, not as rejecting this or that particular exposition of truth, but as being enemies of truth itself.

Once more. A vague notion exists, I believe, in some minds, that the honor of God is somehow implicated in and compromised by the disgraceful altercations to which Christianity has given birth. The fact that he does not interfere to suppress them creates a feeling of uneasiness and distrust, as if the revelation were not in reality from him. Such persons would do well to remember that God gives us truth, as he gives us everything else, not to our acceptance, but to our acquisition. Even the truths of revelation are expected to do us as much good by exercising our fairness of mind, and our love of truth, in the acceptance and interpretation of his Word, as by the light they give. Consult the analogies of nature. In the legislation of Heaven, there is nothing corresponding to Acts of Uniformity. Reflection, and a proper understanding of the world and human nature must convince all, I think, that these dissensions and controversies, though an evil as often conducted, are yet necessary to balance or expel still greater evils. Certain it is, that there never has been so little real religion in the Church, nor so many scandalous excesses and immoralities, as in times when controversy was hushed. In our own day what has led men to search the Scriptures with such intense interest, what has moved them to engage in many noble enterprises, what has led to increased watchfulness, decorum, and fidelity in ministers and private Christains? I cannot help thinking, that among the causes which have brought about what is most bright and promising in the present aspect of things, a high place should be assigned to our contentions, and, I may even add, to the jealousies and rivalships which these contentions have engendered. These are not, perhaps, the highest or the purest motives from which a man can act; but it is certainly better that we should be "provoked" to love and good works, to useful and noble exertion, even by such motives, rather than be given up to indifference, self-indulgence, and a general laxity of manners.

Still, the great practical difficulty, some may insist, remains: amidst this multitude of partial and discordant views, which are we to adopt? To say that we should "prove all things and hold fast that which is good," is a sufficient answer to theologians; but only a few are theologians: others, that is, the bulk of Christians, are not in a condition to "prove all things." Neither will it do to say, that we should select what is common to all these views, and hold to that. For who is to tell us what is common to all these views? and who knows but that what is common to them all to-day, may have to submit to modification to-morrow, as other and more extreme views may be disclosed? Besides, suppose that we have obtained what is common to all views, and that this is absolutely true, it is nevertheless but the skeleton of truth, without life or power. To the question, then, Which among the various partial and discordant views you are to adopt, this is my answer, — Adopt *your own;* hold fast *your own.* Allowing others to have their views, be faithful and just to your own view; endeavoring, of course, to enlarge it from day to day, but adhering to it, meanwhile, and reverencing it, as one view at least of truth, and of that side of truth which is turned towards you, and which, therefore, you must be presumed to be most concerned to know.

Above all, remember that, though *we* are divided,

*Christ* is not divided. We all drink from the same "Spiritual Rock," and that Rock is Christ. There is a living tie of faith, submission, and love which binds us all, if not to one another, at least to one and the same living Head. Again I say, though we are divided, Christ is not divided; and this is our hope; "an anchor of the soul, both sure and steadfast, and which entereth into that within the vail." Our views are still partial, and therefore discordant; but we must believe that they will become less and less so, for they are views of Him who "is the same yesterday, to-day, and forever." What we know not here, we shall know hereafter: the day is coming when, for those who love Christ sincerely, that which is in part shall be done away, and they shall know even as they are known; and there shall be one fold and one Shepherd.

# THE DAY OF JUDGMENT.

AND I SAW THE DEAD, SMALL AND GREAT, STAND BEFORE GOD: AND THE BOOKS WERE OPENED: AND ANOTHER BOOK WAS OPENED, WHICH IS THE BOOK OF LIFE: AND THE DEAD WERE JUDGED OUT OF THOSE THINGS WHICH WERE WRITTEN IN THE BOOKS, ACCORDING TO THEIR WORKS. — Revelation xx. 12.

It belongs to man, in which he would seem to differ essentially from the inferior animals, to make himself and his own thoughts an object of thought; not only to know what he is doing, but to be able to review his conduct and compare it with an ideal standard of expediency and right; in one word, to call himself to account. Not only is he able to do this, but through his intellectual and moral constitution it is forced on him as a practical necessity. In every human mind, according to its measure of activity and self-consciousness, this process of self-judgment is continually going on; and no small part of our happiness and misery on earth is traceable to it, — that is to say, to the pleasures of self-approbation, and the pains of remorse. There is, therefore, an important sense in which the whole of human life is one continued Day of Judgment.

Moreover, the self-judgment here referred to is understood and felt to be of an authority and sanction higher than that of man. We cannot shake off the conviction that there is a divine, as well as a human, element in conscience. The opinion which we form as to what is right in any particular instance, is a mere human opinion. It may be true, and it may be false; one thing to-day, and another thing to-morrow. But the sense of obligation under which we are all laid to judge ourselves by some acknowledged standard of right, and to bring ourselves into conformity to it as we best can, is not human. It does not depend on our own will. It is the decree of our nature; and our nature is the decree of God. It is the voice of God speaking to us through the human faculties, ordained by him for that purpose. Who can believe that God has so made us, that we cannot help judging ourselves by the law of right, without believing, at the same time, that he intended us to be judged, and rewarded or punished according to that law?

On looking round, however, we see that this law is very far from being universally applied, or fully carried out *in the present life*. Nothing is easier than to say, that virtue is its own reward, and vice its own punishment. So perhaps it would be, if the natural and legitimate tendencies of virtue and vice were never obstructed, or turned aside; but, as things go in this world, we know that in point of fact they are obstructed and turned aside in a thousand ways; and the consequence is, that in cases without number the wicked prosper, and the righteous are trodden down. Let no one think to shake this conclusion by insisting that the tendencies of virtue and vice, referred to above, are natural and eternal, whilst the obstacles to their becoming effect in this world are accidental and temporary. It is enough for the argument to know, that the obstacles in question, whether accidental and temporary or not, will last as long as this life lasts. Thus much being conceded, it follows incontestably, that, if there is ever to be a perfectly righteous retribution, we must look for it beyond the grave. Clement of Rome has handed down a tradition in the Church, that the Apostle Peter was so much impressed by this view of the subject as to be in the habit of exclaiming, "God is just; therefore, the soul is immortal."

By such natural intimations as these, almost every people, with or without the aid of revelation, have been led to entertain, with more or less distinctness and confidence, the presentiment of "a judgment to come." Even in Homer there are unmistakable traces of a popular belief in a future state of existence, where the fate of the individual is made to turn, more or less, on his previous character, and especially on his conduct towards the gods. The same is also laid down as a practical doctrine of great moment by the best among the pagan philosophers and moralists; and sometimes, as in the apologue of Erus the Pamphylian, given in Plato's Republic, in language bearing a striking resemblance to that used four hundred years afterwards in the New Testament. A brave man, having fallen in battle, was permitted to return to the earth on the twelfth day, in order to warn the living by a revelation of what he had seen. He had seen the dead arraigned, and when the judges, to borrow the words of the apologue, " gave judgment, they commanded the just to go on the right hand, and upwards through the heaven, having fitted marks on the front of those that had been judged; but the unjust they commanded to the left, and downwards, and these likewise had behind them marks of all that they had done."

There are those, I am aware, who make no account of pagan notions of a future retribution, on the ground that they neither amounted to a proper faith, nor had the influence of a proper faith. We are told, for example, that Cicero, though he insists on the doctrine in his philosophical writings, takes occasion in more than one instance to deride or disown it in private correspondence with his friends. The argument, however, is not of much weight; for, in the first place, what Cicero derides and disowns is often, not the fact of a future retribution, but the popular superstitions respecting it; in the second place, even if his misgivings occasionally go deeper, is it without precedent that very good and pious men should be subject at times to moods, during which they can hardly be said to believe in anything? and, lastly, the individual selected as a representative may be objected to, for it has never been understood that Cicero was a very good, and much less a very pious or religious man, even for the age in which he lived. If, then, a still broader ground should be taken; if it should be contended that the life of pagans cannot be reconciled with a sincere belief in a righteous retribution, I freely admit the difficulty: but it is a difficulty which does not end with the pagans. I ask you to reconcile, if you can, the actual life of Christendom itself with the general acceptance of that doctrine. Probably the solution of the difficulty is the same in both cases. As a general rule, men do not act out their opinions, their theories, their real convictions, certainly not with much strictness, whatever they may be: they act out their passions, propensities, and habits; and these again depend, in no small measure, on organization, and on the customs and institutions of society, that is to say, on physical and local causes, many of which it is impossible either to trace or explain.

From the pagans we pass to the Jews, among whom Christianity arose. Moses, their great Lawgiver, aimed to establish what is called a theocracy, that is a government of God *upon earth*, in which perfect righteousness was to be fulfilled. Of course, in such a state of things, as they had a *present* Divine judgment, there was the less occasion to appeal to a *future* Divine judgment. Nevertheless, I cannot help thinking that those who go so far as to deny a distinct recognition of another world in the Old Testament, and even in the earlier parts of it, must find extreme difficulty in explaining certain passages, especially such traditions as those respecting the translation of Enoch and Elijah. Be this, however, as it may, there can be no doubt that in the time of our Lord the great body of the Jewish people had become believers in the doctrine of a future state of rewards and punishments. In the apocryphal "Book of Wisdom," supposed to have been written about a century before Christ, we find a passage on this subject which might have come from an apostle: "But the souls of the righteous are in the hand of God, and there shall no torment touch them. In the sight of the unwise they seem to die; and their departure is taken for misery, and their going from us to be utter destruction; but they are in peace. For though they be punished in the sight of men, yet is their hope full of immortality; and having been a little chastised, they shall be greatly rewarded: for God proved them, and found them worthy of himself."

Accordingly, the doctrine of a future state of retribution cannot be accounted a Christian doctrine in the sense of being first taught in Christianity. How, then, it may be asked, are we to understand that passage in St. Paul's Second Epistle to Timothy, in which he speaks of "the appearing of our Saviour Jesus Christ, who hath abolished death, and hath brought life and immortality to light through the Gospel"? I answer, that to bring a subject "to light" does not necessarily mean to make it known for the first time, but to make it more generally and fully known, — to illustrate it, to clear it up, to set it in its true light, so that all may see it as it is. And this is precisely what Christianity has done for "life and immortality." It has given us new evidence of the facts in the case; it has enabled us to see these facts in new lights, and under new aspects and relations: so that the whole doctrine, in itself considered, has become substantially a new doctrine.

This being the case, it remains for me to speak of what may properly be considered as *peculiar* and *original* in the Christian doctrine of the judgment to come.

In the first place, I attach but little, if any, importance to the distinction insisted on by Bishop Butler. According to him, "all which can positively be asserted to be matter of mere revelation, with regard to the future judgment, seems to be, that the great distinction between the righteous and the wicked shall be made at the end of this world; that each shall *then* receive according to his deserts."\* On the contrary, the whole doctrine of *a day* of judgment — of a single day or a set time for all mankind — seems to me to have originated in the mistake of construing passages literally which were intended to be understood figuratively. If we insist on construing these passages literally, consistency would seem to require us to go further still. We must believe not merely in a day, but also in a place, — nay, more, in real books, in a real consultation of records; in short, in all the paraphernalia of a human tribunal. Let me not be suspected of objecting to or undervaluing those representations of Scripture which bring up the vision of all mankind standing before the judgment-seat of Christ, "that every one may receive the things done in his body, according to that he hath done, whether it be good or bad." In no other way would it be possible sufficiently to impress the imagination and the feelings with that greatest and most solemn of realities, — namely, that you and I, and every one that lives,

---

\* *Analogy*, Part I. Chap. II.

will have to answer in the spirit for what is done in the body. It is only necessary, that, in our sober thinking, we should not confound the truth which is conveyed under the images in question with the images themselves.

On the whole, the most natural and Christian view would seem to be, that, with every individual, as soon as this life ends the next life begins. Else how could our Saviour say to the penitent thief on the cross, "To-day shalt thou be with me in paradise"? or Paul, of Christians generally, "We are confident, I say, and willing rather to be absent from the body, and to be present with the Lord"? or Stephen exclaim in the agonies of death, "Lord Jesus! receive my spirit"? Without pretending, therefore, to be wise above what is written, I think we may safely hold, that the day of judgment to every individual will be the day of his death. It will *begin then;* by what processes and instrumentalities it will be carried on, and how or when it will end, are among the secret things which belong to the Lord our God. If you wish to be told the details of what is to be in the life to come, you must not go to the Gospel; you must go to the Koran, which is full of it. As regards everything pertaining to the form and manner — or, so to speak, the outward appearance — of the invisible world, what most distinguishes Christianity when compared with other and false religions, — what indeed, on the negative side, may be regarded as *peculiar* and *original* in it, — is, not the fulness of the information it conveys, but its discreet and solemn reserve. In the not very frequent allusions to the subject the language is purposely varied, so that the most cursory reader might not fall into the mistake of understanding it to the letter. One thing, however, is put beyond question, — happiness to the good, misery to the bad; that is, all that can give moral effect to the revelation: not a word, not a syllable, either to stimulate or gratify an idle and impertinent curiosity.

But these things are comparatively of small moment. What chiefly and essentially distinguishes the Christian doctrine of the final judgment has nothing to do with the time and circumstances of that event; it relates to the principle, to the law by which everything is then to be determined. "Who will render to every man according to his deeds: to them who, by patient continuance in welldoing, seek for glory and honor and immortality, eternal life; but unto them that are contentious, and do not obey the truth, but obey unrighteousness, indignation and wrath; tribulation and anguish upon every soul of man that doeth evil, — of the Jew first, and also of the Gentile; but glory, honor, and peace to every man that worketh good,

— to the Jew first, and also to the Gentile; for there is no respect of persons with God." The same ground is also taken by another apostle: "Then Peter opened his mouth and said, 'Of a truth I perceive that God is no respecter of persons; but in every nation he that feareth him, and worketh righteousness, is accepted with him.'" A multitude of such passages might be cited from the apostolic writings; and they do but reassert what our Lord himself had expressly taught in the Sermon on the Mount: "Not every one that saith unto me, Lord, Lord, shall enter into the kingdom of heaven; but he that doeth the will of my Father which is in heaven. Many will say to me in that day, 'Lord, Lord, have we not prophesied in thy name? and in thy name have cast out devils? and in thy name have done many wonderful works?' And then will I profess unto them, I never knew you: depart from me, ye that work iniquity."

We are so accustomed to language like this in the New Testament as to be hardly in a condition to see in it anything *peculiar* or *original*. But where will you find its parallel? Certainly not in any of the thousand forms of polytheism which have prevailed in the world. I do not say, I have no right to say, even of these, certainly not of the best of them, that they entirely exclude moral ideas or a moral accountability. But need I remind you how often even the purest of them represent justice as interfered with by jealousies and rivalships among the Divinities themselves, or by partiality or favoritism for particular communities or particular individuals? how often they speak of the anger of the gods as directed, not against unrighteousness, but against some personal slight or neglect? And what shall I say of Judaism? Every thoughtful reader must be struck with the lofty tone of monotheistic morality pervading the Old Testament; but it was never understood to come up to the Christian standard; it is expressly said in the Sermon on the Mount not to do so. Judaism is marred throughout — sometimes in principle, and still oftener in spirit — by the narrowness and arrogance of a people educated in the belief that God was *their* God in a sense in which he was not the God of all mankind. Nowhere but in Christianity will you find it distinctly laid down, as of Divine authority, that every man is to be judged at last by what he has himself done, whether it be good or bad.

Let us now go one step further, and ascertain, if we can, precisely what is meant when it is said, that men are to be judged "according to their deeds." I believe there are those who interpret it to mean, that a sort of moral account current is opened with every man, as soon as he comes to years of discretion, in which he is credited for all his virtues and charged with all his sins, and that he will be rewarded or punished in the end for each particular act. Mr. Locke must have entertained some such notion when arguing that, before a man can be justly punished in the next life for the sins committed here, those sins must be brought to his remembrance; that is, he must be conscious of having committed those particular sins. And so Coleridge, who, after advancing the conjecture that "the resurrection body" may so stimulate the memory, as to bring before every human soul the collective experience of its whole past existence, adds: "And this, — this, perchance, is the dread Book of Judgment, in whose mysterious hieroglyphics every idle word is recorded." All such speculations originate, as it seems to me, in the common error of pushing too far the analogy between the human and the Divine administrations of justice. The distinction here to be taken into view is sufficiently obvious. We were told long ago, that "the Lord seeth not as man seeth; for man looketh on the outward appearance, but the Lord looketh on the heart." If, therefore, there is one thing clearer than any other in Christian ethics, it is this, — that every man is to stand or fall according to what he is in himself; — not by what he *does*, except in so far as it expresses what he really *is*. Acts of worship in a hypocrite, munificent gifts merely for the name of it, solemn make-beliefs of the would-be worshipper of God and the world at the same time, go for nothing. The question continually returns, What is the man *in himself?* Not that the language used in Scripture in speaking of the final judgment is to be excepted to or set aside, in any manner or degree. It is still as true as ever that we shall all be judged at the last " according to what we have done, whether it be good or bad," because this *will have made us to be what we are;* nevertheless everything at the Judgment Day will depend on what we *are*. There is, therefore, no occasion for the nice balancing of accounts, item by item, referred to above; neither is there any occasion for a miraculous memory to enable us to call to mind every thought we have indulged, every word we have uttered, and every action we have performed. It will be enough, if we know in what moral and spiritual state *all these have left us;* and to know this it will be enough, if we are made conscious of what we are.

This view of the case — distinctly apprehended and firmly held — will help to reconcile an apparent discrepancy in the Scriptures as to *the person of the Judge*. Thus, in one place we are told that "*God* shall bring every work into judgment, with every secret thing, whether it be good or whether it be evil." In another place it is said, " the Father judgeth no man, but hath committed all judgment to *the Son*." And, in still another place, our Lord himself is represented as saying: "And if any man hear my words, and believe not, I judge him not: for I came not to judge the world, but to save the world. He that rejecteth me, and receiveth not my words, hath one that judgeth him; *the Word that I have spoken*, the same shall judge him at the last day." Now there is plainly no contradiction, no difficulty here, provided only that we dismiss the imagination of a formal trial, and make the future judgment to consist in the fact, that every soul will become happy or miserable at death, according to its conscious deserts. The judgment thus understood, we may say with equal truth, looking at the subject under different points of view, that God is the Judge, that Christ is the Judge, or that the Gospel is the Judge. God is the Judge, inasmuch as all justice has its origin and foundation in the absolute holiness and rectitude of the Divine nature. Christ is the Judge, inasmuch as he is the dispenser of Divine justice on earth; it is in and through Him that this justice is made known among men, and applied to human affairs. And finally, the Gospel is the Judge, inasmuch as it is the expression of the Divine justice, that is, it sets forth the laws and conditions of spiritual life and spiritual death, according to which every soul will take its appropriate place in the eternal world.

The last-mentioned statement makes it necessary to glance at one question more. We say, every soul will take its appropriate place in the next life; but why do so in the next life, any more than in this?

There may be agencies and appliances to carry into effect the righteous retributions of eternity, of which, with our present faculties and experience, we can form no conception. But it is hardly necessary to resort to what may be termed the argument from ignorance. There is one thing which we *know*. We know *why* it is that a righteous retribution is not more generally reached in the life that now is. We know, for example, why it is that a mean man lifts up his head in good society; why it is that a designing politician often passes for a sincere patriot; why it is that showy manners often go for more than substantial virtues; why it is that, in the struggle for wealth and honor, the bad man often succeeds, and the good man often fails. It is because *the purely moral* aspect of things has comparatively little to do in determining our condition here. It is because a multitude of influences, having little of nothing to do with virtue or vice are constantly at work in this world to modify the opinions entertained of us by others, and even by ourselves. Here things are not as they seem. We walk in " a vain show." It is only necessary to suppose, therefore, that death will have the effect to strip off these disguises; it is only necessary to assume that this imposing but hollow masquerade will come to an end, and then every soul will *seem to be what it is, and take its place accordingly*. Glimpses are sometimes given us of what is to be expected when the world is judged in righteousness, and the secrets of all hearts are laid bare; and it is always, as our argument would lead us to anticipate, when for some reason moral causes have become for the time all in all. It is when man forgets everything else, and thinks only of his relations to a holy and merciful God; — as in the joy and peace of the new convert, and in the remorse and despair of the stricken soul. Let such a state of things become general, universal, and the dark and perplexing riddle of human destiny is solved: — the judgment is past; heaven and hell have begun!

It may be said, that the guilty soul will still be in the hands of a compassionate God; and this is true. Beware, however, of making compassion in God what it often is in man, — a mere tenderness, I had almost said, a mere weakness. Nor is this all. We must not expect in the next world what is incompatible with its nature and purpose. We are placed here *to make a beginning*. We can begin here what course we please; and if we do not like it, we can go back, and begin again. Are you sure it will be so in the world to come? Why first a world of probation and then a world of retribution, if after all both are to be equally and alike probationary? Let us not run risks, where the error, if it be one, is irretrievable, and the stake infinite. How much better to be able to say, with the Apostle, "Therefore we are always confident, knowing that, while we are at home in the body, we are absent from the Lord: we are confident, I say, and willing rather to be absent from the body, and to be present with the Lord. Wherefore we labor, that, whether present or absent, we may be accepted of Him"

THE END.

Cambridge: Stereotyped and Printed by Welch, Bigelow, & Co.

www.ingramcontent.com/pod-product-compliance
Lightning Source LLC
Chambersburg PA
CBHW051246300426
44114CB00011B/911